Reader's Handbook

A Student Guide for Reading and Learning

Great Source Education Group
a Houghton Mifflin Company
Wilmington, Massachusetts

www.greatsource.com

AUTHORS

Laura Robb Powhatan School, Boyce, Virginia
Author Laura Robb, author of *Reading Strategies That Work* and *Teaching Reading in Middle School*, has taught language arts at Powhatan School in Boyce, Virginia, for more than 30 years. She is a co-author of the *Reading and Writing Sourcebooks* for grades 3–5 and the *Summer Success: Reading* program. Robb also mentors and coaches teachers in Virginia public schools and speaks at conferences throughout the country on reading and writing.

Margaret Ann Richek Northeastern Illinois University, Chicago, Illinois
Contributing Author Margaret Ann Richek is a professor of education at Northeastern Illinois University. Her specialty is the teaching of reading. She is a former teacher in Chicago and the metropolitan Chicago area. She consults extensively for school districts. Her publications include a series of ten co-authored books, *Vocabulary for Achievement* (Grades 3-10), *The World of Words: Vocabulary for College Students*, and a co-authored text, *Reading Problems: Assessment and Teaching Strategies*. Her work is also featured in *Vocabulary Strategies That Boost Students' Reading Comprehension*.

Vicki Spandel Writing specialist Vicki Spandel was co-director of the 17-member
Contributing Author teaching team that developed the 6-trait model for writing instruction and assessment. She is the author of more than 30 books for students and teachers, including *Daybooks of Critical Reading and Writing* (for grades 3-5) and *Write Traits Classroom Kits*. Vicki has been a language arts teacher, award-winning video producer, technical writer, journalist, freelance editor, and scoring director for numerous writing assessments. As lead trainer for Write Traits, she works as a writing consultant and visiting teacher throughout the country and develops a wide range of instructional materials for use in grades K-12.

Editorial: Developed by Nieman Inc. with Phil LaLeike
Design: Ronan Design: Christine Ronan, Sean O'Neill, Maria Mariottini, and Victoria Mullins
Illustrations: Mike McConnell

Printed in the United States of America
International Standard Book Number: 0-669-49010-5 (hardcover)
1 2 3 4 5 6 7 8 9—QWT—08 07 06 05 04 03 02

International Standard Book Number: 0-669-49009-1 (softcover)
1 2 3 4 5 6 7 8 9—QWT—08 07 06 05 04 03 02

READERS AND REVIEWERS

Pam Baglien
Sunnyside Elementary School
New Brighton, MN

Jackie Bledsoe
Jamieson Elementary School
Detroit, MI

Alina (Mac) Boruszko
Thomas Edison
  Elementary School
Morton Grove, IL

Christy Clanton
Callaway Elementary School
Panama City, FL

Geraldine Clare
Normandy Village
  Elementary School
Jacksonville, FL

Evelyn Clark
Normandy Village
  Elementary School
Jacksonville, FL

Kathleen Costley
Normandy Village
  Elementary School
Jacksonville, FL

Karen Crema
E. H. Greene Intermediate School
Cincinnati, OH

Bonnie Diamond
Tripp School
Buffalo Grove, IL

Cheryle Ferlita
Hillsborough County Schools
Tampa, FL

Barbara Forrest
Franklin Elementary School
Burlingame, CA

Mary Jo Fries
Newport School
Wadsworth, IL

Debra Fritz-Fanning
John J. Pershing Magnet School
Chicago, IL

Rosalie Fruchter
Dixon Elementary School
Chicago, IL

Fern Funk
Clarence Culver School
Niles, IL

Kathy Tuchman Glass
Glass Educational Consulting
Woodside, CA

Dr. Laura Guzman
St. Anthony School
Grand Rapids, MI

Dr. Carol Hallman
Ross Local School District
Hamilton, OH

Elaine Hanson
Edina, MN

Janet Ichida
Kennedy Elementary School
Schiller Park, IL

Steve Jozwiak
Rhodes School District 84.5
River Grove, IL

Claudia Katz
Edison Elementary School
Ferndale, MI

Dr. Kim Katz
Hoover Elementary School
Hazel Park, MI

Gerry Kulans
Audubon Elementary School
Chicago, IL

Merrilee Larson
Metro ESCU
Minneapolis, MN

Kim Levy
Wilmot Elementary School
Deerfield, IL

Debbie McArdle
Blue Ash Elementary School
Cincinnati, OH

Alex McCune
Symmes Elementary School
Loveland, OH

Karen McIntosh
Athens Middle School
Athens, IL

Dr. Judylynn Mitchell
West Salisbury
  Elementary School
Salisbury, MD

Barbara Montcalm
Clarence Culver School
Niles, IL

Amanda Moore
Waller Elementary School
Youngstown, FL

April D. Nauman
Northeastern Illinois University
Chicago, IL

Barbara (Dee) Pringle
South Londonderry
  Elementary School
Londonderry, NH

Allison Pryharski
El Rincon School
Culver City, CA

Julie Richter
Newport School
Wadsworth, IL

Gary Rohwer
Summit Charter Academy
Modesto, CA

Karen Schild
Newport School
Wadsworth, IL

Pat Schiller
Washington School
Glenview, IL

Beth Schmar
Emporia State University
Emporia, KS

Dr. Frank Serafini
University of Neveda
Las Vegas, NV

Laura Singer
Northbook School
  District 27
Northbrook, IL

Mindy Siperly
Portage Park School
Chicago, IL

Diane Siska
Hawken Lower School
Lyndhurst, OH

Dee Smith
Brian Piccolo Specialty School
Chicago, IL

Alicen Starek
Buffalo Grove, IL

Louise Stompor
Kennedy School
Schiller Park, IL

Jane Suminski
Luther Burbank
  Elementary School
Milwaukee, WI

Deann Umlauf
Lapeer Community Schools
Lapeer, MI

Vickie Weiss
City School
Grand Blanc, MI

Eleanor Wollett
Lenawee Intermediate
  School District
Adrian, MI

Julie Zambuto
Kennedy School
Schiller Park, IL

Contents

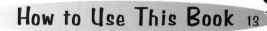

1 Introduction......20

2 The Reading Process......26

3 Reading Know-how.....34

4 Reading Textbooks......56

6 Reading Fiction......210

Sentence before   Key Words   Sentence after

Reader's Almanac......520

A Strategy Handbook............521

B Reading Tools.......................544

C Word Parts: Prefixes, Suffixes, and Roots........560

Acknowledgments......566

Author and Title Index....568
Skills and Terms Index....570

How to Use This Book

As a student, you have to read all kinds of material. You juggle test directions, novels, and textbook lessons. You read news stories, poems, websites, and much more. You have to read fast, stay organized, and know what you've read. Then, you have to remember it all at test time.

You have a big job. This handbook can help make your life a whole lot easier.

This handbook tries to help you in a few simple ways. Here are its goals.

1 Model Good Reading

You know how to read, but this handbook shows you how the most successful readers read. The first goal of this handbook is to model good reading. The reading model is simple, clear, and broken down into easy-to-follow steps of things to do before, during, and after reading. Try using these steps and watch your reading improve.

2 Teach Reading Strategies

You don't need a brand-new brain to become better at reading. What you need is the right reading strategies and tools. A second goal of this handbook is to teach you these strategies and tools and to show them in action.

3 Introduce Different Kinds of Readings

You have to read textbooks, biographies, newspapers, plays, graphics, tests, folktales, essays, poetry, and more. These readings all have different purposes, and they are all organized differently. You can't read them all the same way. A third goal of this handbook is to show you how to approach different types of readings in a way that will give you the best results.

Uses for the Handbook

Here's how you can use this handbook.

1 As a Guide

If you're unsure about how to read your science text, a novel, an essay, or something else, look it up in this handbook. You'll find easy, to-the-point lessons on how to handle different types of readings.

2 For Mini-lessons

If you need a mini-lesson about something like the meaning of a term or how to read a graph, check in the handbook. You'll find lots of suggestions and examples. Dip into the handbook to find whatever you need.

3 As a Desk Reference

What's the difference between a plot and a theme? Look it up in this handbook. The Elements sections contain lists and examples of all the key terms you need to know. Another section, the Almanac, collects the book's reading strategies and all the reading tools you'll need in one handy, easy-to-use reference.

4 For Different Types of Readings

The handbook is full of real-world readings you encounter every day, from web pages to tests to textbooks. You'll see helpful tips on all of them. Check them out!

Book Organization

In this handbook, you'll see four different kinds of lessons.

1 Reading Lessons

These lessons show you how to follow a step-by-step reading process to read different kinds of materials—from textbooks and websites to novels and poems.

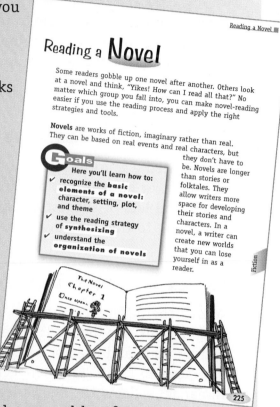

Reading a Novel

Some readers gobble up one novel after another. Others look at a novel and think, "Yikes! How can I read all that?" No matter which group you fall into, you can make novel-reading easier if you use the reading process and apply the right strategies and tools.

Novels are works of fiction, imaginary rather than real. They can be based on real events and real characters, but they don't have to be. Novels are longer than stories or folktales. They allow writers more space for developing their stories and characters. In a novel, a writer can create new worlds that you can lose yourself in as a reader.

Goals

Here you'll learn how to:
✔ recognize the basic elements of a novel: character, setting, plot, and theme
✔ use the reading strategy of synthesizing
✔ understand the organization of novels

The Novel
Chapter 1
Once upon...

225

Each reading lesson includes several key features:

- list of **goals** that tell what the lesson is about

- **preview checklist** that tells you what to look for in a particular type of reading

- one **reading** and another **rereading strategy** to help you find the information you want

- several **reading tools** to help you keep track of information

- information on **how the text is organized**

- **summing up** box that highlights what you should remember

2 Focus Lessons

These lessons are brief close-ups of a single subject. They take a closer, more detailed look at one kind of reading or a specific element, such as setting or theme.

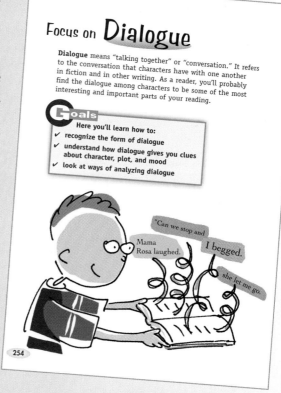

Each focus lesson starts with a list of **goals**. Most include several **helpful tips**, **reading strategies**, or **reading tools** to try. Each lesson concludes with a brief **summary**.

Elements Mini-lessons

These mini-lessons explain all of the key terms related to a particular type of writing.

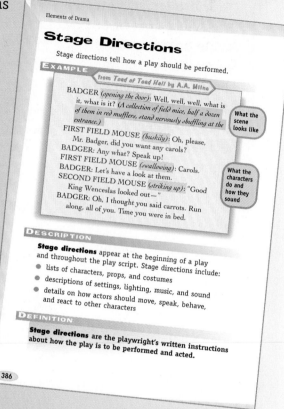

Elements of Drama

Stage Directions

Stage directions tell how a play should be performed.

EXAMPLE

from Toad of Toad Hall by A.A. Milne

BADGER (*opening the door*): Well, well, well, what is it, what is it? (*A collection of field mice, half a dozen of them in red mufflers, stand nervously shuffling at the entrance.*)
FIRST FIELD MOUSE (*huskily*): Oh, please, Mr. Badger, did you want any carols?
BADGER: Any what? Speak up!
FIRST FIELD MOUSE (*swallowing*): Carols.
BADGER: Let's have a look at them.
SECOND FIELD MOUSE (*striking up*): "Good King Wenceslas looked out—"
BADGER: Oh, I thought you said carrots. Run along, all of you. Time you were in bed.

What the scene looks like

What the characters do and how they sound

DESCRIPTION

Stage directions appear at the beginning of a play and throughout the play script. Stage directions include:
- lists of characters, props, and costumes
- descriptions of settings, lighting, music, and sound
- details on how actors should move, speak, behave, and react to other characters

DEFINITION

Stage directions are the playwright's written instructions about how the play is to be performed and acted.

386

Each elements mini-lesson starts with an **example** of the term. Then, you'll find a **description** and a short **definition** of what the term means.

Reader's Almanac

The Reader's Almanac collects three kinds of information for easy reference: descriptions of reading strategies, examples of reading tools, and lists of word parts.

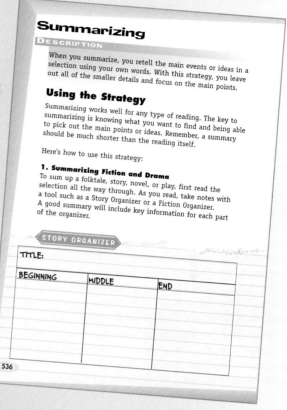

Summarizing

DESCRIPTION

When you summarize, you retell the main events or ideas in a selection using your own words. With this strategy, you leave out all of the smaller details and focus on the main points.

Using the Strategy

Summarizing works well for any type of reading. The key to summarizing is knowing what you want to find and being able to pick out the main points or ideas. Remember, a summary should be much shorter than the reading itself.

Here's how to use this strategy:

1. Summarizing Fiction and Drama
To sum up a folktale, story, novel, or play, first read the selection all the way through. As you read, take notes with a tool such as a Story Organizer or a Fiction Organizer. A good summary will include key information for each part of the organizer

STORY ORGANIZER

TITLE:

BEGINNING	MIDDLE	END

536

■ The **Strategy Handbook** explains in detail each of the 11 reading strategies used in the handbook.

■ The **Reading Tools** section describes and gives examples of 30 tools used throughout the lessons.

■ The **Word Parts** section lists common prefixes, suffixes, and Greek and Latin roots.

Introduction

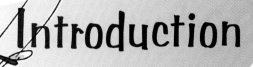

What Is Reading?

Why You Read

What Happens When You Read

Introduction

Let's start by thinking about what reading is. How would you define reading?

What Is Reading?

You can think of reading in a number of different ways. By comparing reading to other things you know about, you can understand it better.

Reading Is a Tool

Like a hammer or saw, reading is a tool that can help you do a number of jobs. You can learn about computers or the rules of hockey, bake a cake from a recipe, or find a few jokes with which to entertain your friends.

Reading Is a Skill

Like swimming or biking, reading is a skill. You get better at it the more you practice. The more you read, the better you get at it.

Reading Is an Ability

Like speaking or seeing, reading is an ability or power. It adds to your ability to think, to learn, and to imagine. Once you can read, you can learn more.

Reading Is a Process

Like writing, reading is a process that you do over a period of time. It's not an act that you do for an instant and then stop. It's an activity that takes time.

Why You Read

You may not always know why you start to read something. Someone asks you to read a book or a chapter, and you begin to read without thinking about it. Still, each time you read something, you have a *reason* for reading. You read for fun, to get information, to learn, or just for something to do.

Here are six good reasons to read:

1   **Fun**—Reading is lots of fun. You read magazines, mystery stories, emails from friends, and more just for fun.

2   **Information**—Reading helps you to learn about the world. You can find and read facts about anything that interests you, from rock stars to dinosaurs.

3   **Meaning**—Reading helps you to explore subjects that add meaning to your life—history, poetry, great ideas, helpful advice, and more. Through reading, all of the knowledge in the world is open to you.

4   **Depth**—Reading expands your mind, makes you smarter, and builds your understanding of people and ideas. This can help you to think about your life and make good personal choices.

5   **Art**—Reading helps teach you what is beautiful and clever and smart.

6   **Ease**—Reading is something that you do without thinking, because you need it to get around in the world every day.

23

What Happens When You Read

Reading is a process that takes place over time. Some kinds of reading—like recipes or schedules—take only a few minutes. Other kinds of reading—like novels or long books—can take an hour or even a few days. So what happens while you read?

Visualizing Reading

Think about what happens when you read. Take 15–20 minutes right now to draw what you think happens when you read. Follow the directions below. Don't worry about how your artwork looks!

Try these simple steps:

1. Close your eyes.

2. Think about what happens when you read a book.

3. Picture the steps you take as you read.

4. Now open your eyes. Sketch what happens when you read. Use one picture or several pictures, like a comic strip.

5. When you finish, look at your sketches. What do they tell you about how you read?

The Reading and Writing Process

Writing is a process with several steps, and reading is too. To call reading an act isn't accurate. Reading is a lot like writing—a process.

When you write, you answer a lot of questions. To create a piece of writing, you think about purpose and subject, length, main point, and details. You answer questions about organization, content, accuracy, and correctness.

Writing can seem difficult unless you break it down into small steps. Here are the main steps in writing:

1. Prewriting
2. Drafting
3. Revising
4. Editing and Proofreading
5. Publishing

To get the most out of reading, you answer questions and follow a series of steps, too. This next part of the handbook will tell you how the reading process works.

The Reading
Process

- **Before Reading**
- **During Reading**
- **After Reading**

The Reading Process

Here is a description of the reading process used in this handbook. It includes three simple stages: Before Reading, During Reading, and After Reading.

Before Reading

You're flying along on your bike and come to a busy street corner. What do you do? You don't just charge into traffic. First, you stop to look where you're going. Then, you decide how and when to cross the street.

Before you read, you do the same thing. You stop to figure out where you're going. You think about how to get there. In reading, this means that you will:

A. Set a Purpose

B. Preview

C. Plan

A Set a Purpose

Before reading, think about what you're going to read and why you're reading it. You'll have different purposes for reading a homework assignment, a recipe, and a new novel by your favorite author.

Think about your reading purpose—whatever it is—and put it into one or more questions. Examples might be, "What is *The Midnight Fox* about? What will happen in this novel?"

B Preview

Next, look at the reading itself and try to learn a little bit about it. This step doesn't have to take a long time. All you need is a few minutes. You can preview a news article quickly. But previewing a social studies chapter or a novel will take longer, if you do the job right.

When you preview, you're trying to get an overview of the reading and some idea about what to expect. Try to figure out how long the reading is, how it's organized, and what it's about. Your preview helps you to decide about *how* you want to read.

C Plan

Planning is important. You can't make a kite without drawing a design for it and getting the right tools and materials. Planning means thinking about the best way to reach your goal. It also means thinking about which tools to use to get the job done.

You can approach reading that way, too. For each reading, come up with a plan and the right tools. Suppose you're reading a science assignment and your reading purpose is to learn about ocean currents. You'll probably use note-taking as a plan—or strategy—for remembering this information. As tools, you might use Key Word Notes or Process Notes.

Other kinds of readings will call for different strategies and different tools.

During Reading

Now you're ready to read. During reading, you'll do two things.

D. Read with a Purpose

E. Connect

D Read with a Purpose

It's easy to feel a little lost when you read. You run into a sea of information—names, dates, characters, events, maps, charts, photos, and more. What are you supposed to do with all of it? You can't remember everything.

That's why you need to read with a purpose. Keep your reading purpose in mind as you read. A purpose tells you why you're reading and what to look for. A purpose for reading can help keep you on track so you won't get lost.

E Connect

Imagine that you're reading
a story about a boy named Carey. When he loses his
dog, you feel terrible. You remember
how awful you felt when your
cat got lost once.

Guess what? You've
just connected with
the reading. You've
compared what you're
reading with what
you already know and have experienced.
You sympathize with the character. Now
the story probably has more meaning for you.

You can connect with all
kinds of readings—
folktales, social studies,
science, news stories,
websites, and more. Just think
about what you already know
and how you feel about the
new things you're learning.

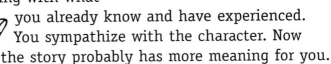

To connect, ask yourself these
questions as you read:

- Has something like this ever happened to me?
- Have I seen or read something like this before?
- What do I think about this?
- How do I feel about this?
- What about this is important or meaningful to me?

After Reading

After reading, you stop for a moment to think about what you've just read. Take some time to ask yourself, "What did I learn? What did I want to learn? Did I get the information that I was after?"

F. Pause and Reflect

G. Reread

H. Remember

F Pause and Reflect

During this step, you review your original purpose in reading. Are your questions answered? Do you have new questions? What part of the reading confused you? Were you unclear about anything?

G Reread

Sometimes you can't answer all of your questions without returning to reread the selection. Sometimes you need to reread a part that confused you. If you're reading something for fun—like a comic strip or a story—you may not reread it. But textbook chapters, some fiction and poetry, nonfiction, and directions often need rereading.

When you reread, do it with a purpose in mind. Choose a reading strategy and tools that will help you to get answers to your questions. Rereading is a way of getting more from your reading or patching up the holes in your understanding. By going back and reading a little more about a character or scene, you can develop a deeper and better understanding of it.

 Remember

Do you ever have trouble remembering things that you've read? If you take a few steps after reading to remember what you've read, you can solve that problem.

The key is to do something with the information you read and translate it into your own words. Try taking notes, making an organizer, summarizing, or simply telling a friend about what you've learned. Remembering is always easier if you "make the information your own."

 umming Up

To sum up, the reading process has these steps:

Before Reading

- **Set a purpose.**
- **Preview the reading.**
- **Plan a reading strategy.**

During Reading

- **Read with a purpose. Look for information that fits your purpose.**
- **Create a personal connection to the reading.**

After Reading

- **Pause, reflect, and look back to see if you found information that fits your purpose.**
- **Reread to find out things you might have missed the first time.**
- **Remember what you learned.**

Predicting

Evaluating

Comparin

Reading Know-how

- Essential Reading Skills
- Reading Actively
- Reading Paragraphs
- Kinds of Paragraphs
- Ways of Organizing Paragraphs

Reading Know-how

You may not know it, but you already have a lot of reading know-how. In this chapter, you'll learn how to start using it more often so that you can become a better reader.

Essential Reading Skills

Every day you make inferences and draw conclusions. You compare things. You evaluate situations. You make predictions. These skills help you to choose friends, settle arguments, and make decisions. You can use these same skills to help your reading. Think of these as essential reading skills that you should always have ready.

Making Inferences

Inferences are important because, when you read, you often have to figure things out for yourself. An *inference* is something that you conclude based partly on evidence and partly on your own knowledge. When you make an inference, you read something, add what you know to it, and draw a conclusion.

For example, you read that a character "has tears in his eyes." What do you infer about the character?

MAKING INFERENCES

What I Read +	What I Know Already =	What I Infer
A character has tears in his eyes.	People with tears in their eyes often are sad.	The character might be sad.

Drawing Conclusions

When you draw a conclusion, you "put two and two together." You take all of the information that you have and make a judgment about what it means.

Here's an example. Say that you suddenly smell smoke. Next, you *see* smoke. Then, you hear fire engines! What conclusion do you draw? You conclude that a building may be on fire.

DRAWING CONCLUSIONS

FACT 1
I smell smoke.

FACT 2
I see smoke.

FACT 3
I hear fire engines.

▼

CONCLUSION
A building might be on fire.

If you keep track of details and facts as you read, you can put them together to know what's going on. The facts that you pick up as you read also help you predict what happens next.

37

Comparing and Contrasting

When you compare and contrast two things, you think about ways that they are alike and different. This process can help you understand both things better.

You compare things all the time. You compare your grades in science with your grades in social studies. You compare your choices when you're deciding on shoes, clothing, desserts, and movies. Here's how one of those comparisons might look.

SARAH SHOPS FOR SHOES

SARAH WANTS...	PAIR 1	PAIR 2
1. Comfort	No	Yes
2. Style	Yes	No
3. Low price	No	Yes
4. The right color	No	Yes

Sarah buys Pair 2 because it has most of the qualities that she wants.

When you read, you compare and contrast characters, settings, events, and points of view. By doing so, you learn more about them and better understand what they mean.

Try to look at a reading in different ways.

■ How are these stories, characters, or settings alike and different?

■ How would someone of a different age or race feel about this reading?

■ In what ways are these two readings alike and different?

■ How does this work compare with others by the same author?

Evaluating

When you evaluate, you are being a judge.
You give your opinion or rate something.
You decide whether something is
good or bad. You state its
strong or weak points.

Whenever you say what
you like or don't like about
something, you're evaluating.
Whenever you think about
one thing as better or worse
than another, you're
evaluating.

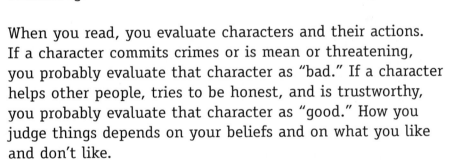

When you read, you evaluate characters and their actions.
If a character commits crimes or is mean or threatening,
you probably evaluate that character as "bad." If a character
helps other people, tries to be honest, and is trustworthy,
you probably evaluate that character as "good." How you
judge things depends on your beliefs and on what you like
and don't like.

Predicting

Can you predict how your parents will react to your asking
them for a second helping of dessert? You probably can.
That's because you know a lot about them and about how
they react to requests.

When you read, you also make predictions. You guess what
will happen next based on what you read and your own
experience. For example, you might preview the covers of
a book to predict what it's about. As you continue reading,
you learn more and adjust these predictions.

Reading Actively

Sometimes people read like robots. Their eyes just run over the pages. Nothing sticks in their brains, and soon they forget what they've read.

Active readers see reading differently. To them, reading is a sport, like soccer or football. Active readers jump into reading and put their minds to work as they read. Reading helps them to learn and develop themselves.

Being an Active Reader

Active readers pay full attention to what they're reading. As they read, they pretend they're in a conversation with the author. They listen and ask questions. They form opinions and connect what they're reading to their lives.

SIX WAYS TO READ ACTIVELY

1 **Mark or highlight** *the text as you read. Use sticky notes or a marker or pen.*

2 **React to and connect with** *the reading. What's the author saying? What does it mean to you?*

3 **Ask questions.** *Why does this character act this way? What's the main idea here?*

4 **Create pictures in your mind** *as you read. Sketch them or make a chart.*

5 **Make things clear** *as you go. Make sure you understand what you're reading.*

6 **Predict** *what will happen. Think ahead. Where is this going? What's likely to happen next?*

How an Active Reader Marks Text

Note how an active reader marked up this passage.

from *Julie of the Wolves* by Jean Craighead George

1 Miyax pushed back the hood of her sealskin parka and looked at the Arctic sun. It was a yellow disc in a lime-green sky, the colors of six o'clock in the evening and **2** the time when the wolves awoke. Quietly she put down her cooking pot and crept to the top of a dome-shaped frost heave, one of the many earth buckles that rise and fall in the crackling cold of the Artic winter. Lying on her stomach, she looked across a vast lawn of grass and moss and **3** focused her attention on the wolves she had come upon two sleeps ago. **4** They were wagging their tails as they awoke and saw each other.

Her hands trembled and her heartbeat quickened, for she was frightened, not so much of the wolves, who were shy and many harpoon shots away, but because of her desperate predicament. Miyax was lost. She had been lost without food **5** for many sleeps on the North Slope of Alaska. The barren slope stretches for three hundred miles from the Brooks Range to the Arctic Ocean, and for more than eight hundred miles from the Chukchi to the Beaufort Sea. No roads cross it; ponds and lakes freckle its immensity. Winds scream across it, and the view in every direction is exactly the same. Somewhere in this cosmos was Miyax; and **6** the very life in her body, its spark and warmth, depended upon these wolves for survival. And she was not so sure they would help.

1. Mark

2. React

I'd be afraid.

3. Ask questions

What is she looking for?

4. Create pictures

5. Make clear

This means many nights.

6. Predict

She'll try to use the wolves to survive.

Finding a Reading Place

You can read anywhere—on a train or a bus, in a doctor's office, or while waiting for a ride home. But it's great if you can find a special reading place that is private and quiet. To be an active reader, you need to concentrate.

A GOOD READING PLACE HAS:

✔ good light
✔ peace and quiet
✔ comfortable chair
✔ pen, pencil, highlighter, or sticky notes
✔ glass of water

Finding Time for Reading

You probably read when you do your homework every night. But you also need time for your own reading. If you plan ahead, you can find time to read every day. Try to read for at least 20 to 30 minutes each day.

This reading is strictly for you. Find things to read that you're interested in—a favorite magazine, a certain type of story, or books by authors that you like. Many people read every night just before they fall asleep. If you do this over the years, you can read thousands of books. This lifelong reading habit can add a lot to your life and to what you know.

Reading Paragraphs

Almost everything you read is made up of paragraphs. If you learn how to understand paragraphs, you'll read more quickly and understand more.

Two main steps in understanding a paragraph are:

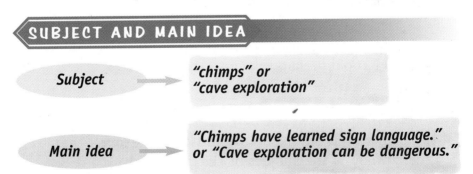

1. **Find the subject.** What is the paragraph about?

2. **Find the main idea.** What does the author say about the subject?

Sentences and paragraphs are the basic units of writing. Most paragraphs have several sentences. Taken together, all of the sentences in a paragraph express one large thought. When you've found that one thought, you've found the **subject** of the paragraph.

Every paragraph also contains a **main idea.** The main idea is what the writer is saying about the subject.

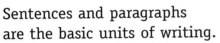

SUBJECT AND MAIN IDEA

Subject ⟶ *"chimps"* or *"cave exploration"*

Main idea ⟶ *"Chimps have learned sign language."* or *"Cave exploration can be dangerous."*

A paragraph does not stand by itself. Every paragraph is related to the other paragraphs around it and to the larger chapter or book as a whole. Each of the paragraphs in the larger work adds a little bit of meaning.

Finding the Subject

When you want to know what's going on in a paragraph, the first thing to look for is the subject. Ask yourself, "What's the main thing being written about in this paragraph?"

Here's where to look for the subject:

1. Look at the title or heading.
2. Look at the first sentence.
3. Look at any names, key words, or repeated words.

With that in mind, read this paragraph.

Title

from "The Cowboys Arrive"

First sentence

As ranching grew in the Southwest in the mid 1800s, a new figure arose—the cowboy. Many cowboy stories tell about brave men who captured wild horses by day and told jokes around campfires at night. But real cowboys worked long hours for little pay. They risked their lives in blizzards to guard herds on the open prairies. They rounded up cattle and branded them by burning their ranch's mark into the animals' hides. And the cowboys drove cattle hundreds of miles to railroads so that they could be shipped across the country.

Repeated words

By using a few simple steps, you can determine that the cowboy is the subject of the paragraph.

Subject: *the cowboy*
First Sentence: *"a new figure arose—the cowboy"*
Repeated Words: cowboy *and* cattle

Finding the Main Idea

If you know the subject of a paragraph, you can find the main idea. Just ask what the author is saying about the subject.

You'll sometimes find a paragraph's main idea in the first sentence or in the last sentence. Other times you'll need to figure out the main idea for yourself.

Main Idea in the First Sentence

from "Split-Screen View" by Susan Mondshein Tejada

Main idea

Subject

Four details

If you've ever tried to swat a fly, you know it's hard to hit. That's because a ❶ fly can detect moving objects extremely well. ❷ Flies view the world through compound eyes — eyes with multiple lenses. ❸ Each lens faces a different direction and views a small part of a scene. ❹ The parts add up to a complete picture in the insect's brain, which tells a fly to fly away fast!

In the first sentence, you learn the subject of the paragraph— the fly. Then you learn what the main idea is—that a fly is "hard to hit." The rest of the paragraph gives details that explain why.

Subject: *a fly*
Main Idea: *Flies are hard to hit.*

Detail 1: *Flies detect moving objects well.*
Detail 2: *They have compound eyes with multiple lenses.*
Detail 3: *Lenses face in different directions.*
Detail 4: *Images are combined in flies' brains.*

Main Idea in the Last Sentence

Sometimes writers like to build up details in a paragraph and then sum them up at the end. When that happens, you'll find the main idea in the last sentence.

Read this example.

from *The Magic Paintbrush* by Laurence Yep

Five details

Reverently he removed the wrapping and held up a black-and-white photo. It seemed to be of someone's **1** living room. On a table sat a big, **2** old-fashioned radio. In front of it **3** a man and woman stood together. The **4** man was in a tuxedo, and the woman was in a fluffy gown. They were **5** holding hands, as if they were about to dance. They were so **Main idea** young, they didn't look like his parents.

This paragraph lists details that the narrator sees in a photo. The last sentence states the main idea—that these people in the photo are his parents.

Subject: *a photo*

Detail 1: *living room*
Detail 2: *old-fashioned radio*
Detail 3: *man and woman standing together*
Detail 4: *dressed in a tuxedo and a gown*
Detail 5: *holding hands and about to dance*

Main Idea: *These two young people in the photo are his parents.*

Implied Main Idea

Sometimes an author doesn't state the main idea. As the reader, it's your job to read the paragraph and figure out what the main idea is.

from "The Birds' Peace" by Jean Craighead George

Four details

On the day Kristy's father went off to war, she ①burst out the back door and ran down the path to the woods. Her ②eyes hurt. Her ③chest burned. She ④crossed the bridge over the purling stream and dashed into the lean-to she and her father had built near the edge of the flower-filled woodland meadow.

This paragraph offers you many details about what Kristy does when her father leaves. But it's up to you, as the reader, to infer how she feels and figure out the main idea. The implied main idea is that Kristy is very upset that her father is going to war.

Subject: *Kristy*
Detail 1: *burst out back door and ran to woods*
Detail 2: *eyes hurt*
Detail 3: *chest burned*
Detail 4: *crossed bridge and dashed into the lean-to*

Implied Main Idea: *Kristy is very upset that her father is leaving for the war.*

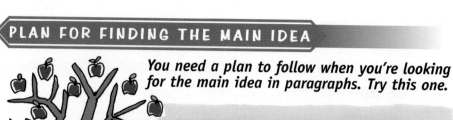

PLAN FOR FINDING THE MAIN IDEA

You need a plan to follow when you're looking for the main idea in paragraphs. Try this one.

1. First, find the subject. Look at:
- the title or heading
- the first sentence
- any names, key words, or repeated words

2. Next, decide what the writer is saying about the subject.
- Ask yourself: "What does the writer say about it in the first sentence?" "What's the writer saying about it in the last sentence?" "What are the details in the paragraph about?"
- Then put together what the writer is saying about the subject. State the idea in your own words.

3. Use a Main Idea Organizer to keep track of what the paragraph is about.
- Write the main idea at the top.
- List details in smaller boxes.
- Then sum it all up. Write the conclusion.

Main Idea:

Detail #1:	Detail #2:	Detail #3:	Detail #4:

Conclusion:

Kinds of Paragraphs

Paragraphs come in all shapes and sizes. Some are lengthy descriptions. Others are short listings of events. Paragraphs perform a number of different jobs. Both as a reader and as a writer, you know about four general kinds of paragraphs.

KINDS OF PARAGRAPHS

Narrative Paragraphs
- *They tell a story or experience.*

Persuasive Paragraphs
- *They express an opinion or viewpoint.*

Descriptive Paragraphs
- *They describe.*

Expository Paragraphs
- *They explain.*

The Trouble with Paragraphs

As a reader, you soon realize that no paragraph is perfectly one kind or another. The paragraphs you read seem to have a little description, a little explanation, and a little something else. For example, look at this paragraph and one reader's notes about it.

from *Freckle Juice* by Judy Blume

Andrew Marcus wanted freckles. Nicky Lane had freckles. He had about a million of them. They covered his face, his ears and the back of his neck. Andrew didn't have any freckles. He had two warts on his finger. But they didn't do him any good at all. If he had freckles like Nicky, his mother would never know if his neck was dirty. So he wouldn't have to wash. And then he'd never be late for school.

> Explanation of Andrew's feelings

> Description of Andrew

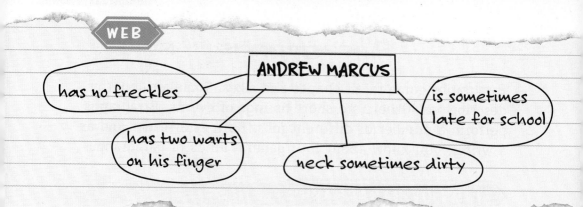

The paragraph is mostly description. You learn what Andrew Marcus is like. But you also begin to learn why Andrew wants freckles and his point of view about why he needs to have them.

Knowing How Paragraphs Are Organized

Why should you worry about what kind of paragraph something is, anyway? The reason is that, as a reader, when you know how a paragraph is organized, you know what's important. In other words, by knowing the *purpose* of a paragraph, you can understand it more easily.

You know that the sentences in a paragraph usually fit together to express one main idea. Once you begin to see that the details are organized in a particular way, you will find yourself understanding the paragraphs you read better, more quickly, and more completely. Knowing the purpose of a paragraph helps you:

1. decide what details are important and how they fit together

2. understand what the author is trying to say

3. remember what you read

Ways of Organizing Paragraphs

Good writers organize the facts and details in a paragraph so that readers can easily understand them. Here are some of the common ways that writers order paragraphs:

- time order
- location order
- order of importance
- cause-effect order
- comparison-contrast order.

Time Order

When writers talk about things that happen, they usually don't skip around. They tell the events in the order in which they happened.

from *America Will Be*

Three time periods

❶ By the 1700s, some Quakers spoke out against slavery. ❷ In the late 1700s, some leaders of the American Revolution argued that slavery did not belong in a nation where "all men are created equal." ❸ By the 1830s, more and more Americans believed that slavery should end. These people were called abolitionists.

It's easy to show the order of these events in a Timeline.

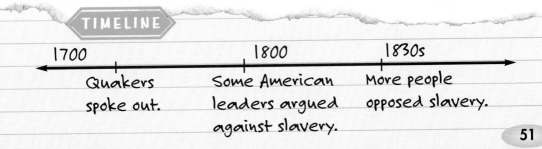

TIMELINE

1700	1800	1830s
Quakers spoke out.	Some American leaders argued against slavery.	More people opposed slavery.

Location Order

When writers describe places, they try to paint a picture in your mind. They set up details in an order that will make sense to you. They may describe things by moving from top to bottom, from left to right, or in a circle.

Sometimes they will describe a scene by moving from outside to inside a house or from far away to close up.

from *Danny the Champion of the World* by Roald Dahl

Four details

The filling station itself had only ① two pumps. There was a ② wooden shed behind the pumps that served as an ③ office. There was nothing in the office except an ④ old table and a cash register to put the money into.

Imagine that you are getting out of a car and walking into the office. You'd move from the gas pumps to the shed and then go inside to the office. It all makes sense.

MAP OF THE SCENE

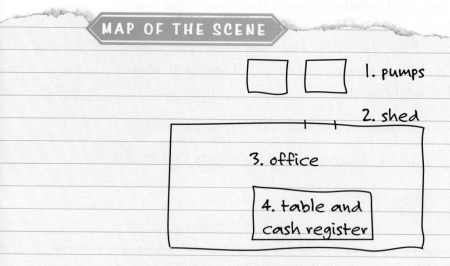

1. pumps

2. shed

3. office

4. table and cash register

Order of Importance

Sometimes a writer begins a paragraph with the least important idea and moves toward the most important idea.

from *Lincoln: A Photobiography* by Russell Freedman

While the North was free soil, it was hardly a paradise for blacks. Racial prejudice was a fact of everyday life. Most Yankee states had enacted strict "black laws." In Illinois, Lincoln's home state, ① blacks paid taxes but could not vote, hold political office, serve on juries, testify in court, or attend schools. They ② had a hard time finding jobs. Often they ③ sold themselves as "indentures" for a period of twenty years—a form of voluntary slavery—just to eat and have a place to live.

Main idea

Three reasons

Here the first sentence states the main idea: Life in the North was not easy for blacks. The author goes on to list three basic reasons to support that idea.

As you can see in the chart below, the reasons are given in order of importance, from the least to the most important.

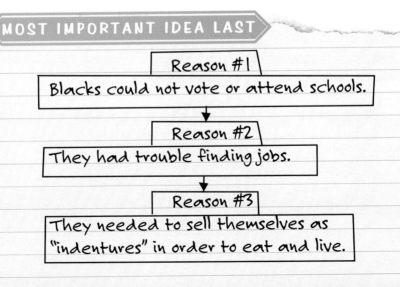

MOST IMPORTANT IDEA LAST

Reason #1
Blacks could not vote or attend schools.

Reason #2
They had trouble finding jobs.

Reason #3
They needed to sell themselves as "indentures" in order to eat and live.

Cause-Effect Order

Often in textbooks, biographies, or other nonfiction, you'll find a paragraph that talks about causes and effects. The writer might begin with the cause and then describe the effects. Or the writer might begin with the effects and then name the cause.

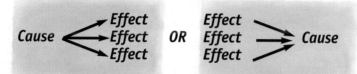

This is sometimes called problem-solution order.

> **from "Blood"**
>
> **Cause**
>
> When a blood vessel in the skin is cut, some ① blood leaks out. However, ② platelets soon clump together at the break in the blood vessel. The platelets give off a substance that causes a tangle of ③ sticky fibers to form. Platelets, fibers, and trapped blood cells clump together to ④ form a clot. . . . The ⑤ clot seals the break in the blood vessel. ⑥ The bleeding stops.
>
> **Six events**

Use an organizer like the one below to keep track of cause-effect order.

CAUSE-EFFECT ORGANIZER

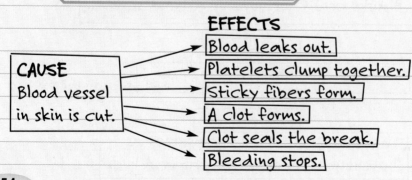

Comparison-Contrast Order

When writers are introducing something that is new, they sometimes compare and contrast it with something the reader knows already. Comparing and contrasting two things can help readers to understand both things better.

from *Scott Foresman Science*

The owl's wing is somewhat like your arm. It has the ①same three parts—the hand, the lower arm, and the upper arm. The owl ② can bend its upper arm the way you can bend your upper arm. The owl flaps its large wings to ③ lift itself into the air.

> Compares wing to arm

> Three details

Because you can move and feel your arm, you understand better how an owl's wing works. The writer wants you to see the comparison as clearly as if it were in a chart.

COMPARISON AND CONTRAST

OWL WING	ARM
3 parts (tip, upper wing, lower wing)	3 parts (hand, lower arm, upper arm)
bends	bends
used to fly	not used to fly

Of course, not all paragraphs will be organized in exactly one of these ways. But knowing the common kinds of organization can make it easier to understand what you read.

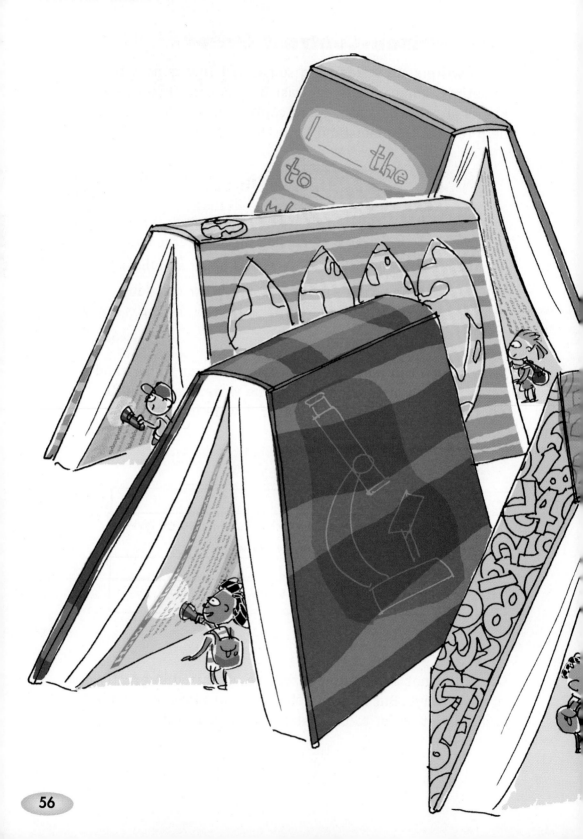

Reading
Textbooks

Reading Different Subjects

Reading Social Studies
Reading Science
Reading Math

Focus on School Reading

Focus on Word Problems
Focus on Questions

Elements of Textbooks

Reading Social Studies

What pops into your head when somebody mentions social studies? Do you picture lots of names, dates, and maps? Or, do you see Washington crossing the Delaware or the Wright Brothers trying out their first airplane? Social studies can be pretty exciting, if you read it the right way. After all, it's the story of us— the human family.

Social studies textbooks try to help you picture the world of the past. They use many resources—words, maps, diagrams, timelines, drawings, and photographs. As you read a social studies textbook, your job is to pull together those pieces into an overall picture of the time period.

Goals

Here you'll learn how to:

✔ read and understand **social studies textbooks**

✔ apply the reading strategy of **using graphic organizers**

✔ understand how **social studies textbooks are organized**

Before Reading

Suppose you were about to read a chapter on the Louisiana Purchase in your textbook. Where should you start?

A Set a Purpose

First, you need a reason or purpose for reading. Here are some possibilities.

- Learn some facts about the subject.
- Find out how the information connects to your life.
- Figure out why the event is important.

Now you can set a purpose for reading this chapter.

Setting a Purpose

- **What is the Louisiana Purchase?**
- **Why is it important to our lives today?**

B Preview

When you preview a reading, you don't read every word. Instead, you look for key information. Use the checklist below to help you preview. Move your finger along the text to touch each checklist item as you find it. Look for:

Preview Checklist

✔ the chapter title and subheadings

✔ any names, dates, or words that are repeated or set in bold type

✔ any pictures, maps, charts, or diagrams and captions

✔ any questions or study guides

Textbooks

L E S S O N   3

PREVIEW

Title

The Next Frontier

THINKING
F O C U S

PREVIEW

Question

What were the main results of purchasing the Louisiana Territory?

PREVIEW

Repeated names

Key Term

• Louisiana Purchase

➤ *The pocket watch contains a portrait of James Monroe, the man who made the decision to purchase the Louisiana Territory.*

PREVIEW

Subheading

PREVIEW

Boldface terms

In 1802, American settlers were moving west into the lands beyond the Appalachians. At the same time, events were unfolding in France that would change the future development of the United States.

Napoleon Bonaparte, the ruler of France, was worried about the French colony of what is now Haiti in the West Indies. He had already sent thousands of troops there to crush a revolt of black slaves. He would need to send thousands more. Napoleon also found himself on the verge of war with Great Britain. Wars cost money, and Napoleon would need lots of it. President Thomas Jefferson worried about the French controlling the Louisiana Territory. He sent James Monroe to Paris to buy New Orleans from France. Owning this Mississippi River port would safeguard American trade.

When Monroe arrived in Paris, he found that Napoleon wanted to sell the entire Louisiana Territory for $15 million. Monroe thought hard—though not about the Indian nations who lived on the land. He worried that he could only spend $10 million. But for just $5 million more he could double the size of the nation. What should he do?

The Louisiana Purchase

Monroe decided to take the risk. On April 30, 1803, he agreed to the **Louisiana Purchase,** in which he bought 828,000 square miles of land west of the Mississippi River.

Find the Louisiana Territory on the map on the next page. The United States bought this land for less than three cents an acre. Compare it with the map on pages 620–621 in the Atlas. What present-day states make up this area?

President Jefferson was happy with Monroe's purchase, but some

Chapter 14

NOTE
Time order

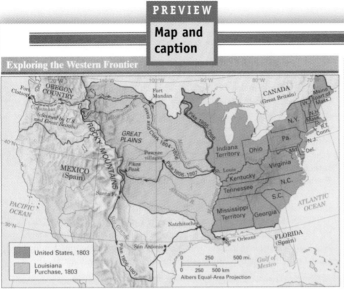

PREVIEW

Map and caption

Exploring the Western Frontier

United States, 1803
Louisiana Purchase, 1803

◄ *The Louisiana Purchase stretched from the Mississippi River all the way to the Rocky Mountains. Note the routes of explorers Lewis and Clark and Pike on this map.*

PREVIEW

Photo and caption

▼ *The official seal of France (below) was attached to the Lousiana Purchase document.*

members of Congress were not. They said the Constitution did not allow the president to buy new territory without permission of Congress. Jefferson urged Congress to agree with his actions.

> This treaty must of course be laid before both Houses. . . . They, I presume, will see their duty to their country in ratifying and paying for it. . . . It is the case of the guardian [adult] investing the money of his ward [child] in purchasing an important adjacent territory, and saying to him when of age, I did this for your good.

President Jefferson knew little about the new territory. New Orleans was a trade center for the frontier west of the Appalachians. Hunters and trappers brought furs to the city by traveling down rivers that fed into the Mississippi.

President Jefferson wondered if one of the rivers flowed to the Pacific Ocean. If so, it would form a trade route across the continent. To explore this territory, Jefferson chose two men. One was Meriwether Lewis, his secretary. The other was William Clark, an army officer. ■

PREVIEW

Question

■ *Why did people in the United States disagree about whether or not the country should buy the Louisiana Territory?*

The Lewis and Clark Expedition ◄ • • • • • • • •

President Jefferson sent Lewis and Clark on an expedition, or journey of discovery. They were to travel up the Missouri River and make their way to the Pacific. They were to map the area as they traveled, and they were to find out as much as they could about the plants and animals living there. To learn more about the Lewis and Clark expedition, see A Closer Look on the following pages.

PREVIEW

Subheading

Moving West

PREVIEW

Repeated names

PREVIEW
Repeated names

How Do We Know?

HISTORY *People today know what happened to Lewis and Clark, because the explorers kept very complete journals. Since the purpose of their expedition was to do research, they took thorough notes on much of what they saw.*

PREVIEW
Question

■ *What was the main goal of the Lewis and Clark expedition?*

Lewis and Clark chose 40 to 50 frontiersmen and hunters for the trip. The group included a black slave named York. In May 1804, the explorers set off from St. Louis in riverboats. They spent the winter with the Mandan Indian tribes in what is now North Dakota. In the spring, they continued the journey. By that time, Sacajawea *(sak uh juh WEE uh)*, a Shoshone, had joined the expedition with her husband.

When the explorers came out of the Rocky Mountains, they met the Nez Perce *(nehz purs)* Indians. They traded with the Nez Perce for fresh supplies. The explorers then built canoes and paddled down the Columbia River. They reached the Pacific in November 1805, after 18 exhausting months.

Lewis and Clark shipped their reports and maps back to President Jefferson. The reports gave Americans a better understanding of the huge territory that was now part of the United States. Lewis and Clark didn't find a river route to the Pacific, but they showed that overland travel was possible. They also laid a foundation for friendly relations with the Indians. ■

REVIEW

PREVIEW
Review questions

1. **FOCUS** What were the main results of the purchase of the Louisiana Territory?
2. **CONNECT** How was the pattern of settlement in the Louisiana Territory similar to the pattern in the Northwest Territory?
3. **GEOGRAPHY** Why was control of the city of New Orleans considered so important to people in the United States?
4. **CRITICAL THINKING** Why did Daniel Boone keep moving westward rather than settle down in one place?
5. **CRITICAL THINKING** Compare Jefferson's decision to send Lewis and Clark on an expedition with the decision by Ferdinand and Isabella to sponsor Columbus. What did both Jefferson and the monarchs hope the explorers would find?
6. **WRITING ACTIVITY** What do you think President Jefferson wanted to know about the Louisiana Purchase? Write a list of five questions he might have asked Lewis and Clark when they returned from their expedition.

C Plan

What did you learn from your preview? You probably picked up information like this:

■ The Louisiana Purchase happened in 1803.

■ The Lewis and Clark expedition came after the Louisiana Purchase.

■ Napoleon, Jefferson, Lewis, and Clark are some of the key people.

Maybe you've already heard of Lewis and Clark. Maybe you live in a state that once was part of the Louisiana Purchase. As you read, compare what you already know with the facts in the lesson.

Textbooks

Reading Strategy: Using Graphic Organizers

Before you read, choose a reading strategy that will help you meet your reading purpose. **Using graphic organizers** can help you to keep track of the details. Graphic organizers are diagrams or charts in which you take notes and group details in a visual way as you read. You'll learn about several organizers in this lesson.

You might start by creating a simple Timeline to keep track of the major events in this chapter.

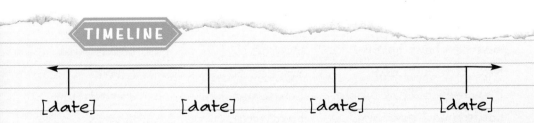

TIMELINE

[date]   [date]   [date]   [date]

During Reading

Your next step is to go back to "The Next Frontier" and read it.

D Read with a Purpose

As you read, look for information related to your reading purpose. Write down important details on sticky notes or in a special section of your notebook devoted to social studies. The first time through, you'll probably take rough notes. That's OK. You can reread for details later on.

As you read, record what you learn in graphic organizers. That's your strategy. Here are some possible graphic organizers you can use for reading social studies.

READING
SOCIAL STUDIES

✔ Timeline
✔ Web
✔ 5 W's and H Organizer
✔ K-W-L Chart
✔ Cause-Effect Organizer

1. Timeline
Social studies textbooks usually list events in the order in which they happened. A Timeline can help you remember the important dates and events in the lesson.

TIMELINE

1802	1803	1804
Monroe plans to buy New Orleans, but Napoleon offers whole Louisiana Territory.	Monroe agrees to Louisiana Purchase.	Lewis and Clark expedition starts.

2. Web

Another useful organizer for taking notes is a Web. With a Web, you put the main topic in the middle and related facts and events around it. A Web helps you to keep related details and ideas together.

Here is a sample Web about the Lewis and Clark expedition.

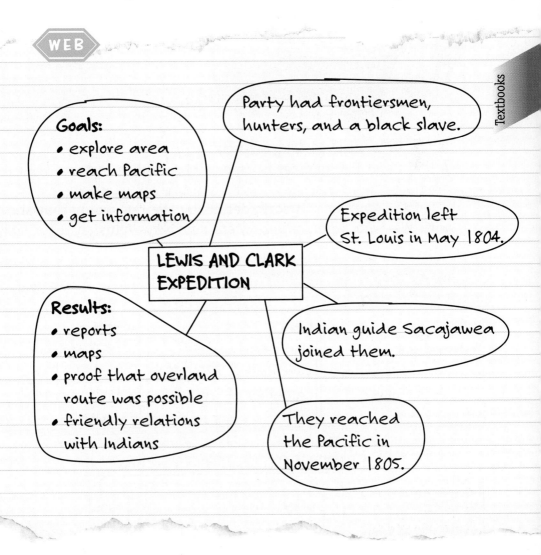

WEB

Textbooks

Goals:
• explore area
• reach Pacific
• make maps
• get information

Party had frontiersmen, hunters, and a black slave.

Expedition left St. Louis in May 1804.

LEWIS AND CLARK EXPEDITION

Results:
• reports
• maps
• proof that overland route was possible
• friendly relations with Indians

Indian guide Sacajawea joined them.

They reached the Pacific in November 1805.

3. 5 W's and H Organizer

A 5 W's and H Organizer is especially useful in history. <u>This organizer helps you make sure that you ask questions about all of the key facts.</u> It sorts details by the five words that start with W—*who, what, when, where,* and *why*—plus an H for *how.*

> ### 5 W'S AND H ORGANIZER

WHO	WHAT	WHEN
• Napoleon • Thomas Jefferson • James Monroe	United States purchased 828,000 sq. miles of land.	• 1802 Monroe goes to Paris. • 1803 deal is made.

SUBJECT: Louisiana Purchase

WHERE	WHY	HOW
from Mississippi River to the Rockies	Napoleon needed money and feared slave revolts. U.S. wanted land and port of New Orleans.	Monroe made decision, and Jefferson got Congress to go along with it.

4. K-W-L Chart

Another organizer you can use for textbooks is a K-W-L Chart. It has three columns—What I **K**now, What I **W**ant to Know, and What I **L**earned. A K-W-L Chart is a good organizer to use with textbooks because it connects the information to questions you have about the subject. The headings of a K-W-L Chart look like this:

K-W-L CHART

WHAT I **K**NOW	WHAT I **W**ANT TO KNOW	WHAT I **L**EARNED

Textbooks

Before you begin reading, try to recall some things you already know about the subject. Write them in the first column. Next, write any questions you have about the subject. Put them in the middle column. As you read, you will probably think of more questions to add.

On the next page is a sample of a completed K-W-L Chart.

WHAT I **K**NOW	WHAT I **W**ANT TO KNOW	WHAT I **L**EARNED
• Lewis and Clark were explorers. • I live in South Dakota, which once was part of the Louisiana Purchase.	1. What was the Louisiana Purchase? 2. Why was this important to America? 3. How does the Louisiana Purchase affect us today?	• In the Louisiana Purchase, the U.S. bought the land between the Mississippi and the Rockies. • It opened up the West to settlers. • Without it, the U.S. would end at the Mississippi!

When you finish reading, go back to your K-W-L Chart. In the last column, write what you learned from your reading. You can also add any further questions that you have. Don't worry if you have some questions that you can't answer.

How Social Studies Textbooks Are **Organized**

Social studies textbooks usually
are organized into one or two
main patterns.

> **1. Time Order**
>
> **2. Topic Order**

1. In Time Order

Most history textbooks are organized in **time order**—that
is, the order in which things happened. Look back at the
chapter "The Next Frontier." Did you see several sentences
with the time-order clues?

In 1802, American settlers
were moving west into the
lands beyond the Appala-
chians. At the same time,

risk. On April 30, 1803, he agreed
to the **Louisiana Purchase,** in which
he bought 828,000 square miles of
land west of the Mississippi River.

Following the time order of a passage
helps you pick out important details.

slave named York. In May 1804, the
explorers set off from St. Louis in
riverboats. They spent the winter

2. In Topic Order

In social studies textbooks, facts and ideas often are arranged
by topic. In "The Next Frontier," for example, the two
subheadings announce the two main topics: the Louisiana
Purchase and the Lewis and Clark Expedition. Even the last
part of "The Lewis and Clark Expedition" section
is organized by topic into four paragraphs.
Each paragraph begins a new topic:

- their mission from
  President Jefferson

- how they started out

- how and where they
  traveled

- the results

Textbooks

E Connect

Active readers make connections with what they read. Connecting means asking yourself questions like these and answering them.

> Has something like this ever happened to me?

> What have I seen or heard like this before?

> What do I think about this?

> How does this make me feel?

> Have I read anything else like this?

Here are some notes one reader made about this passage about Lewis and Clark.

Eighteen months is a long time.

How Do We Know?

HISTORY *People today know what happened to Lewis and Clark, because the explorers kept very complete journals. Since*

Waiting must have been hard. I would have been so eager to get moving again.

Lewis and Clark chose 40 to 50 frontiersmen and hunters for the trip. The group included a black slave named York. In May 1804, the explorers set off from St. Louis in riverboats. They spent the winter with the Mandan Indian tribes in what is now North Dakota. In the spring, they continued the journey. By that time, Sacajawea *(sak uh juh WEE uh)*, a Shoshone, had joined the expedition with her husband.

When the explorers came out of the Rocky Mountains, they met the Nez Perce *(nehz purs)* Indians. They traded with the Nez Perce for fresh

supplies. The explorers then built canoes and paddled down the Columbia River. They reached the Pacific in November 1805, after 18 exhausting months.

Lewis and Clark shipped their reports and maps back to President Jefferson. The reports gave Americans a better understanding of the huge territory that was now part of the United States. Lewis and Clark didn't find a river route to the Pacific, but they showed that overland travel was possible. They also laid a foundation for friendly relations with the Indians. ∎

After Reading

After reading, it's always a good idea to sit and reflect a moment about all that you've just read.

F Pause and Reflect

Now's the time to think again about why you are reading. What were you trying to find out? Did anything confuse you? Take a few moments to look back on what you read and try to answer some questions.

Looking Back

- **Can I name several key people, places, and dates mentioned in the chapter?**
- **Do I have notes or graphic organizers that cover the whole chapter?**
- **Is there anything that puzzles or confuses me?**

G Reread

Good readers reread all the time. They reread sections or parts that confused them because they know almost no one gets everything in the first reading. But your second reading of a social studies lesson can usually be more relaxed. Now you know the general outline of the information.

On your second reading, use a different reading strategy. Try one that helps you find out more about the meaning of the Louisiana Purchase and its connection to today.

Looking for Cause and Effect

Looking for cause and effect helps you to make links between events. The original event is the *cause*. The result is the *effect*. Finding cause and effect is very important in reading social studies. For example, what were the effects resulting from the Louisiana Purchase?

To show cause and effect in social studies, use a Cause-Effect Organizer like the one below. This organizer works well for history because history writers tell *what* happened and *why* it happened. That is, they tell what caused each main event and what its effects were.

CAUSE-EFFECT ORGANIZER

EFFECTS

U.S. gets land west of Mississippi to Rockies.

CAUSE

Napoleon sells Louisiana Territory to U.S.

Lewis and Clark open trail to Pacific.

New Orleans passes from French to American rule.

France now has no territory in America.

Remember

Do you have a hard time remembering events in social studies? Think about how what you're reading about connects with what you know already and with your own life.

What if . . .

How would your family's life be different if the Louisiana Purchase had never happened? Write in your journal or notebook about three or four ways that your life might be different.

 umming Up

When you read a social studies textbook, remember to use the reading process and to apply the reading strategy of **using graphic organizers.** Decide on the kind of tools that will be helpful, such as:

- ■ Timeline
- ■ Web
- ■ 5 W's and H Organizer
- ■ K-W-L Chart
- ■ Cause-Effect Organizer

As you read, look also for **the way social studies writing is often organized**—*in time order or in topic order.* After reading, use the rereading strategy of **looking for cause and effect.**

Reading Science

Why do plants grow every spring? What causes lightning? Could people live on the moon? Your science textbooks can give you the answers to these questions.

Science teaches you facts about how our world and the universe work. Science also shows you a scientific way of thinking. Reading science is sort of like an adventure in thinking like a scientist.

Goals

Here you'll learn how to:

✔ read and understand **science textbooks**

✔ apply the reading strategy of **note-taking**

✔ understand the **organization of science textbooks and science writing**

Before Reading

When you read science textbooks, you learn a lot of new terms and new facts. For example, you can learn the parts of a plant or a definition of *erosion*. But terms and facts by themselves don't explain how nature works. Often, you need to learn a process that explains how something works or the solution to a problem.

A Set a Purpose

When you read science, go beyond *what* happens to *why* and *how* it happens. Here are some questions to ask as you preview and read part of a science chapter called "What Is the Life Cycle of a Flowering Plant?"

Setting a Purpose

- What is the life cycle of a flowering plant?
- What key facts or steps do I need to know?

B Preview

Before you read, preview to learn about what you will be reading. Note especially the subject of the chapter. Look for these items as you preview:

Preview Checklist

✔ the title and any subheadings

✔ any bulleted notes, introduction, or review information

✔ any words that are repeated or in large or bold type

✔ any photos, maps, graphs, or diagrams and the words that are with them

Textbooks

PREVIEW
Bulleted notes

PREVIEW
Title

PREVIEW
Introduction

What's the Big Idea

You will learn:

- how plants grow from seeds.
- about the mature stage of a flowering plant's life cycle.

Lesson 4

What Is the Life Cycle of a Flowering Plant?

All living things have a life cycle. Yes, even you! When you were born, you were a baby. In a few years, you will be a teenager! **Wow!** Your parents are adults. These are some of the stages in your life cycle.

PREVIEW
Subheading and words in bold

Glossary

dormant (dôr′mənt), the resting stage of a seed

Plants Grow from Seeds

PREVIEW
First paragraph

The bean seeds in the picture are hard and dry. These seeds are in the resting stage, or are **dormant**. Seeds that are dormant will not begin to grow. Seeds can be dormant for a few days or a few weeks. Some seeds are dormant for years.

A dormant seed will begin to grow if it has water, oxygen, and the right temperature. The pictures on the next page show how a bean seed begins to sprout, or germinate. The first three pictures show stages of growth from a dormant seed to a sprouting seed. Find the new leaves and the root. The fourth picture on the page shows a young seedling—with leaves, stem, and roots.

◀ These beans can grow into bean plants. Some black beans are eaten in foods, such as black bean soup.

PREVIEW
Photo and caption

PREVIEW

Subheading

NOTE

Steps in a process

Life Cycle of the Bean Plant

1

Dormant Seed
The dormant seed takes in water and the seed coat gets soft. If the seed has enough oxygen and the right temperature, it will begin to germinate.

2

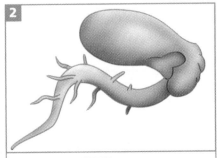

Germinating Seed
First a root pushes through the seed coat and grows downward.

3

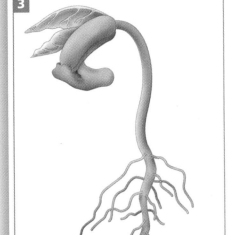

Germinating Seed
The top part of the root grows upward and becomes the stem. The stem carries the seed coat and the seed leaves with it. The seed coat falls off. The seed leaves provide food for the plant. Two small leaves begin to grow from between the seed leaves.

4 **Seedling**
When the stored food in the seed leaves is used up, they dry up and drop off. More leaves grow from buds on the stem as the plant grows taller. The new leaves can trap energy from sunlight and make sugar. Plants use the energy in the sugar to grow.

PREVIEW

Diagrams and words with them

A 27

PREVIEW

Repeated word

Textbooks

PREVIEW
Subheading

Mature Stage of a Plant Life Cycle

With time, young seedlings can grow into mature plants like the one in the picture. To become mature plants, the seedlings need water, air, and the right temperature. They also need sunlight for energy. Many plants also need to grow in soil.

When you eat green beans, you are eating the fruits of the bean plant. ▼

PREVIEW

Picture and caption

After a few weeks, the bean plant is full grown. Then the plant blooms. The flowers are pollinated and grow into bean pods, or fruits. Inside the bean pods, new bean seeds grow.

PREVIEW

Last paragraph

When the seeds are full grown, the fruits dry up. Farmers then remove the seeds from the dry fruits. These beans are dormant and will remain so until they have what they need to grow. The bean plant also dries up and dies. When the new bean seeds are planted, they will continue the life cycle of the bean plant.

Lesson 4 Review

1. How does a bean plant grow from a bean seed?

2. What do seedlings need to grow into mature plants?

3. **Main Idea**
   What is the main idea of the first paragraph on this page?

PREVIEW

Review questions

A28

Plan

So, what did you learn in your preview? You probably learned information like this:

■ Many plants grow from seeds.

■ This lesson tells about steps in the life cycle of a bean plant.

■ The lesson includes pictures and information about how beans grow.

Now you're about ready to read the selection in-depth. But first you need a plan for reading science lessons. Which reading strategy will work best?

Textbooks

Reading Strategy: Note-taking

Note-taking helps you to understand and remember what you're reading. Good readers take notes before, during, and after reading a selection. As they read, they watch for important information and write it down. There are several types of notes that you can take.

Class and Text Notes can be really helpful for reading science. Class and Text Notes allow you to connect what you read about with what your teacher says in class. To get started, divide a paper in two columns like this:

CLASS AND TEXT NOTES

CLASS NOTES	TEXT NOTES

During Reading

Now go back and read the part of the chapter "What Is the Life Cycle of a Flowering Plant?"

D Read with a Purpose

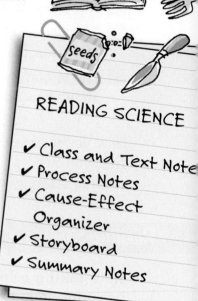

As you read, remember your reading purpose and your strategy of note-taking. Take notes in a separate part of your notebook that you have set aside for science.

READING SCIENCE

✔ Class and Text Notes
✔ Process Notes
✔ Cause-Effect Organizer
✔ Storyboard
✔ Summary Notes

You also can use several kinds of note-taking tools to organize information in science. Here are a few examples of different kinds of notes you may want to try. Find one that works for you.

1. Class and Text Notes

Use Class and Text Notes to group key ideas from class with ideas and details from your text. Divide your notebook in half. On the left, write down key terms and ideas your teacher mentions in class. On the right, write notes from your textbook about the same terms and ideas.

CLASS AND TEXT NOTES

CLASS NOTES	TEXT NOTES
what seeds need to grow	water, oxygen, and the right temperature
dormant seed	• means "resting" • can be dormant a day or a year

2. Process Notes

Process Notes work well when you want to keep track of a series of steps, stages, or events. You number the steps of the process and draw arrows between them. This organizer is a good choice for writing down the main stages of any process.

PROCESS NOTES

Life Cycle of the Bean Plant

1. Seed needs water, air, and the right temperature to grow.

2. Seed first grows downward (root).

3. Germinating seed then grows upward (stem, leaves).

4. Seedling grows taller, with more leaves.

5. Mature plant blooms and develops bean seeds.

6. If bean seeds are planted, they continue the life cycle.

Textbooks

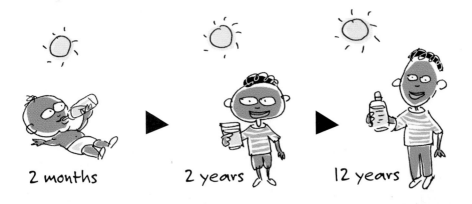

2 months   2 years   12 years

3. Cause-Effect Organizer

Scientists often try to understand cause and effect. The Cause-Effect Organizer is a tool you can use to show what conditions cause something to happen. The example here shows several sets of causes and effects.

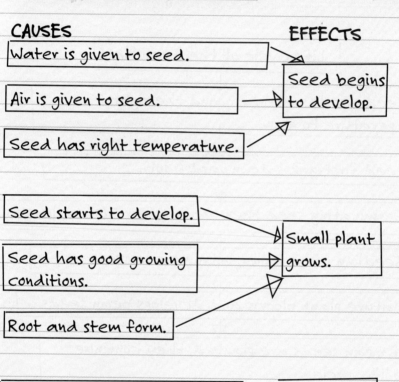

CAUSE-EFFECT ORGANIZER

CAUSES | EFFECTS

Water is given to seed.

Air is given to seed. → Seed begins to develop.

Seed has right temperature.

Seed starts to develop.

Seed has good growing conditions. → Small plant grows.

Root and stem form.

Leaves trap energy.

More leaves and branches form. → Plant grows bigger and bigger.

How Science Textbooks Are Organized

Science textbooks show you how scientists think about the world. You want to learn to think about science in the same ways that scientists do.

Scientists consider things like cause-effect order, how things can be grouped or classified, problem-solution order, and steps in a process. They ask questions like these:

> *What causes plants to grow? (cause-effect)*

> *What kinds of plants are there? (classification)*

> *How can a plant grow in dry, hot weather? (problem-solution)*

> *What is the life cycle of a flowering plant? (process)*

Textbooks

You'll find most science textbooks present information this way. That's part of how they help you think like a scientist.

The science chapter shown in this lesson presents a process. It explains what happens in each stage or step of the process. You can draw the stages of a scientific process in a Storyboard.

⟨ S T O R Y B O A R D ⟩

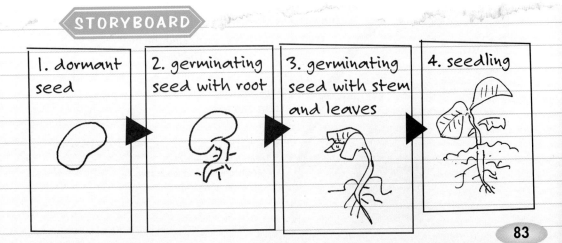

1. dormant seed

2. germinating seed with root

3. germinating seed with stem and leaves

4. seedling

E Connect

Science is much easier to read and understand if you make a personal connection with what you are reading.

To connect with what you read, ask yourself:

1 *What does this topic have to do with my life?*

3 *What do I see or know that is like what's described?*

2 *Why is this an important subject for me to know about?*

Here are some personal connections one reader made while reading the lesson.

These seeds are in the resting stage, or are **dormant.** Seeds that are dormant will not begin to grow. Seeds can be dormant for a few days or a few weeks. Some seeds are dormant for years.

A dormant seed will begin to grow if it has water, oxygen, and the right temperature. The pictures on the next page show how a bean seed begins to sprout, or germinate. The first three pictures show stages of growth from a dormant seed to a sprouting seed. Find the new leaves and the root. The fourth picture on the page shows a young seedling—with leaves, stem, and roots.

These are like the seeds I planted in cups and put in the window.

Are the pine cones I collect dormant?

◀ *These beans can grow into bean plants. Some black beans are eaten in foods, such as black bean soup.*

After Reading

A science chapter is usually packed with new terms, facts, and big ideas. If you're like most readers, you don't always understand all of them right away.

F **Pause and Reflect**

Review your purpose for reading. Think back over the lesson. What parts do you need to read again?

Textbooks

Looking Back

- ■ **Do I understand what the main topics are?**
- ■ **Can I explain the key terms or processes?**
- ■ **Do I understand how the writing is organized?**

In science lessons, the pictures are often the most important way of making processes clear. Can you remember the pictures showing the life cycle of plants, step by step?

If you can't answer questions like these about the reading, you need to do some rereading. It's perfectly normal to reread. Few readers pick up everything the first time through.

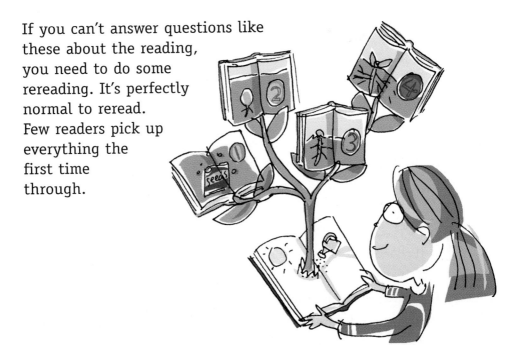

G Reread

Your second reading of the science lesson can be more focused than the first. Now you can reread specifically for points that you didn't quite get on the first reading.

A new reading strategy can also help make sure you really understand the ideas of the lesson.

Rereading Strategy: Paraphrasing

Paraphrasing means using your own words to state what you have read, seen, or heard. Think of it as explaining something to a friend or family member. Paraphrasing is a helpful strategy to use with diagrams and pictures. It allows you to put science processes and pictures into your own words.

In a science notebook, one reader wrote these notes about the life cycle of a flowering plant.

SUMMARY NOTES

LIFE CYCLE OF A FLOWERING PLANT

1. In the first stage, there's just a seed. To grow, it needs air, water, the right temperature, and maybe soil.

2. In the second stage, the seed starts to grow. First, it grows a root down into the soil.

3. In the third stage, the seed starts to grow upward. It forms a stem and leaves.

4. In the fourth stage, the seedling is growing more leaves and using sunlight for energy. It flowers and produces seeds of its own.

Remember

Even after reading a chapter, you need some help to remember it. Here's a way to make the lesson your own.

Do an Activity

You can make the science you read about "come alive" by doing an experiment or trying a related activity. For example, try growing a plant from seeds at home. Draw a sketch of what your plant looks like and compare what you see every week to what's pictured in your book.

Summing Up

When you read a science lesson, use the reading process and the strategy of **note-taking.** You can choose from many different kinds of note-taking tools:

- Class and Text Notes
- Process Notes
- Cause-Effect Organizer
- Storyboard
- Summary Notes

Remember that science writing uses **four kinds of order:** cause-effect, classification, problem-solution, and process. **Paraphrasing** is a good strategy for rereading because it helps you to describe a science process in your own words.

Textbooks

Reading Math

When you open your math book to do an assignment, chances are that you're not thinking about reading. If you're like most students, math and reading might seem like totally different subjects.

The truth is that reading is very important when you study math. In a math textbook, you read lots of things—numbers, symbols, word problems, definitions of key terms, and descriptions of ways to do problems in math. In reading math, all of these details count!

Goals

Here you'll learn how to:

✔ read about **math concepts and processes**

✔ use the reading strategy of **visualizing and thinking aloud**

✔ understand the **organization of math textbooks**

Before Reading

When you do math problems, you march along from step to step. Each step builds on the step before. Each chapter of a math textbook also builds on the earlier chapters. That makes it all the more important that you understand each chapter as you go along.

A Set a Purpose

So how do you read math textbooks? Begin by setting a purpose. With any math lesson, you can ask key questions like these:

Setting a Purpose

- **What are the key terms I should know in this lesson?**
- **What's the main idea of the lesson?**
- **How do I check my answers when doing this type of problem?**

B Preview

Next, do a quick preview of the lesson. Look for the lesson's subject, the examples, and any explanation. Use the Preview Checklist below. Look for:

Preview Checklist

✔ the main title and any subtitles or headings

✔ any introduction to the lesson

✔ any example problems and their solutions

✔ any key terms that are underlined or in boldface type

✔ any boxed items or questions in the margins

Textbooks

PREVIEW
Main title and introduction

LESSON 5 — Divide by a Unit Fraction

You will learn how to divide by a fraction with a numerator of 1.

Review Vocabulary
unit fraction

Learn About It

Mr. Perez has 6 oranges. He cuts each one in half and offers half an orange each to some students. To how many students can Mr. Perez give each half an orange?

Find how many halves are in 6 oranges.

Divide. $6 \div \frac{1}{2} = n$

PREVIEW
Example problem and solution

Find $6 \div \frac{1}{2}$.

There are 2 halves in 1 whole.
So there are 12 halves in 6 wholes.

$6 \div \frac{1}{2} = 12$

Since $6 \times 2 = 12$, dividing by $\frac{1}{2}$ gives the same result as multiplying by 2.

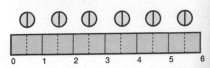

This number strip also shows that $6 \div \frac{1}{2} = 12$.

Check your answer using multiplication.

$12 \times \frac{1}{2} = 6$

Solution: Mr. Perez can give half an orange to each of 12 students.

PREVIEW
Boldface term

To divide a number by a **unit fraction** like $\frac{1}{n}$, multiply the number by the denominator, n.

PREVIEW
Boxed item

Another Example

PREVIEW
Example problem and solution

What is $1\frac{1}{2}$ divided by $\frac{1}{4}$?

$1\frac{1}{2} \div \frac{1}{4} = \frac{3}{2} \times 4$

$\qquad = 6$

The number strip shows that there are 6 fourths in $\frac{3}{2}$.

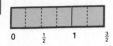

Explain Your Thinking

▶ Why does dividing by a unit fraction result in a quotient that is always greater than the number divided?

▶ Use number strips to explain how $10 \div \frac{1}{2}$ and 10×2 are related.

PREVIEW

Headings • • • •

Guided Practice

Divide. Use a number strip to show the answer. Check your answer with multiplication.

1. How many thirds are in 2?

2. How many fifths are in 2?

Divide. Check your answers.

3. $1 \div \frac{1}{4}$ **4.** $\frac{2}{3} \div \frac{1}{6}$ **5.** $2\frac{2}{5} \div \frac{1}{10}$

Ask Yourself

• Did I write the dividend and the divisor in the correct order?

• Did I multiply by the denominator of the unit fraction?

PREVIEW

Questions in margins

Independent Practice

Match each question with a number strip. Then write division sentence to answer the question.

6. What is 3 divided by $\frac{1}{4}$?   **7.** What is 3 divided by $\frac{1}{2}$?   **8.** What is 3 divided by $\frac{1}{6}$?

a   b.   c.
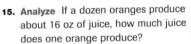

Find each quotient. Check your answers.

9. $4 \div \frac{1}{3}$ **10.** $3 \div \frac{1}{8}$ **11.** $\frac{4}{5} \div \frac{1}{5}$ **12.** $2\frac{3}{4} \div \frac{1}{4}$ **13.** $1\frac{1}{4} \div \frac{1}{4}$

Problem Solving • Reasoning

14. If each section of three oranges is about $\frac{1}{12}$ of one orange, how many sections are there?

15. Analyze If a dozen oranges produce about 16 oz of juice, how much juice does one orange produce?

16. Logical Thinking The U.S. produces more oranges than Spain but fewer than Brazil. China produces more than Spain but fewer than the U.S. List the countries from greatest to least by production of oranges.

17. Write About It If freezing rain destroyed $\frac{1}{9}$ of an orange grove and 100 trees were destroyed, how many trees were in the orange grove? Use a drawing to explain your thinking.

PREVIEW

Practice problems

Mixed Review • Test Prep

Compare. Write >, <, or = for each ●. *(pages 66–68, 162–164, 336–338)*

18. $12 + 3$ ● $3 + 14$ **19.** $1.4 - 0.6$ ● $2 - 1.5$ **20.** $10 \div 4$ ● $2 + \frac{1}{2}$

㉑ How many decimal places would you expect to find in the product $7 \times 0.7 \times 0.07$? *(pages 408–413)*

   A 4   **B** 3   **C** 1   **D** none

Textbooks

C Plan

What did you learn from your preview? You probably learned things like this:

- This lesson is about dividing by a fraction.
- *Unit fraction* is a key term in this lesson.
- Both number problems and word problems use fractions.

Think about what you already know about fractions. Have you studied them before? Review any terms and rules that might be helpful with this lesson. Then, choose a strategy or plan for meeting your reading purpose.

Reading Strategy: Visualizing and Thinking Aloud

When you visualize, you think in pictures or images that you draw. If you talk out loud at the same time, you often can "talk your way through" a math problem. That can help you think through the steps needed to solve the problem. This makes **visualizing and thinking aloud** a great strategy for math lessons.

VISUALIZING

The illustration of Mr. Perez cutting his six oranges helps you to picture the problem. You can see that he is dividing six things in half, one at a time.

Review Vocabulary

unit fraction

During Reading

Now you're ready to go back and do a detailed reading of the lesson.

D Read with a Purpose

Read slowly. Pay special attention to each example problem.

■ Read each example problem. Be sure you understand it.

■ Apply the reading strategy of visualizing and thinking aloud.

Next, try solving the example problem for yourself.

1. Solve the Example Problem

When you visualize, you make a mental picture or image of a problem. You might also sketch it on paper. As you do this, it helps to think aloud about what you're reading. This reading strategy of visualizing and thinking aloud can help you "see" the problem and help you hear yourself walking through the steps to solve it.

Here is an example of how to use visualizing and thinking aloud to solve the first problem in this lesson.

OK. In this problem, Mr. Perez cuts 6 oranges in half. The problem asks how many students can get half an orange.

First, I know there are two halves in 1 orange. So, I'll use that number to figure out how many halves are in 6 oranges.

1 orange divided by ½ equals 2 halves.

½   ½

6 oranges divided by ½ equals 12 orange halves.
If I divide 6 oranges in half, I get 12 halves.

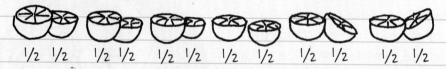

½ ½   ½ ½   ½ ½   ½ ½   ½ ½   ½ ½

That means that 12 students can each get half an orange.

$$6 \div ½ = 12$$

2. Work a Practice Problem

Visualizing can be very helpful in math. Drawings can help you see ideas like numbers. Now try to visualize and think aloud with a practice problem from the chapter.

$$4 \div 1/3$$

> **VISUALIZING AND THINKING ALOUD**

The division sign means "split into." Divided by 1/3 is the same as splitting into thirds. All right. Let me draw a number strip with four equal parts.

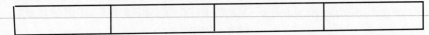

Now I'll see how many thirds I get in one of those parts. I'll divide the space for one of the units into three equal parts. I get three thirds.

I'll do the same thing with the other three units. I get three thirds in each of them.

When I count the sections in the number strip, I've got 12.

1	2	3	4	5	6	7	8	9	10	11	12

There are 12 parts in all. So $4 \div 1/3$ equals 12. The book says to check the answer by multiplying the number 4 by the bottom number of the fraction, 3. So, that means

$$4 \div 1/3 = 12.$$
$$4 \times 3 = 12.$$

To be sure that you understand this lesson, reread the example and try making diagrams of your own. Then check your understanding with some practice problems.

How Math Textbooks Are Organized

Understanding how a reading is organized will make it easier to pick out key information. Math lessons usually are organized in similar ways. Most lessons in math textbooks have these main parts:

MAIN PARTS OF A MATH LESSON

Main Part	What It Shows
① Title and introduction	Main idea or concept of lesson
② Example problems	Model of type of problem in this lesson
③ Process for solving problems	Steps used to solve all problems of this type
④ More practice	More examples and practice in using the problem-solving process you've learned
⑤ Photos, illustrations, and graphics	Information to help you understand the problem or the process

You probably noticed some of these parts when you previewed the sample lesson. Look back again at the first page of the lesson and find each of these lesson elements.

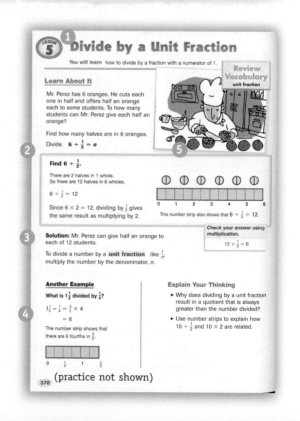

(practice not shown)

378

E Connect

It's not hard to make personal connections to math lessons. You use math concepts every day. To connect with a math lesson, ask yourself, "What does this have to do with me?"

Think of some fractions from your everyday life.

To make a problem more interesting and easier to understand, try connecting it to your life. One way to do that is to use a sticky note to make a connection to something you know.

EVERYDAY EXAMPLES OF FRACTIONS

Textbooks

✔ You're 5 feet, 1/4 inches tall.
✔ You put 1 1/2 cups of milk in macaroni and cheese.
✔ You are 3/4 of the way through a book.
✔ You're watching the final half of a basketball game.

Learn About It

Mr. Perez has 6 oranges. He cuts each one in half and offers half an orange each to some students. To how many students can Mr. Perez give each half an orange?

Review Vocabulary
unit fraction

This reminds me of dividing up pizza into a certain number of slices.

After Reading

After reading a math lesson, take some time to think about what you have learned.

F Pause and Reflect

Math lessons can be tough. You preview, read, and try to solve the problems. Sometimes even then you have to go back and review. That's OK.

Review the pages with your reading purpose in mind.

Looking Back

- **Can I name the key terms in this lesson?**
- **Do I know the main idea of this lesson?**
- **How do I solve this type of problem and check my answers?**

Did you meet your reading purpose? Did you understand the example problem?

If not, go back to reread any parts of the lesson that confused you. Rereading can help to fix the key terms, main idea, and other concepts from the lesson firmly in your mind. Rereading also strengthens your understanding of the process for solving problems.

G Reread

There's a lot going on in most pages of a math textbook. Math lessons are packed with information, abstract ideas, symbols, and numbers. One reading is often not enough. Try a different strategy when you go back to reread.

Rereading Strategy: Note-taking

Note-taking is a great strategy in math. When you take notes, you write down all of the most important things you learned in a lesson. Note-taking can help you meet your reading purpose.

Taking Key Word Notes for each lesson is a great way to review important information and prepare for a test. Start by creating two columns, one for key words or topics, and another for your notes. For every lesson, write down the key terms, the main ideas, the example problem, and how to solve and check it. You may also want to include your reading strategy and similar problems that your teacher solves in class or that you make up yourself. See the example below.

Textbooks

KEY WORD NOTES

DIVIDE BY A UNIT FRACTION

KEY WORDS OR TOPICS	NOTES
Key term	unit fraction
Example problem	$6 \div 1/2 = n$
How to solve problem	Divide 6 by $1/2 = 12$ Result is same as multiplying by 2.
How to check answers	Check answers using multiplication. $6 \div 1/2$ is the same as $6 \times 2 = 12$
Reading strategy	Try visualizing and thinking aloud. Use sketches or number strip to "see" divisions.
Other sample problems	Find $3 \div 1/4 = 3 \times 4 = 12$.

Remember

The final step in reading math is remembering it. If you have previewed, read, and reread the lesson, you have a much greater chance of being prepared for math homework and tests. But will you remember it in the future? Here's an idea that can help you remember math material.

Write Sample Test Questions

Make up sample test questions using index cards. Write one question or problem on each card and put the answer on the back. Exchange the cards with a friend, and check each other's answers. When you practice answering sample math questions, taking real math tests gets easier.

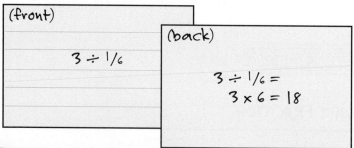

(front)

$3 \div 1/6$

(back)

$3 \div 1/6 =$
$3 \times 6 = 18$

Summing Up

When you read a math lesson, remember to use the reading process and to apply the reading strategy of **visualizing and thinking aloud.** Try creating organizers or making notes like these:

- Diagrams or Sketches
- Key Word Notes
- Think Alouds

Pay attention to the **five main parts of a math lesson:** the title and introduction; example problems; the process for solving problems; practice exercises; and photos, illustrations, and graphics. The rereading strategy of **note-taking** will help you to remember what you have learned.

Focus on Word Problems

Do math word problems give you trouble? If so, you're not alone. Math word problems are hard for many students. If you have difficulty with word problems, pay attention. Help is on the way!

Believe it or not, solving word problems isn't as hard as it looks. You need to know how to approach them and which reading and math strategies to use.

Goals

Here you'll learn how to:

✔ **use a four-step plan to solve word problems**

✔ **apply the reading strategy of visualizing and thinking aloud**

Before Reading

Take your time reading math word problems. Read the problem slowly, looking for what you know and what you have to find out.

Previewing Word Problems

To solve word problems, you have to sort through all of the information given. When you first see a problem, try to find the main question—the information that the problem asks for. Next, find the key facts that are given. These facts often are listed out of order. Also, there may be some extra information.

Try previewing this problem for the main question and the key facts.

SAMPLE PROBLEM

PREVIEW
Key facts

Olivia Hayes took her five younger brothers and sisters to a carnival. For spending money, she gave each of them $5 less than the next older child. If the oldest brother got $25, how much did the youngest child receive?

PREVIEW
Main question

You probably noticed that the key facts involve numbers and that the main question is at the end of the problem. That happens a lot. You need to sort out the information you're given from the question you're asked.

As you get ready to solve this problem, you'll need a good reading strategy. One excellent strategy to use with word problems is visualizing and thinking aloud.

Reading Strategy: Visualizing and Thinking Aloud

Numbers and pictures are both ways of making ideas easier to understand. So it's not surprising that drawing a problem and **visualizing** it in your mind can help you see it. If you **think aloud** as you draw, you can often "see and talk your way through" a word problem.

During Reading

After your quick preview, it's time to solve the problem. As you begin, follow this four-step plan.

FOUR-STEP PLAN FOR WORD PROBLEMS

Step 1 Read. Read the problem several times until it makes sense.

Step 2 Plan. Think of a way you can get the answer.

Step 3 Solve. Use a math or reading strategy to solve the problem.

Step 4 Check your work. Be sure your answer makes sense.

Step 1 Read.

Read the word problem again. If it helps you, say it out loud in your own words. Next, be sure you can pick out the key facts and the main question. Ignore any numbers you do not need. Then use your reading strategy of thinking aloud.

OK. I'll find the main question. There it is at the end: "How much did the youngest child receive?"

Now, what are the key facts? The numbers are probably important. There are 5 children. The oldest one gets 25 dollars, and each one after that gets 5 dollars less. The word "less" gives a clue that it's a subtraction problem.

Step 2 Plan.

By now you understand the problem well enough to plan how you will solve it. You know you will be using subtraction. Use the strategy of visualizing to picture the problem. For example, make a quick sketch of the five children.

Step 3 Solve.

You can often "see and talk your way through" a word problem. Try solving this problem. Here's how one reader solved the sample problem.

THINK ALOUD

1. OK. The oldest boy gets 25 dollars.
2. The second oldest child gets 5 dollars <u>less</u>.
   That's 25 minus 5, which equals 20.
3. The third one gets 20 minus 5, which is 15.
4. The fourth gets 15 minus 5, which is 10.
5. That leaves only 10 minus 5, which is 5 dollars,
   for the youngest. That's what the problem asked—
   How much did the youngest child get?

Step 4 Check your work.

Remember to check your answer. Since you used subtraction to solve the problem, check it with addition. Solving the problem in another different way is a good way to check your answers. Use visualizing and thinking aloud to check your work, too.

SAMPLE PROBLEM

Olivia Hayes took her five younger brothers and sisters to a carnival. For spending money, she gave each of them $5 less than the next older child. If the oldest brother got $25, how much did the youngest child receive?

VISUALIZING AND THINKING ALOUD

To check my answer, I should add. Let's work backward. I'll start with 5, which I think is the answer. If the youngest had 5 dollars, 5 plus 5 equals 10. Then, if the next kid had 10 + 5, that equals 15. Then, if the next oldest had 15 + 5, that equals 20. Then, if the last kid had 5 more dollars, that 20 plus 5 equals 25. That's it. The oldest child started with 25 dollars, which is what the problem states.

$5 $10 $15 $20 $25

After Reading

After working through word problems, review your work. Some problems will be harder than others. You may get an answer that just doesn't make sense. Or you may not even be sure where to start. Don't give up. Reread the problem again. Work through the four-step plan. Sometimes it helps to talk through a problem with a partner. Often you can make small mistakes in the way you write a problem, even though you know the answer. Take the time to check your work.

Make notes about what methods worked best for you. Write these down in the math part of your notebook. That way, you'll remember what to do the next time you've got a page of problems to solve.

Textbooks

Summing Up

- When you first see a word problem, start by reading the question carefully. Then look for the key facts and the main question.

- Use the strategy of visualizing and thinking aloud to find the answer.

- Use the four-step plan to solve word problems: read, plan, solve, and check.

Focus on Questions

In textbooks, you'll find questions all over the place. Questions appear in titles, headings, and margins. Questions appear at the ends of lessons, chapters, and units. They help you to review or test what you've learned.

You are absolutely surrounded with questions. Among them are short-answer questions, multiple-choice questions, essay questions, and true-false questions.

All of these questions ask for a response from you. *Fact questions* ask you to answer with specific details. *Critical thinking questions* ask you to draw conclusions or think critically.

Goals

Here you'll learn how to:

✔ **read and answer questions in your textbooks**

✔ **use the reading strategy of skimming**

✔ **check your answers**

With so many questions around, you should probably learn a few ways to handle them.

Before Reading

Believe it or not, the two tips that can help you the most with questions may seem obvious:

▮ Read each question carefully.

▮ Read the material the question is based upon.

All too often, students forget to do these obvious things. That's the first place to start. But, things are seldom that simple.

Textbooks

Preparing to Answer Questions

With textbook questions, your reading purpose is to understand what questions say, what they ask for, and how to find the answers.

Before you read a textbook chapter or test, quickly preview the questions. Size them up. How many questions are there? What types of questions are they? How difficult do they look? A preview will help you know what to look for to find the answers.

PREVIEW Key words

PREVIEW Type of question

PREVIEW Five questions

REVIEW

1. **FOCUS** What are the major landforms of the United States?
2. **GEOGRAPHY** Describe the climate of the deserts of the Southwest.
3. **CONNECT** Look at the landforms in the pictures on page 12–13. Which areas might have been easier for early European ethnic groups to settle?
4. **CRITICAL THINKING** Do you think it would be more fun to live in the mountains or near a river? Why?
5. **CRITICAL THINKING** Write a paragraph describing the landforms and the climate where you live. If you live in a city, write about the land nearby.

With any textbook questions, **skimming** is a very useful strategy. When you skim, you glance quickly over the text looking for key words or specific information. Once you spot your key words, you begin reading.

During Reading

You've already previewed the sample questions. Now read them again word by word. To answer questions correctly, you have to read them carefully.

PLAN FOR READING QUESTIONS

1. *Read the question carefully.*

2. *Ask, "What is this question asking me to do?" Fact questions ask for information that's in the text. Critical thinking questions ask you to combine information from the text with what you know already.*

3. *Ask, "What information do I need to answer this question?"*

4. *Note the key words in the question and circle them. To find the answer, skim the material the question is based on, looking for the same key words. Once you find the key words, read the sentences around these key words carefully. Try to read at least one sentence before and one sentence after the key words.*

Answering Fact Questions

Now try this plan and strategy on some specific questions. Read the question. Then break it down until you know what it is asking you to find.

Question 1

> 1. **FOCUS** What are the major landforms of the United States?

◄ STEPS FOR QUESTION 1

1. *Read the question.*

2. *What is the question asking?*   to name the major U.S. landforms

3. *Information needed?*   names of landforms (facts)

4. *Key words?*   major landforms

To answer the question, skim the textbook chapter looking for the key words *major landforms*. Look first at the chapter title and introduction:

"Landforms of the United States"

Next, look at the main headings:

"The Desert" "The Mountains" "The Plains"

By looking only at them, you have found the right answer.

Textbooks

Question 2

Now read the next question. Think about how to answer it.

> 2. **GEOGRAPHY** Describe the climate of the
>   deserts of the Southwest.

Use the same steps to break down what it is asking you
to find. Circle or highlight the key words as shown above.

STEPS FOR QUESTION 2

1. *Read the question.*	
2. *What is the question asking?*	to describe climate of the Southwest's deserts
3. *Information needed?*	climate description
4. *Key words*	climate, deserts, Southwest

To answer the question, skim the lesson looking for the three
key highlighted words. If you did that, you would zero in
on this paragraph in the text under the heading "The Desert."

NOTE
Key words

> The desert is a place with a dry and often very hot
> climate. The climate is the type of weather, including
> temperature, rainfall, and wind, that is most common for
> an area. The climate of the desert is so dry that sometimes
> months go by without a single drop of rain falling. Few
> plants or animals can live in the desert. Deserts cover
> much of the southwestern United States.

NOTE
**Information
to use in
answer**

By reading the sentences in and around the key
words from the question, you can easily find the
answer. This is a fact question, so you can find the answer
"right there" in the text. The climate is dry and hot, with
very little rain falling.

Answering Critical Thinking Questions

Now try your plan and strategy on a critical thinking question.

Question 3

For this type of question, you combine information from the text with what you already know. Read through this sample critical thinking question.

> 3. **CONNECT** Look at the landforms in the pictures on page 12–13. Which areas might have been easier for early European ethnic groups to settle?

STEPS FOR QUESTION 3

1. *Read the question.*

2. *What is the question asking?*   to identify landforms and which are easiest to settle

3. *Information needed?*   information about landforms

4. *Key words?*   landforms, easier, settle

Once you're sure you understand the question, you need to find the landform pictures. Look at them carefully, and don't forget to read the captions.

▲ The Rocky Mountains, pictured above, are over 3,000 miles long. This mountain range is just one of many landforms in the United States.

▲ In the Plains, crops like corn, wheat, and soybeans spread for miles on the flat, treeless land.

To answer this question, you need to find information in the pictures and make a decision about it. In other words, you put the information you find with what you already know.

CRITICAL THINKING QUESTIONS

What I Learn + What I Already Know

The pictures in the book show a mountain range and the plains. You know mountains are rocky and hard to travel across. You also may know that the plains are flat lands where many crops grow. Which of these sounds like it would be easiest to live in?

This is where what you know comes in. If you are like most people, you would say the wide, open spaces of plains would be easiest to live in. They are easy to travel, and they make good farmland. Not only can you answer the question, but you can also give two good reasons why you think your answer is right.

After Reading

After answering a group of questions, stop to reflect. Review both the questions and your answers.

Here are some tips for checking your answers:

- Be sure your answer is clear and easy to read.
- Be sure your answer matches what's found in the text. Fix any mistakes in spelling, capitalization, or punctuation.
- Be sure you answered the question. Sometimes you need to read the question again to be sure you've included all the necessary information.

Textbooks

Summing Up

- **Remember to read the question carefully and the material on which it is based.**
- **Look for key words in questions. Then, skim to find the key words and read a few sentences around them.**
- **Look for the answers to fact questions "right in the text." For critical thinking questions, combine what you learn in the text with what you already know.**

Elements of Textbooks

You spend a lot of time in school with textbooks, so it's good to know what they offer.

Like the parts of a bicycle, each part of a textbook has a specific purpose. A glossary collects key terms for you. Illustrations and photos make information easier to understand. Headings highlight the main ideas. The index helps you to find things fast. Each element has a part in helping you learn.

Here's an overview of common elements in textbooks.

Elements of Textbooks

Glossary

Most textbooks have a glossary at the back of the book. A glossary lists key terms and their definitions.

EXAMPLE

Glossary

A **acid rain** (AS ihd rayn) rain that carries certain kinds of pollution (p. 396).

adapt (uh DAPT) to change in order to survive in a new environment (p. 19).

aeronautics (air uh NAW tihks) the science of building and operating aircraft (p. 247).

aerospace (AIR oh spays) a word used to describe businesses that make airplanes (p. 337).

agribusiness (AG ruh bihz nihs) a large company that raises and sells agricultural products (p. 298).

amendment (uh MEHND muhnt) a change made to the Constitution. (p. 122).

aquifer (AK wuh fur) a huge underground collection of water (p. 261).

archaeology (ahr kee AHL uh jee) the study of artifacts to learn how early people lived (p. 268).

architecture (AHR kih ek chur) the art of designing buildings (p. 306).

artifact (AHR tuh fakt) something that people from the past made, used, and left behind (p. 268).

assembly line (uh SEHM blee lyn) a method of manufacturing goods in which the thing being made moves from worker to worker and everyone does one job. (p. 107).

astronaut (AHS truh nawt) a person who is specially trained to travel in space (p. 247).

blizzard (BLIHZ urd) a storm with heavy snowfall and high winds (p. 145).

bluegrass (BLOO gras) music with roots in English, Irish, and Scottish fiddle music (p. 235).

blues (blooz) slow, often sad songs (p. 232).

border (BAWR dur) the line that divides one country, state, or region from another (p. 58).

boundary (BOUN duh ree) a line that marks the border of a country, state, or region (p. 56).

C **canal** (kuh NAL) a waterway made by people (p. 152).

capital (KAP ih tl) a city where a state or country's government is located (p. 153).

cash crop (kash krahp) a crop that a farmer grows only to sell (p. 366).

chamber of commerce (CHAYM bur uhv KOM urs) a group of business people who work together to make their companies more successful (p. 351).

citizen (SIHT ih zun) a person who has the same rights as everyone else in their country (p. 123).

civil war (SIHV uhl wawr) a war fought between two groups or regions of a nation (p. 214).

clear-cutting (klyr KUT ing) cutting down all the trees in one area of a forest (p. 362).

climate (KLY miht) the usual pattern of weather

Key word

Definition

Pronunciation

DESCRIPTION

To make terms easy to look up, the **glossary** lists the key terms in alphabetical order. Each key word is defined, and sometimes a glossary includes a pronunciation for each word. Use the glossary to look up key terms in your textbooks. Knowing the meaning of the words in the glossary will help you better learn and understand the subject.

DEFINITION

A **glossary** is an alphabetical listing of key words from the book, along with pages where the words appear.

Headings and Titles

Headings and titles are the "headlines" of a textbook. They appear in large or brightly colored type at the beginning of units, chapters, lessons, and subheadings within the lessons.

EXAMPLE

DESCRIPTION

Headings of a textbook usually outline the content. The size of a heading shows its importance. A big idea becomes a big heading. The first big heading is usually called the **title.** Chapter headings are bigger than lesson headings. Lesson headings are bigger than the subheadings. Inside a chapter, the headings list the main ideas and outline the content. You can use the headings to help you take notes.

DEFINITION

Headings and titles name the units, chapters, lessons, and parts within lessons. They are generally printed in large, bold type to make them stand out.

Illustrations and Photos

Illustrations and photos give information in the form of a picture or drawing. They add color and brightness, but they also help "tell the story." Illustrations and photos work with the words and headings of a textbook to help teach the material.

EXAMPLE

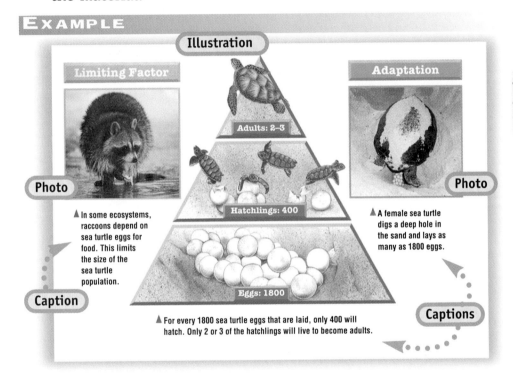

Illustration

Limiting Factor

Adaptation

Photo

Photo

Adults: 2–3

Hatchlings: 400

Eggs: 1800

▲ In some ecosystems, raccoons depend on sea turtle eggs for food. This limits the size of the sea turtle population.

▲ A female sea turtle digs a deep hole in the sand and lays as many as 1800 eggs.

Caption

Captions

▲ For every 1800 sea turtle eggs that are laid, only 400 will hatch. Only 2 or 3 of the hatchlings will live to become adults.

Textbooks

DESCRIPTION

A textbook's **illustrations and photos** provide information and add visual interest to the book. They give you a quick way to preview the material. They also can show enlarged views of items that you can't easily see any other way. The *captions* (text) with illustrations and photos usually explain the content or purpose of the illustration.

DEFINITION

Illustrations and photos show information in a visual way.

Index

Most textbooks include an index at the back of the book. The index helps you find information.

EXAMPLE

Index entry

Index subentry

Page numbers

A Abu Simbel, temple of, *p73*
Acadia, Canada, 212–213
   Acid rain, 396, *c396–c397*,
   396–397
Adaptation to environment, 19, 263,
   326–327
Adopt-a-Stream Program, *p397*
Aerospace industry, 337
Africa
   cultural influences on U.S., 86, 221,
   231, 232, 243
   droughts, 433
   enslavement, 84, 151, 212
African-Americans
   civil rights, *c123*, 130
   enslavement, 84, 151, 212
   equal opportunity, 88–89, 117
   heritage, 231, 232–233, 234, 243
   jobs, 291
   Great Migration, 100
   segregation, 88, 117

Andes, the, 418, 419
Andrews, John, 381, 382, *p382*, 385
Andropov, Yuri, 125
Angel Island, California, 85, 348
Anglin, Erin, 340–341
Antarctic Treaty, 449
Antarctica, 29, 419, 448–449, *m449*,
   m475. *See also* South Pole.
Anthony, Susan B., *p113*, 123
Appalachian Highlands, 63
Appalachian Mountains, 34, *m38*, 39,
   m41, 55, *m62*, *m63*, 144, 180, 200,
   212, 260, 399, 408
Appleseed, Johnny. *See* Chapman, John
Aquifer, 261
Arabic alphabet, 69, *m69*
Arcata Marsh and Wildlife Sanctuary, 398
Archaeology, 268
Arches National Park, 37, *p37*
Architecture, 306–311, *p307*, *c309*, *p310*,
   p311, 312

DESCRIPTION

The **index** is an alphabetical listing of the key names, terms, events, and topics in the textbook. Sometimes a main topic will include listings of subtopics. Each index entry includes one or more page numbers where you'll find information on that topic. Use the page numbers to help you find pages that refer to the topic you looked up. Think of the index as a way to help you find things in the textbook.

DEFINITION

An **index** is an alphabetical list of words with page numbers that show where names, terms, events, and topics appear in the book.

Maps

Maps often appear in social studies, literature, and science textbooks, giving all kinds of information.

EXAMPLE

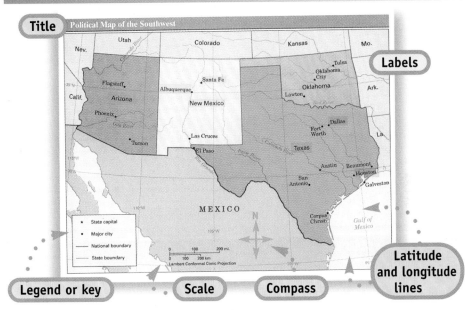

Title

Political Map of the Southwest

Labels

Legend or key

Scale

Compass

Latitude and longitude lines

DESCRIPTION

There are many different types of **maps**, all with different types of information. *Physical maps* show the earth's features, such as mountain ranges and rivers. *Political maps* may show these features but also will show locations of political units, such as countries, cities, and towns. Every map has certain main parts. The *map title* tells you the map's subject. The *map legend*, or key, tells you what the map's symbols or colors mean. The *map's scale* shows you how to measure distances on the map. The *latitude* and *longitude* lines show north-south and east-west location.

DEFINITION

Maps are reduced drawings of the whole world or part of the world. They present information in visual form.

Previews

Most textbooks have previews at the beginning of a unit or chapter. The purpose of these preview pages is to prepare you for the pages ahead.

EXAMPLE

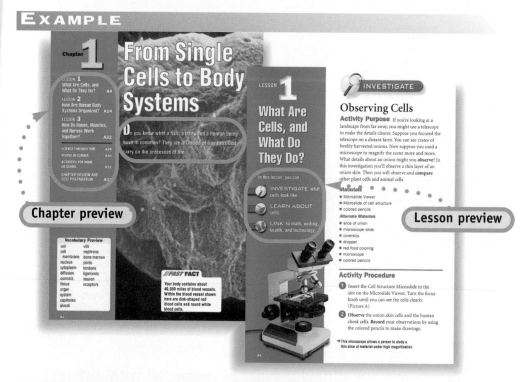

Chapter preview

Lesson preview

DESCRIPTION

You'll find **previews** at the beginnings of textbook units and chapters. Previews introduce the major points of the unit, chapter, or lesson and ask the key questions that you will read about. Previews often appear as short text paragraphs. They may also be lists of key terms, questions, outlines, or even photos or diagrams. Some previews combine all of these things.

DEFINITION

A **preview** is an opening part of a book, unit, chapter, or lesson that summarizes the material to come. Its purpose is to help you look ahead to plan your reading.

Study Questions

Study questions appear throughout textbook units, chapters, and lessons.

EXAMPLE

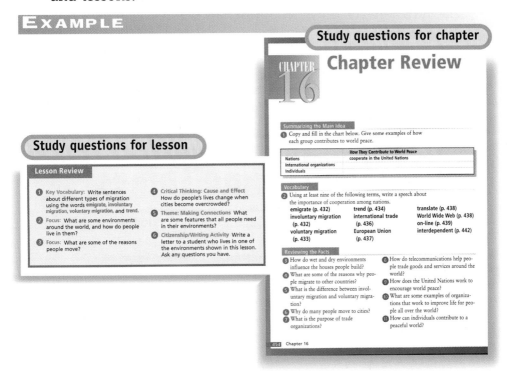

Study questions for chapter

CHAPTER 16

Chapter Review

Summarizing the Main Idea
1 Copy and fill in the chart below. Give some examples of how each group contributes to world peace.

	How They Contribute to World Peace
Nations	cooperate in the United Nations
International organizations	
Individuals	

Study questions for lesson

Lesson Review

1 Key Vocabulary: Write sentences about different types of migration using the words emigrate, involuntary migration, voluntary migration, and trend.

2 Focus: What are some environments around the world, and how do people live in them?

3 Focus: What are some of the reasons people move?

4 Critical Thinking: Cause and Effect How do people's lives change when cities become overcrowded?

5 Theme: Making Connections What are some features that all people need in their environments?

6 Citizenship/Writing Activity Write a letter to a student who lives in one of the environments shown in this lesson. Ask any questions you have.

Vocabulary
2 Using at least nine of the following terms, write a speech about the importance of cooperation among nations.

emigrate (p. 432)
involuntary migration (p. 432)
voluntary migration (p. 433)
trend (p. 434)
international trade (p. 436)
European Union (p. 437)
translate (p. 438)
World Wide Web (p. 438)
on-line (p. 439)
interdependent (p. 442)

Reviewing the Facts
3 How do wet and dry environments influence the houses people build?
4 What are some of the reasons why people migrate to other countries?
5 What is the difference between involuntary migration and voluntary migration?
6 Why do many people move to cities?
7 What is the purpose of trade organizations?
8 How do telecommunications help people trade goods and services around the world?
9 How does the United Nations work to encourage world peace?
10 What are some examples of organizations that work to improve life for people all over the world?
11 How can individuals contribute to a peaceful world?

454 Chapter 16

Textbooks

DESCRIPTION

Study questions appear at the ends of lessons, chapters, and units. Usually you will find two kinds of questions:

● ones that ask you to recall the facts

● ones that ask you to draw conclusions, apply what you've learned, and use other critical thinking skills

Use study questions to guide you in reviewing and thinking about the material.

DEFINITION

Study questions appear at the end of a lesson, chapter, or unit to help you to recall facts, apply the material, and think critically about what you've read.

Table of Contents

The table of contents is like a map of your textbook. It presents an outline, or overview, of the book. It also gives page numbers for units, chapters, and lessons, telling you where to find everything.

EXAMPLE

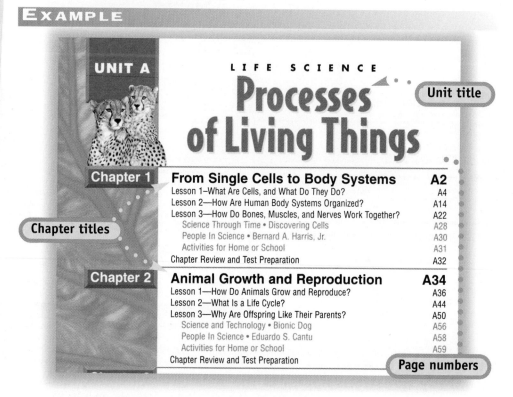

UNIT A

LIFE SCIENCE

Processes of Living Things

Unit title

Chapter titles

Page numbers

DESCRIPTION

A **table of contents** outlines the main topics in the textbook. The unit titles announce the big ideas or main points. Under units come smaller sections, such as chapters and then lessons. Also listed are special features, reviews, and tests.

DEFINITION

A **table of contents** lists the major parts of a book along with their page numbers. Use it to help you locate things in the book and see how everything is organized.

Text (Plain, Boldface, and Italics)

The text in a book is the single largest element. Different kinds of text styles are used to send different signals about the content.

DESCRIPTION

EXAMPLE

Most of the text in a textbook (like this sentence) is printed in plain type. Words or phrases that the authors wish to emphasize are printed in **boldface type** or in *italic type*. **Boldface terms** are words printed in heavy or darker type or in color. Boldface usually signals key words. Type printed in *italics* often is used in picture captions and for book titles and other elements that need to stand out.

Textbooks

LESSON 3

Wetlands: A Resource

Main Idea Wetlands are an important part of the natural environment.

Plain text

Y our boat slides quietly through the coffee-colored water of the swamp. Cypress trees grow crowded together along the water's edge. Their branches block most of the sunlight. Their roots stick up out of the water like bent knees. It's so quiet that you think you must be the only one around.

Suddenly you hear a rustle. A white and black bird that's taller than you rises from the grass with a fish in its mouth. It's a wood stork, and it has just caught its dinner in the Okefenokee National Wildlife Refuge in Georgia.

Key Vocabulary
wetlands
ground water
endangered species

Key Places
Okefenokee Swamp
Everglades

Italic text

The Wetlands of the South

Lily pads float around the base of cypress trees in Okefenokee Swamp, at the beginning of the Suwannee River.

Focus *Why are the South's wetlands so important?*
The Okefenokee (oh kuh fuh NOH kee) Swamp is a large wetland in the South. A wetland is a place where the ground is soaked with water for at least part of the year. Swamps, marshes, and bogs are types of wetlands.

Wetlands are usually near lakes, rivers, or the ocean. Water from the Okefenokee Swamp, for example, flows into the St. Marys and Suwannee (suh WAH nee) rivers. Water in the Everglades, a large wetland in Florida, comes from Lake Okeechobee. From the Everglades, water flows into the Gulf of Mexico and Florida Bay.

Wetlands act like a gigantic sponge. They absorb water that falls as rain. This water then trickles underground and helps keep up the supply of ground water. Ground water is water beneath

Boldface text

DEFINITION

The text in a textbook can be styled as plain, boldface, or italic type. The style and color of type sends you signals about how you read the content.

Reading
Nonfiction

Reading Kinds of Nonfiction

Reading a Magazine Article
Reading a News Story

Ways of Reading Nonfiction

Focus on Personal Essays
Focus on Persuasive Writing
Focus on Biography
Focus on Real-world Writing

Elements of Nonfiction

Reading a **Magazine Article**

Whatever you like to read about—from sports to nature to music to famous people—there's sure to be a magazine about it. Most magazines try to catch your eye and excite your interest as you flip through the pages. Magazines use interesting titles, photos, and special features to pull you in and get you reading.

Goals

Here you'll learn how to:

✔ recognize the basic parts of **magazine articles**

✔ use the reading strategy of **questioning the author**

✔ understand the **organization of magazine articles**

Before Reading

You read magazines in different ways, depending upon your purpose. Sometimes you're reading just for fun. In that case, you can zip through an article. Other times, you want to learn something from what you're reading. In that case, you read at a slower pace and use the reading process.

A Set a Purpose

Most of the time your purpose for reading a magazine article is simple and direct. Here you'll read an article about oil drilling in Alaska called "Alaska: The Lost Frontier?" You can use the title to help set your reading purpose.

Setting a Purpose

■ **What do I need to know about Alaska, the lost frontier?**

■ **Why is this important?**

B Preview

To get an overview of what's in an article, preview it using the Preview Checklist below. Look for:

Preview Checklist

✔ the title and any headings

✔ the first and last paragraphs

✔ any photos, captions, or other special features

✔ any words repeated or in bold

Nonfiction

PREVIEW
Title

ALASKA
THE LOST FRONTIER?

The U.S. is the most oil-hungry country on Earth. Is Alaska paying too high a price to feed that hunger?

by Alexandra Hanson-Harding

PREVIEW
Photo

PREVIEW
First paragraph

Alaska's North Slope may not look like much. It is a vast, seemingly empty stretch of tundra far above the Arctic Circle. But this frozen land, which stretches from the Brooks mountain range to the Arctic Ocean (*see map*), has hidden riches.

It is home to polar bears, huge herds of caribou, and other wildlife. It is also home to the largest oil field in the U.S.

Alaska has been called America's Last Frontier. Now some people fear that oil drilling and development will turn it into a *lost* frontier.

Big Money

PREVIEW
Heading

In the 1960s, a huge underground oil reservoir was discovered beneath the North Slope's Prudhoe Bay. Since the 1970s, companies that include BP Amoco and Arco have been pumping billions of barrels of oil from there.

The oil has brought many benefits to Alaskans—and not just to those who work for the oil companies. Because of oil revenues, Alaskans do not pay state income or sales taxes. In addition, each Alaskan shares in the oil profits from a special account called the Alaska Permanent Fund. This year, the payout was more than $1,500 per person.

Alaskans aren't the only Americans who benefit from the oil. People in the lower 48 states use it for heating, energy, and transportation. As BP Amoco representative Ronnie Chappell told *JS*, "Oil is a wonderful product. It's how we keep our homes warm, how we get our children to school. It's why we have bananas at an affordable price."

Chappell points out that a lack of affordable oil last winter caused a great hardship for people in the Northeast. Now, the price of gasoline is at a record high throughout the U.S. Affordable sources of oil, most people agree, are essential.

The Hunt for New Oil

Oil production at Prudhoe Bay reached its peak in the 1980s. Since then, there has been a slow decline. Now, oil companies are looking for other oil deposits in the North Slope.

One place they have been looking is in the National Petroleum Reserves-Alaska. In 1923, the federal government set aside this Indiana-sized area of potentially oil-rich land in case of emergency. For many years it wasn't used. But this past winter, the U.S. government allowed oil companies to begin exploratory drilling there.

Many environmentalists are worried. They say that drilling for oil will harm wildlife. Environmentalists are even more upset about plans to drill for oil on the coastal plain of the Alaska National Wildlife Refuge (ANWR).

The coastal plain is the "biological heart" of the Refuge—home to many plant and animal species. Critics say drilling could cause a host of problems—from oil spills to pollution to destruction of wildlife habitats.

Nonfiction

PREVIEW
Repeated words

PREVIEW
Heading

Native people and some scientists fear that oil drilling will kill off or force the caribou to change their migration paths. These people depend on the caribou for food and clothing.

Bob King, a spokesman for Alaska's Governor Tony Knowles, doesn't think that oil drilling will harm wildlife. As he told *JS,* "Technological improvements over the years have really reduced the **footprint** (effects) of development on the Arctic. A lot is taking place without affecting the tundra."

PREVIEW

Word in bold

Oil Disaster

What damage could an oil spill do? Eleven years ago, Alaskans found out when the oil tanker *Exxon Valdez* crashed, spilling nearly 11 million gallons of oil into Prince William Sound. The world watched, horrified, as thousands of oil-soaked seabirds and other forms of wildlife died.

It was an expensive mistake for Exxon, which had to pay more than $900 million in fines and clean up costs. Today, 11 years later, species like the common loon, the harbor seal, and the killer whale still have not completely recovered.

PREVIEW

Headings

New Danger Offshore?

Recently, a group of Greenpeace activists set up camp on Alaska's Arctic Ocean. They went there to observe a new BP Amoco oil-drilling project called Northstar.

PREVIEW

Repeated word

Greenpeace claims that Northstar is unsafe. "The reason we're focusing on Northstar," says Dr. Iain MacGill, a Greenpeace spokesman, "is that it is the first freestanding offshore oil project on the Arctic Ocean, and what [BP Amoco] is attempting to do is opening up a new frontier, the offshore frontier."

According to MacGill, Greenpeace is particularly concerned about a six-mile-long underground pipeline that Northstar will use to bring oil to the Alaskan mainland. If it leaks, he says, it could be a disaster because clean-up would be difficult.

"This is part of the larger Greenpeace campaign against new oil," MacGill says. "We don't say we can stop using oil today. Our society's built on it. But we can start making the transition away from oil. We already have more oil than we can safely use, if we're going to protect the climate."

Spending $500 million on Northstar, says MacGill, means "you don't spend [enough] on things like solar energy."

Dependence on oil seems to hurt the Arctic environment. According to satellite data, global warming has caused parts of the Arctic to heat up three to five times faster than other areas. This, in turn, causes the ice to thin and changes the natural habitat for creatures like polar bears. It also has harmful effects on the vast Arctic forests.

What for the Future?

BP Amoco's Ronnie Chappell agrees that global warming is harming the Arctic. "We understand that global warming is a problem . . . [and that] there are indications that the use of fossil fuel is a contributing factor."

That's why, he says, BP Amoco is one of the largest manufacturers of solar panels in the world—and one of the largest users. Still, he says, the company needs to provide customers with the fuel they need—"and [at this time] there is no substitute for the product we make."

Greenpeace says oil companies could do much more to develop solar and other forms of energy. Greenpeace also says that instead of drilling for new oil, we should waste less of this precious substance.

Steve Sawyer of Greenpeace told *JS*, "The problem is not production, it's consumption. [We need to] move away from fossil fuels. We don't have enough oil to do that. We waste more energy than anywhere else on the planet."

All Americans can help to make sure that we don't run

PREVIEW
Repeated words

PREVIEW
Heading

Nonfiction

133

out of oil—by conserving energy and not wasting it. We can turn off unneeded lights, turn down the thermostat in winter, and avoid unnecessary car trips.

Until now, much of Alaska's environment has survived relatively unharmed. But it may be our last chance to preserve one of the world's most untouched and beautiful places.

PREVIEW

Last paragraph

ARCTIC OCEAN

RUSSIA

NATIONAL PETROLEUM RESERVE — Barrow

Beaufort Sea

Prudhoe Bay

GATES OF THE ARCTIC NATIONAL PARK AND PRESERVE

Arctic Circle

Trans-Alaska pipeline

ARCTIC NATIONAL WILDLIFE REFUGE

Bering Sea

Fairbanks

ALASKA (U.S.)

CANADA

Anchorage

Area affected by Exxon Valdez oil spill

Valdez

Prince William Sound

Juneau

ALEUTIAN ISLANDS

KODIAK ISLAND

N
W——E
S

Plan

What did you learn in your preview?

- The article is about oil drilling in Alaska.
- It gives a lot of facts about oil drilling, global warming, and saving wildlife.

Now think about your reading purpose. You're after information about Alaska, but you also want to know *why* the author wrote this article.

Reading Strategy: Questioning the Author

Try the strategy of **questioning the author.** When you
question the author, you think about decisions the author
made when he or she was writing. As you read, you might
ask yourself questions like these:

*Why did the author
include these photos
and features?*

*Why did the author
include these details?*

*What am I supposed to
conclude from reading this?*

*What point is the
author trying to make?*

Nonfiction

You need to make inferences and
draw conclusions as you
read. The author probably
gave you enough information in the article so that you can
infer answers to these questions.

During Reading

Now you are ready to read the magazine article.

D Read with a Purpose

Open your reading journal and keep it next to you. As you
go back and read, write the questions that come to you in
the left-hand column. Write the answers to those questions
on the right-hand side of your journal. This is the beginning
of an Inference Chart.

Try to come up with at least one question for the author
for each page of the magazine article. On the next page
are questions one reader wrote for the first part of "Alaska:
The Lost Frontier?"

QUESTIONS	MY CONCLUSIONS
page 1 Why does the article start out with a picture of caribou and geese near an oil pipeline?	
page 2 Why does the article mention drilling on the Alaska Wildlife Refuge?	
page 3 Why does the article include so many facts? Why is global warming brought up?	

Coming up with several questions—and trying to answer them—will help you make sense of what the author is saying.

Making Inferences

As a reader, you often have to figure things out for yourself. You have to put "two and two together." Or, to put it another way, you have to "read between the lines." Both expressions mean that you have to take what you learn in your reading and combine it with what you already know.

What I learn from reading	+	*What I already know*	=	*What I infer*

When you do that, you make an inference. An Inference Chart like the one on the next page helps you focus on specific parts of a reading and make inferences about them.

INFERENCE CHART

QUESTIONS	WHAT I CONCLUDE
Why does the article start out with a picture of caribou and geese near an oil pipeline?	The photo shows people need oil, but animals also need a place to live in Alaska. The scene looks scary. It makes me feel worried for the animals. The photo really grabs my attention.

By thinking through questions as you read, you can get more from the article and understand it better.

Drawing Conclusions

When you question an author, often you need to look closely at the text to find the answers. For example, let's say you want to know why the article mentioned drilling on the Alaska National Wildlife Refuge. Find the part where the Alaska National Wildlife Refuge was mentioned and read it carefully. Why did the author include these facts?

Nonfiction

from "Alaska: The Lost Frontier?"

Many environmentalists are worried. They say that drilling for oil will harm wildlife. Environmentalists are even more upset about plans to drill for oil on the coastal plain of the Alaska National Wildlife Refuge (ANWR).

The coastal plain is the "biological heart" of the Refuge—home to many plant and animal species. Critics say drilling could cause a host of problems—from oil spills to pollution to destruction of wildlife habitats.

NOTE
Key words

The author brought up oil drilling on the Refuge to emphasize the possible dangers to plants and animals.

Evaluating

As you read, you evaluate what you read and make judgments. You decide whether or not you like the article, whether you believe what the author is saying or not, and whether you want to continue reading more or just stop. For instance, let's say you notice all the different facts and statistics the author of "Alaska: The Lost Frontier?" includes. What's your judgment of all of the information?

If you're like most readers, you probably are impressed by the specific information in the article. Use a Double-entry Journal to help you evaluate important parts of a text. Write the quotations in the first column. Next, write your thoughts about them in the second column.

DOUBLE-ENTRY JOURNAL

QUOTES	MY THOUGHTS
"Because of oil revenues, Alaskans do not pay state income or sales taxes. In addition, each Alaskan shares in the oil profits from a special account called the Alaska Permanent Fund."	I never thought about how important oil must be to the people in Alaska. The author seems to know a lot about the issues.
"Many environmentalists are worried. They say that drilling for oil will harm wildlife."	The words "worried" and "harm" make me side with the environmentalists.

How Magazine Articles Are Organized

Like most writing, magazine articles do not follow one neat set of rules. They can be organized in all kinds of ways. One clue to the way writing is organized is the headings.

What did you notice when you previewed the headings in the article about Alaska?

- Big Money
- The Hunt for New Oil
- Oil Disaster
- New Danger Offshore?
- What for the Future?

Nonfiction

These headings all are different topics. Once you see that they're topics, you can tell how the article is organized. Then use reading tools that help you keep track of the topics and understand the article more easily.

Topic Order

As you read, get in the habit of paying attention to headings. Use note-taking tools such as a simple Web or a more detailed Thinking Tree to help you keep track of the different topics. Here are examples of them.

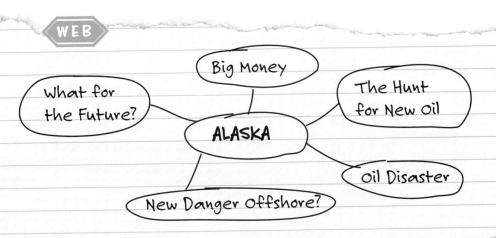

WEB

Big Money
What for the Future?
The Hunt for New Oil
ALASKA
Oil Disaster
New Danger Offshore?

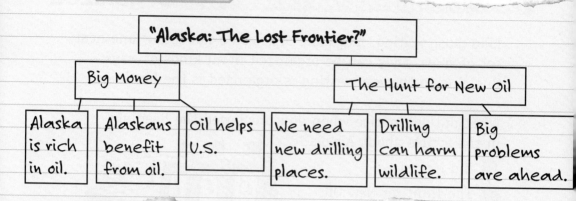

When taking notes with a Thinking Tree, first list the title. Each time you come to a new heading, start a branch for it. Try to write 2 to 3 things under each heading. The example above shows a Thinking Tree for the first two headings.

E Connect

As you read a magazine article, be sure to pay attention to your own feelings and reactions. For example, here is the way one reader connected with the article.

from "Alaska: The Lost Frontier?"

My dad turns off lights when we visit my grandparents' house.

All Americans can help to make sure that we don't run out of oil—by conserving energy and not wasting it. We can turn off unneeded lights, turn down the thermostat in winter, and avoid unnecessary car trips.

Until now, much of Alaska's environment has survived relatively unharmed. But it may be our last chance to preserve one of the world's most untouched and beautiful places.

I saw pictures of Alaska on the news. I would love to go there.

After Reading

After reading, stop and consider what you've read. Now is the time to think about all that you've read and to fill in the parts you'd like to know more about.

F Pause and Reflect

Think for a moment about your reading purpose. Do you have answers to these questions?

Looking Back

- What have I learned about this subject?
- Are there parts that I don't understand?
- Why is this subject important?

G Reread

Rereading is always a good idea if you're unclear on any important points or if you have unanswered questions. For example, do you understand why global warming is a problem and why it's hurting Alaska? For example, you might want to do some rereading to answer that question.

Rereading Strategy: Reading Critically

Try using a new reading strategy. When **reading critically,** you look at the evidence that the author uses to support his or her viewpoint. Then, you can decide whether or not the author presents the argument in a fair way.

Critical Reading Chart

You can analyze the information that an author gives in a Critical Reading Chart. This organizer asks key questions about how an author presents and supports an argument.

CRITICAL READING CHART	
1. IS THE MAIN IDEA OR VIEWPOINT CLEAR?	Yes. Oil drilling can hurt Alaska's wildlife and environment. We should develop new types of energy and stop global warming.
2. WHAT EVIDENCE IS PRESENTED?	Facts about oil drilling and views of many people
3. ARE THE SOURCES RELIABLE?	Yes. Oil companies, native people, Greenpeace, and Alaska's governor
4. IS THE EVIDENCE CONVINCING?	Yes. There are lots of facts.
5. IS THERE ANOTHER SIDE TO THE STORY?	The other side is the importance of oil and oil company arguments. That is explained fairly.

Filling out a Critical Reading Chart can help you evaluate what you're reading. It can also help you make sense of a specific detail. For instance, by reading critically you can focus on why the author brings up global warming. The use of so much oil may be making global warming worse. Bringing up the effects of global warming is important to the author because it helps support the idea that we shouldn't do so much oil drilling.

Remember

The key to learning is remembering what you have read. It's easy to remember something when it has meaning in your own life. Here is a way to apply what you learned about "Alaska: The Lost Frontier?"

Find Ways You Can Help

Use the Internet and the library to learn more about global warming, its causes and effects. Write a short journal entry about what you learn, including a list of four or five ways that you can help slow global warming.

Summing Up

Whenever you read a magazine article, remember to use the reading process and apply the reading strategy of **questioning the author.** Pay attention to **how magazine articles are organized in topic order** and use tools like these:

- ■ Inference Chart
- ■ Double-entry Journal
- ■ Web
- ■ Thinking Tree
- ■ Critical Reading Chart

The rereading strategy of **reading critically** will help you to evaluate the author's evidence.

Nonfiction

Reading a News Story

"Who won the basketball game last night?" "Did you read about the tornado?" When you want up-to-the-minute news, you read a news story.

News stories tell you what's going on in your town or city and all around the globe. You'll find news stories in newspapers, in magazines, and on the Internet. They can give you information to help with class assignments, or they can help you to form opinions and make decisions.

Goals

Here you'll learn how to:

✔ recognize the major parts of a **news story**

✔ use the reading strategy of **summarizing**

✔ understand the **organization of news stories**

Before Reading

Every day, newspapers, magazines, and the Internet offer a lot of news stories. People don't read all of them. They quickly scan the headlines to find stories that interest them. Then they read these stories in detail.

A Set a Purpose

When reading news, you mainly want to get facts. Here, for example, are some possible reasons for reading the sample news story "Earthquake Disaster."

Setting a Purpose

■ **What is the "Earthquake Disaster"?**

■ **What are the main facts about it?**

Nonfiction

B Preview

Luckily for you, news stories are easy to preview. They're built to give you information fast. The Preview Checklist below tells you where to look in the story for information. Use it to preview the news story "Earthquake Disaster."

Preview Checklist

✔ the headline (title) and author
✔ the opening paragraphs, or "lead"
✔ any headings or repeated words
✔ any photos and captions, maps, charts, tables, or diagrams

Earthquake Disaster

Soldiers search through rubble for survivors as a man grieves.

ARCTIC OCEAN

GORDA PLATE

EURASIAN PLATE

ASIA

PACIFIC PLATE

PHILIPPINE PLATE

CAROLINE PLATE

FIJI PLATE

Major earthquake zone

Plate boundary

AUSTRALIA

INDO-AUSTRALIAN PLATE

PACIFIC OCEAN

ANTARCTICA

Thousands of people were trapped under the rubble of their homes when a disastrous earthquake struck India on January 26. The quake, which killed more than 18,000 people, is the worst to hit that country in 50 years.

The quake registered 7.9 on the Richter (RICK-ter) scale, a 10-point number system that measures the force of earthquakes. Any quake over 6.0 can cause great damage, especially if it hits near a city.

Relief teams dug through the rubble to find survivors. Now, the need is for tents to temporarily house people who lost their homes.

Where will the next quake strike? Unlike hurricanes, floods, and some other natural disasters, scientists have not found a way to predict when and where an earthquake will strike.

When Plates Go Bump

What causes earthquakes? Scientists have developed a theory called *plate tectonics* to explain why most earthquakes occur. The theory says that the Earth's crust, or outer surface, consists of about 10 large, rigid plates and 20 smaller ones.

These plates are in constant motion. They move slower

"Earthquake Disaster," continued

Nonfiction

PREVIEW

Map

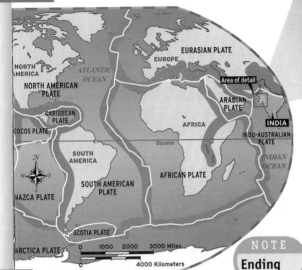

PAKISTAN
0   200 Miles

⦿ Town affected
   by the quake

Hyderabad
Badin
EPICENTER   I N D I A

Bhuj Surendranagar
Gulf of Kutch   Rajkot
Arabian Sea   Surat

Area of detail

EURASIAN PLATE
EUROPE

NORTH AMERICA
ATLANTIC OCEAN

NORTH AMERICAN PLATE

CARIBBEAN PLATE
COCOS PLATE

ARABIAN PLATE

AFRICA   INDIA

INDO-AUSTRALIAN PLATE

Equator   INDIAN OCEAN

SOUTH AMERICA

AFRICAN PLATE

SOUTH AMERICAN PLATE

NAZCA PLATE

SCOTIA PLATE

ARCTICA PLATE   0   1000   2000   3000 Miles

4000 Kilometers

NOTE

Ending

PREVIEW

Repeated words

than molasses, but when they bump into each other, watch out!

Most quakes occur when two or more moving plates get stuck together. Pressure builds up as the plates try to move but cannot. When they finally shift, they release a huge amount of energy in the form of earthquakes.

Most earthquakes occur along the boundaries of these massive plates. The world map shows the plates' boundaries and major earthquake zones. The inset map shows the location of the recent quake in India.

Questions

Study the maps and table to answer the following questions.

1. The January 26 earthquake in India was east of what city on the map?
_____

2. The quake was near India's border with what country?
_____

3. The quake was the worst to strike India in how many years?
_____

4. The quake occurred near the junction of which three plates?
_____
_____

5. On which plate is the U.S.?

6. Which coast of North America is more likely to be hit by a quake?

7. The North American plate meets the African and Eurasian plates under which body of water?

8. Where did the most deadly quake since 1985 strike?
_____

9. Where did the most powerful quake since 1985 strike?

10. Where will the next big quake hit?
_____

India, 2001

DEADLIEST QUAKES	1985-2001		
YEAR	LOCATION	DEATHS	SIZE*
1985	Mexico	9,500	8.1
1988	Armenia	55,000	7.0
1990	Iran	40,000+	7.7
1993	India	9,748	6.3
1995	Japan	5,500	6.9
1998	Afghanistan	4,700	6.9
1999	Turkey	17,200	7.4
2001	India	18,000+	7.9

*Measured on the Richter scale.

MARCH 12, 2001

PREVIEW

Photo and table

Nonfiction

C Plan

Your preview probably gave you information like this:

- An earthquake in India killed more than 18,000 people.
- The article explains the causes of earthquakes.
- A photo shows the scene of the earthquake.
- Earthquakes have something to do with plates.

A plan, or strategy, will help you gain an understanding of the news event or issue.

Reading Strategy: Summarizing

Summarizing means restating the main events or ideas of what you're reading in your own words. You summarize whenever you tell a friend about a news story or report on one in class. To summarize an article, you describe the subject and then create a list of the most important details.

Use a 5 W's and H Organizer like the one below to help pull together key facts from the story.

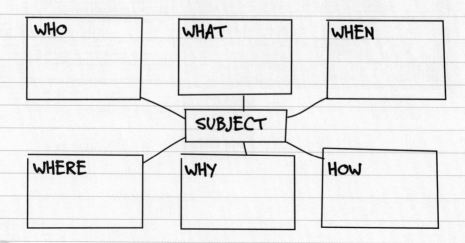

5 W'S AND H ORGANIZER

WHO · WHAT · WHEN · SUBJECT · WHERE · WHY · HOW

During Reading

Now you are ready to read "Earthquake Disaster."

D Read with a Purpose

As you read, take notes on the facts you are looking to find. Try using one of the reading tools below or on the next few pages. These tools can help you summarize a news story.

1. 5 W's and H Organizer

Filling in a 5 W's and H Organizer makes it easy to focus on the key information.

Nonfiction

5 W'S AND H ORGANIZER

WHO
- Thousands were trapped.
- More than 18,000 people died.

WHAT
- An earthquake struck.
- It was 7.9 on the Richter scale.
- It was India's worst quake in 50 years.

WHEN
January 26, 2001

SUBJECT: Earthquakes

WHERE
India

WHY
- Earthquakes are natural disasters.
- Scientists still can't predict when or where they will strike.

HOW
A scientific theory called plate tectonics explains the causes of earthquakes.

2. Web

You might also consider another kind of reading tool, such as a Web. <u>With a Web, you start with the topic and organize supporting information around it.</u> Make your Web as simple or as detailed as you want.

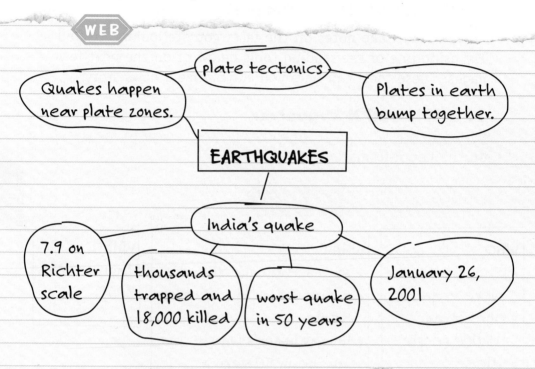

WEB

plate tectonics

Quakes happen near plate zones.

Plates in earth bump together.

EARTHQUAKES

India's quake

7.9 on Richter scale

thousands trapped and 18,000 killed

worst quake in 50 years

January 26, 2001

3. Main Idea Organizer

Another way to summarize the article is with a Main Idea Organizer. With this tool, you pick out the main idea, record the most important supporting details, and state a conclusion.

MAIN IDEA ORGANIZER

TITLE: "Earthquake Disaster"

MAIN IDEA: An earthquake struck India.

DETAIL:	DETAIL:	DETAIL:	DETAIL:
The quake happened on January 26, 2001.	Thousands were trapped, more than 18,000 killed.	It registered 7.9 on the Richter scale.	Scientists use the theory of "plate tectonics" to understand why quakes happen.

CONCLUSION:
This was a very serious earthquake.

Nonfiction

How News Stories Are Organized

Knowing how news stories are organized makes it easier to find key information. Most news stories have the same basic parts. Look back to the story and find each part.

1. **Headline**—the story's title, which tells the subject

2. **Caption and Photo**—information next to a news story photo

3. **Lead**—the story's first paragraph, which sums up the most important information

4. **Body**—the story's middle section, which provides more details

5. **Ending**—the story's conclusion, which may suggest further thought about the subject

1. *Headline*
2. *Caption and Photo*
3. *Lead*
4. *Body*
5. *Ending*

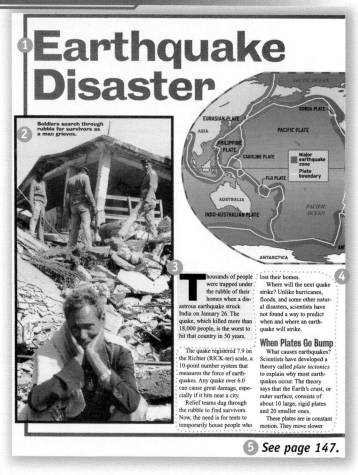

Earthquake Disaster

Soldiers search through rubble for survivors as a man grieves.

Thousands of people were trapped under the rubble of their homes when a disastrous earthquake struck India on January 26. The quake, which killed more than 18,000 people, is the worst to hit that country in 50 years.

The quake registered 7.9 on the Richter (RICK-ter) scale, a 10-point number system that measures the force of earthquakes. Any quake over 6.0 can cause great damage, especially if it hits near a city.

Relief teams dug through the rubble to find survivors. Now, the need is for tents to temporarily house people who lost their homes.

Where will the next quake strike? Unlike hurricanes, floods, and some other natural disasters, scientists have not found a way to predict when and where an earthquake will strike.

When Plates Go Bump

What causes earthquakes? Scientists have developed a theory called *plate tectonics* to explain why most earthquakes occur. The theory says that the Earth's crust, or outer surface, consists of about 10 large, rigid plates and 20 smaller ones.

These plates are in constant motion. They move slower

5. *See page 147.*

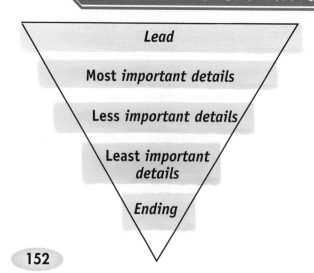

Lead

Most *important* details

Less *important* details

Least *important* details

Ending

You can picture a news story as an upside-down pyramid. The story's most important information is in the **lead,** or first paragraph or two. As you read through the article, the details become less and less important.

E Connect

A big part of reading the news is the personal connection you make with a story. Try to connect with each news story you read. That shouldn't be too hard, given that you picked it out in the first place!

One way to record your reactions to a story is to make notes next to the important parts of the article. Also try asking yourself questions like these:

What else do I know about this place?

What have I heard or read about that's similar?

How would I feel if something like this happened to me?

Nonfiction

Then, make notes of your reactions on sticky notes or mark and underline the article as you read.

from "Earthquake Disaster"

Thousands of people were trapped under the rubble of their homes when a disastrous earthquake struck India on January 26. The quake, which killed more than 18,000 people, is the worst to hit that country in 50 years. *(See article on pp. 12-15.)*

The quake registered 7.9 on the Richter (RICK-ter) scale, a 10-point number system that measures the force of earthquakes. Any quake over 6.0 can cause great damage, especially if it hits near a city.

Relief teams dug through the rubble to find survivors. Now, the need is for tents to temporarily house people who lost their homes.

Where will the next quake strike? Unlike hurricanes, floods, and some other natural disasters, scientists have not found a way to predict when and where an earthquake will strike.

When Plates Go Bump

What causes earthquakes? Scientists have developed a theory called *plate tectonics* to explain why most earthquakes occur. The theory says that the Earth's crust, or outer surface, consists of about 10 large, rigid plates and 20 smaller ones.

These plates are in constant motion. They move slower

This is really scary.

I feel sorry for them!

After Reading

Most people read news stories quickly. Sometimes, you may want to double-check some facts or use the information from the article in some way. As a result, you might want to go back to the article again for rereading.

F Pause and Reflect

After a first reading, think about whether you achieved your original purpose. Ask yourself a couple of questions to help you reflect on what you got out of your reading.

Looking Back

■ **Can I state the main idea in my own words?**

■ **Do I understand how the article is organized?**

■ **Do I know enough key details to answer the *who, what, where, when, why,* and *how* questions?**

G Reread

You may not be clear about some of the facts of the story. That's why it often helps to look back and do some rereading using a new strategy. Another reason is that some news stories don't always report the facts without a slant or bias. They may try to tell you only one side of a story. You often need to return to a news story to read it critically.

Rereading Strategy: Reading Critically

Reading critically means looking beyond the facts and details in a story to their real meaning. As a critical reader, you should:

■ decide whether the facts are accurate

■ evaluate the point that the writer is making

■ consider other points of view

The questions in a Critical Reading Chart guide you in analyzing the facts, opinions, and evidence in nonfiction. Use this kind of chart whenever you want to evaluate the quality of a news story or other reading. Here's how one reader evaluated "Earthquake Disaster."

Nonfiction

CRITICAL READING CHART

QUESTIONS	MY EVALUATION
1. Is the main idea or viewpoint clear?	Yes. The story reports facts on the disaster and explains why earthquakes happen.
2. Is the story well supported by evidence?	Yes. The story gives a lot of facts and statistics.
3. Is the evidence convincing?	Yes, but specific sources are not given for this story. This writer seems good.
4. Is there another side to the story?	No. The article gives only facts on the disaster.

Do you agree with this evaluation? This reader felt that the article reports facts fairly and that it doesn't give an opinion. If you're not sure about the evidence or source, check the story's facts against those in news stories from other sources.

H Remember

Think about the facts and your own reactions to this news story. To help you to remember what you have read, try one of the ideas below.

1. Talk about It

Talk with your friends and family about news events, such as the earthquake in India. Ask them what they know about life in India. What kind of area was struck by this disaster? Talk about the effect that this event will have on people.

2. Email a Friend

Email a friend with information and comments about this disaster. Summarize the article and tell your friend what you learned and how you feel about the event.

Summing Up

When you read a news story, remember to use the reading process and to apply the reading strategy of **summarizing.** Look for the **lead** and the upside-down **pyramid organization.** Then, decide on the kind of graphic organizers that will be helpful, such as:

- 5 W's and H Organizer
- Web
- Main Idea Organizer
- Critical Reading Chart

After reading, use the strategy of **reading critically.** This will help you to determine if the article is reporting the news fairly and without bias.

Focus on Personal Essays

Do you read essays in magazines and newspapers? An **essay** is a short work of nonfiction that focuses on one subject.

Most essays are one of two types: expository or narrative. In an *expository* essay, a writer explains a specific subject, often giving a lot of information. In a *narrative* essay, a writer tells a story about a personal experience, usually expressing an opinion or viewpoint. In this lesson, you'll read a personal essay about a young girl's experience on a school bus.

Goals

Here you'll learn how to:

✔ **determine a writer's purpose**

✔ **read an essay for the main idea and details**

✔ **look at the organization of different kinds of essays**

Nonfiction

SCHOOL BUS

Before Reading

Before reading any essay, it's useful to know a few things about why authors write essays in the first place.

Find the Author's Purpose

Essay writers write to inform you, to entertain you, or to persuade you of something—or some combination of these purposes. How can you tell what a writer's purpose is? Well, sometimes the author tells you why he or she is writing. At other times, readers have to figure out what the purpose is.

AUTHOR'S PURPOSE

The Purpose Might Be . . .	If the Author Uses . . .
to inform	■ *definitions* ■ *instructions* ■ *statistics* ■ *a "teaching" tone*
to persuade	■ *strong language* ■ *an "arguing" tone*
to entertain	■ *humor* ■ *colorful language* ■ *a "conversational" tone*

When you read an essay, you want to know:

■ its subject, or what it's about

■ what the author says about the subject

■ how you feel about the author's message

Now preview "The Bus Ride" by Christine Nichols. Start by reading the title and the first and last paragraphs. Then, skim the rest of the essay. Look for repeated names, words, or phrases.

The Bus Ride
by Christine Nichols

It was Wednesday afternoon. I sat waiting anxiously at my desk. It was almost time to leave school. That meant it was almost time to go on the bus. I hated the bus. Big sixth-graders sat in the back. They always bullied us third-graders. Butterflies began forming in my stomach as I quickly jogged to my locker.

Today, I was late. It was my turn to clean the chalkboard. I grabbed my books out of my locker and shoved them into my bag. The halls were deserted except for a few kids hurrying to the door. As I walked out into the warm May sunshine, my fear ceased for a moment as I enjoyed the beautiful afternoon; but it left as soon as it came when I spotted the bus.

When I climbed the big, black steps onto the bus, I prayed that there would be an empty seat left up front; but there wasn't. Every single seat was filled with two people. I walked toward the back hoping to find an empty seat. The kids around me were happily talking; I wished I could be one of them. Why, why wasn't there an empty seat? It wasn't fair. Suddenly I spotted an empty seat. The only problem was, it was right smack in the middle of the sixth-graders. I tried to look around me for another place to sit, but there was none. The bus started moving so I had to sit down.

The radio was playing "Bye, Bye, Bye" by 'N Sync. All of the sixth-grade girls around me started singing, while the boys were groaning. Happily, I sat back in my seat. None of them had noticed me yet.

NOTE
Second event

As we were getting off the highway, the boy sitting in front of me turned around. He had one green eye and one blue. His blond hair hung over his eyes as if to hide them.

"Hey, what are you doing back here? The back of the bus is for sixth-graders only." At first, I didn't know what to say. Then, I realized I should just tell the truth.

PREVIEW
Repeated phrase

"I had to stay after school and clean the chalkboard, which made me late, and there was nowhere else to sit by the time I got here."

"So, you're a teacher's pet? I don't like teachers' pets; in fact, I hate teachers' pets!"

I wished that someone would help me, that the bus driver would hear what was going on; but he didn't. By now, everybody in the back of the bus was quiet, waiting for the boy's next move. Or perhaps, they simply did not want to get involved.

"I like your little baby overalls and your pink flowered shirt. Who picked them out for you? Your mommy? I bet you wish she was here right now, don't you, don't you?"

NOTE
Third event

That was the last straw. I had been so nervous for so long that I started to cry. Tears were streaming down my face that reminded me of a warm spring rain. I couldn't help myself. I wanted to stop and fight back but I couldn't.

PREVIEW
Repeated words

Just when I thought I couldn't cry anymore, a tall blond-haired, blue-eyed girl wearing practically the same outfit as me sat down next to me. She gave me a big hug and said, "You can stop crying now, it will be OK."

NOTE
Fourth event

"The Bus Ride," continued

She turned to the boy and said, "Stop picking on innocent little girls. She told you why she sat back here; I'm sure she would have sat up front if she could have. As for the outfit, I'm wearing practically the same thing and I don't look like a baby, do I?"

NOTE
Fifth event

The boy just sat there stunned. He opened his mouth to speak, but nothing came out. People around us started cheering for this mysterious girl sitting next to me. The boy slumped down into his seat.

PREVIEW
Last paragraph

The rest of the bus ride home the girl (named Hannah) and I became quick friends. When I got off the bus that afternoon I was on top of the world.

Nonfiction

161

During Reading

In your preview, you learned that the essay is about Christine's experience on a school bus and that Christine was bullied by a sixth-grader.

Read for the Main Idea

Now read the essay carefully. Start by finding out exactly what happened on the bus ride. After you pin down the details of Christine's experience, you can think about what happened.

1. Story String

One way to keep track of what happens is to record the main events in a Story String. This organizing tool is especially useful when you want to keep track of a number of events.

STORY STRING

> 1. Christine has to stay after school and clean the chalkboard.

> 2. She is late for the bus and can't find a seat.

> 3. The only seat left is among the sixth-grade bullies.

> 4. A boy bullies her for sitting in the back. She feels helpless and cries.

> 5. Another girl defends her and tells off the bully.

> 6. Christine makes a new friend and feels great that someone helped her.

2. Main Idea Organizer

Now you know exactly what happened on Christine's bus ride. What point is she trying to make in this essay? To answer that question, try to come up with a **main idea** that you feel summarizes or makes sense of all the other details in Christine's story. The essay describes details about a bus ride (the subject), but what's the point the author is trying to make? The bus is just *where* the experience happens. The main idea is different from the subject. The main idea is the statement, or point, the author is trying to make.

A Main Idea Organizer is set up to help you pull together the supporting details and state a main idea. Here is a Main Idea Organizer one reader created for "The Bus Ride."

Nonfiction

MAIN IDEA ORGANIZER

MAIN IDEA: Kids who are bullied need help from others.			
DETAIL #1 Christine hates the bus.	**DETAIL #2** She is afraid to sit with the sixth-graders.	**DETAIL #3** She is bullied to tears by a boy.	**DETAIL #4** Another girl sees her crying and helps her.
CONCLUSION: It's important to stick up for people who need help.			

Do you agree that the main idea of "The Bus Ride" is that kids need help from bullies? Or would you have stated the main idea differently—maybe something about how everybody needs friends? Because the author never directly stated what her main point is, it's up to you to read between the lines. What's important is that you can support your main idea statement with details from the essay.

How Essays Are Organized

Making sense of an essay will be easier once you recognize how many essays follow one of these patterns.

1. **Narrative Essay Organization**
2. **Expository Essay Organization**

1. Narrative Essay Organization

Many personal essays, such as "The Bus Ride," are narratives. They tell a story and a series of events in chronological order: first this happened, then this, and so on. If the author states the main point, it is often told in the last few paragraphs.

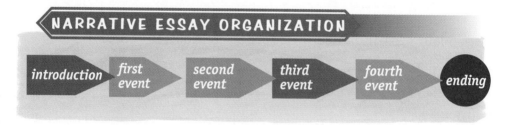

NARRATIVE ESSAY ORGANIZATION

introduction → first event → second event → third event → fourth event → ending

2. Expository Essay Organization

Expository essays usually have three parts: introduction, body, and conclusion. The main idea is commonly stated in the introduction or conclusion.

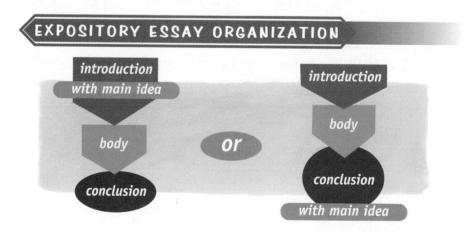

EXPOSITORY ESSAY ORGANIZATION

introduction with main idea → body → conclusion

or

introduction → body → conclusion with main idea

After Reading

After reading, pause and think about the essay. You may decide to go back and reread any parts that aren't clear to you. As you reread, focus not just on what the author is saying but also on your own reactions to it.

Reread and Reflect

After you finish reading "The Bus Ride," ask yourself how you feel about it. Use a Double-entry Journal to record your reactions to important quotes or ideas in an essay. Here are one reader's reactions to part of "The Bus Ride."

Nonfiction

DOUBLE-ENTRY JOURNAL

QUOTES	MY THOUGHTS
"Big sixth-graders sat in the back. They always bullied us third-graders."	I feel sorry for her. I know what it feels like to be bullied.
"By now, everybody in the back of the bus was quiet, waiting for the boy's next move."	Christine is alone, and no one helps.
"She gave me a big hug and said, 'You can stop crying now, it will be ok.'"	This girl is nice. She isn't afraid to stand up for Christine.

After reading, you'll want to remember what you've learned. It's easy to remember something when it has meaning in your own life. Try recording your personal reactions to the ideas in "The Bus Ride."

Remember

What are your experiences with bullying? Why do you think it happens? How do you feel about it?

Record your ideas about the essay and these questions in a journal entry. Your responses will help you remember the essay and get more from your reading of it.

Summing Up

- In reading a personal essay, note whether the author's purpose is to inform, to persuade, to entertain, or some combination of these purposes.

- As you read an essay, first find the subject. Then, look for the main idea and details.

- After reading, ask yourself how you feel about what the author said.

Focus on Persuasive Writing

You see persuasive writing all the time. Ads promise that you'll be happier if you buy certain clothes or go to certain movies. Articles try to talk you into believing something. Speeches try to persuade you to change your mind or do something.

In persuasive writing, a writer gives an opinion or argues for a certain idea. The writer's goal is to explain why the reader should think, act, or feel the same way he or she does.

Goals

Here you'll learn how to:

✔ **identify the topic and the author's viewpoint**

✔ **recognize the three parts of an argument**

✔ **use the strategy of reading critically to evaluate an author's viewpoint**

Nonfiction

Before Reading

With any kind of reading, start with a preview.

Find the Topic

As you preview the editorial on the next page, look for the topic of the reading. Start by reading the title and the first paragraph. Then skim the reading, looking for repeated words and phrases. Ask yourself, "What is this piece of writing about?"

"Why I Will Never Cut My Hair" by Gurdeep Sareen

When I was in kindergarten, I was an outsider. Every day at school, kids would gawk [stare] at me and snicker at my long hair. No one, not even my teacher, was there by my side to help me through my pain and anguish.

So the abuse continued, both verbally and physically.

There were times when the abuse was just too much and I was ready to cave in and cut my hair. But I couldn't turn my back on my parents. They were the ones who gave me the courage to be who I am and to ignore the malicious ignorant comments of others.

Sikhs [believers in a religion of India] believe that nothing God gives them should be changed. This is why we don't cut our hair. By keeping my hair long and staying a true Sikh, I have kept my uniqueness in a world where uniqueness is becoming extinct. I am glad to be unique.

Many people go through life with a feeling that they don't fit in. They are discriminated against because they are too tall or too short, too smart or too dumb, too dark or too light. Almost all people have had times when they have felt they didn't belong—a time when you feel distant from everyone else.

But I encourage everyone—whether it be the way they dress, talk or even laugh—to be themselves.

Reach within and find who you really are.

Then be that person.

What did your preview tell you about the topic? The title says Gurdeep Sareen won't cut his hair. The first paragraph mentions teasing in school because of his "long hair." These things tell you the topic.

Understand the Parts of an Argument

Most good arguments have three basic parts.

PARTS OF AN ARGUMENT

Part of Argument	Meaning
1. Viewpoint	*A statement or belief that the author wants to explain or support.*
2. Support	*Facts, figures, examples, and opinions that support the viewpoint. A good argument has at least three reasons supporting it.*
3. Opposing viewpoint	*The author defends the viewpoint against objections that other people might have.*

Nonfiction

Recognizing the three parts of an argument will make it easier for you to follow what the writer is saying. Look for them when you read Sareen's editorial more closely. As you read, try to be a critical reader.

Reading Strategy: Reading Critically

When you **read critically**, you size up the author's views and arguments. Critical reading means asking questions like these:

What is the viewpoint?

How good is the author's evidence?

What are the author's sources?

Are the sources believable?

What is the other side of the story?

During Reading

Now go back and read Gurdeep Sareen's editorial closely.

Find the Author's Argument

Start by taking notes on what Sareen is saying. Think about how he has organized his writing and what message he's trying to communicate to readers. Here is a Nonfiction Organizer one reader made to sort out what Sareen says.

NONFICTION ORGANIZER

TITLE:	"WHY I WILL NEVER CUT MY HAIR"
INTRODUCTION:	School kids tease Sareen about his long hair, and no one defends him.
BODY:	Sareen was unhappy for a long time because kids were mean to him. His parents helped him to be true to himself. In the Sikh religion, they don't believe in cutting their hair.
CONCLUSION:	Sareen tells everyone to be "who you really are."

Following what the writer says is the first step to understanding persuasive writing. Next, look critically at the argument Sareen makes. Sort out the main parts of the argument. Set up an Argument Chart to record this information.

ARGUMENT CHART

1 VIEWPOINT	2 SUPPORT	3 OPPOSING VIEWPOINT

Nonfiction

1. Author's Viewpoint

First, figure out Gurdeep Sareen's viewpoint. To find it, ask yourself, "What is Sareen saying about the topic?" Remember, the writer might not state the viewpoint in the beginning. It could be in the middle or even the end. Write your ideas in the Viewpoint column.

2. Support

Next, think about how Sareen supports his argument. What facts, experiences, examples, or opinions does he use to back up his viewpoint?

3. Opposing Viewpoint

Now think about what an opposing viewpoint might be. What argument might someone use against Sareen? Sometimes authors don't state any opposing views to their argument. Look in Sareen's editorial for any opposing viewpoint.

Here's an Argument Chart summarizing the three parts of "Why I Will Never Cut My Hair."

TOPIC: Sareen's long hair and trouble in school

VIEWPOINT	SUPPORT	OPPOSING VIEWPOINT
Every person should be his or her unique self.	• Kids teased Sareen because of his long hair. • His parents taught him to be himself and ignore those who are mean to him. • Sareen tried to be himself in a world where everyone tries to fit in. • Many other people have felt that they don't fit in or belong.	Kids feel that everyone should fit in.

Connect with the Reading

How do you feel about Gurdeep Sareen's viewpoint? Record your reactions to Sareen's argument in a Double-entry Journal. First, write quotes from the editorial in the Quotes column. Then write your thoughts about the quotes on the right.

QUOTES	MY THOUGHTS
"By keeping my hair long and staying a true Sikh, I have kept my uniqueness. . . ."	Sareen tries to be strong and follow what he believes. I admire him.
"But I encourage everyone—whether it be the way they dress, talk or even laugh—to be themselves."	This is a great idea, even though it can be very hard to do. What if the school had rules about long hair?

After Reading

After reading, make sure that you understand the author's argument. Now it is time to evaluate the argument and develop your own opinion.

Evaluate the Argument

Evaluate the argument, keeping in mind your critical reading questions. Was Sareen's point clear? Did he support it well? A Critical Reading Chart like the one below can help you judge persuasive writing.

CRITICAL READING CHART

1. Is the viewpoint clear?	Yes. He's trying to persuade people to "be themselves." He says that in the last three sentences.
2. What evidence is presented?	He uses his own personal experiences. He also mentions his parents' ideas.
3. Does the evidence seem reliable?	I think he is telling the truth about how he was teased and how he felt. What he says about his religion is probably true.
4. Is the evidence convincing?	He's just giving his opinion, but I agree with him. Everyone probably does know what it's like to try and fit in.
5. Is there another side of the story?	Sometimes it's not easy to "find out who you really are." And what if you would get in trouble for sticking up for what you believe in? Maybe some schools have rules about how long a boy's hair can be.

Decide How You Feel

You are now ready to decide how *you* feel about the author's viewpoint. One good way to do this is by writing a journal entry of your own, arguing for or against Sareen's views.

JOURNAL ENTRY

I think the author did a good job of telling how he felt. It is stupid and mean to pick on people because they look different. I agree that people do not all have to be all alike. I never realized how important having long hair could be to someone. I can see why Sareen wouldn't want to cut it.

Summing Up

- Writers try to persuade readers to agree with their opinions and change how they think, act, or feel about a topic.

- Effective arguments are made up of three parts—a viewpoint, the support, and the opposing viewpoint.

- Reading critically can help you to understand and evaluate arguments.

Focus on Biography

How do you learn more about a famous person's life? You read a **biography.** In a biography, an author called a *biographer* tells the life story of a real person, the *biographical subject.*

Biographies give information about the subject's character and the time period in which he or she lived. The purpose of a biography is to create a portrait, or complete picture, of the subject. Many biographies also include diary pages, photos or pictures, and other personal materials.

oals

Here you'll learn how to:

✔ **keep track of events and key details**

✔ **use the strategy of looking for cause and effect**

✔ **understand how biographies often are organized**

Nonfiction

Before Reading

You may be reading a biography either because you're curious or because your teacher assigned it. Either way, first decide on a purpose for reading. Some possible purposes are to learn about the key events in the subject's life, to find out what kind of person he or she was, and to learn why he or she was important.

Before reading, preview the biography to get some general information about the subject. Start by looking at the front cover and the table of contents of a biography of Abraham Lincoln.

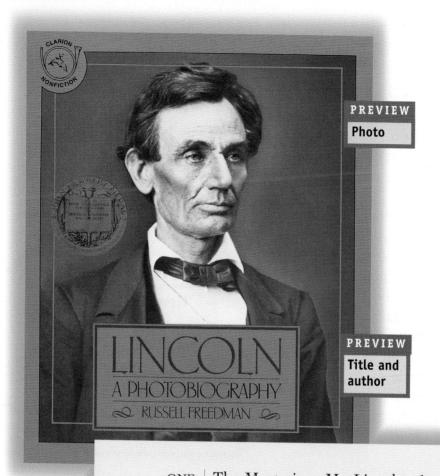

PREVIEW
Photo

LINCOLN
A PHOTOBIOGRAPHY
RUSSELL FREEDMAN

PREVIEW
Title and author

PREVIEW
Table of contents

During Reading

Your quick preview gave you some information about Lincoln's background and childhood. You learned that Lincoln went from "backwoods boy" to the White House. How did this happen? To find out, pay attention to what Lincoln was like and how he developed into a leader. Now read the passage carefully and with your reading purpose in mind.

Read for Key Events

Most biographies describe a subject's life events in time order. That means they tell the events in the order in which they happened. Many biographies begin with the birth and family history of the subject and follow the person from childhood to adulthood.

Now read two passages about Lincoln's childhood. Look for the key events and dates.

Nonfiction

from *Lincoln: A Photobiography* by Russell Freedman

He was born near Hodgenville, Kentucky, on February 12, 1809, in a log cabin with one window, one door, a chimney, and a hard-packed dirt floor. His parents named him after his pioneer grandfather. The first Abraham Lincoln had been shot dead by hostile Indians in 1786, while planting a field of corn in the Kentucky wilderness.

NOTE
Lincoln's birth

NOTE
Grand-father's death

Thomas Lincoln [Abraham's father] was thinking about moving on again. Lately he had heard glowing reports about Illinois, where instead of forests there were endless prairies with plenty of rich black soil. Early in 1830, Thomas sold his Indiana farm. The Lincolns piled everything they owned into two ox-drawn wagons and set out over muddy roads, with Abraham, just turned twenty-one, driving one of the wagons himself. They traveled west to their new homesite in central Illinois, not far from Decatur. Once again, Abraham helped his father build a cabin and start a new farm.

NOTE
Moved to Illinois

Record what you learned in a Timeline. This reading tool is useful for keeping track of events in a biography.

TIMELINE

1786	1809	1830
Lincoln's grandfather shot by Indians in Kentucky	born on February 12	moved to Illinois

Form a Portrait of the Subject

There's more to reading a biography than just learning dates. You also want to learn all you can about Lincoln as a person. As you read two more parts of Lincoln's biography, look for key facts about him and insights into his character.

from *Lincoln: A Photobiography*

NOTE
How he looked

Abraham was growing up fast, shooting up like a sunflower, a spindly youngster with big bony hands, unruly black hair, a dark complexion, and luminous gray eyes. He became an expert with the ax, working alongside his father, who also hired him out to work for others. For twenty-five cents a day, the boy dug wells, built pigpens, split fence rails, felled trees. "My how he could chop!" exclaimed a friend.

NOTE
What he did

The passage above gives you details about what Lincoln looked like and what kind of work he did. Read on to find out more about Lincoln and the kind of person he was.

Nonfiction

from *Lincoln: A Photobiography*

Mostly, he educated himself by borrowing books and newspapers. There are many stories about Lincoln's efforts to find enough books to satisfy him in that backwoods country. Those he liked he read again and again, losing himself in the adventures of *Robinson Crusoe* or the magical tales of *The Arabian Nights*. He was thrilled by a biography of George Washington, with its stirring account of the Revolutionary War. And he came to love the rhyme and rhythm of poetry, reciting passages from Shakespeare or the Scottish poet Robert Burns at the drop of a hat. He would carry a book out to the field with him, so he could read at the end of each plow furrow, while the horse was getting its breath.

NOTE
Educated himself

NOTE
Loved all kinds of reading

NOTE
Read while he worked

Thinking Tree

A Thinking Tree can help you take notes as you read. These kind of notes "branch off" in any direction. You can list ideas about the subject at the top of the Thinking Tree and then note the details from the book that support them.

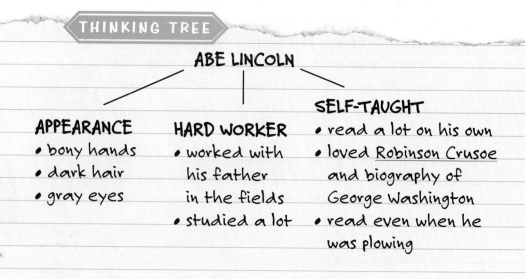

THINKING TREE

ABE LINCOLN

APPEARANCE
• bony hands
• dark hair
• gray eyes

HARD WORKER
• worked with
  his father
  in the fields
• studied a lot

SELF-TAUGHT
• read a lot on his own
• loved <u>Robinson Crusoe</u>
  and biography of
  George Washington
• read even when he
  was plowing

Discover Cause and Effect

When you read a biography, you also need to think about why the subject became the sort of person he or she did. Put the facts together to figure out *why* the subject believed in certain things or made important decisions. What caused him or her to believe a certain idea or make that choice?

In other words, you need to look for **cause and effect.** The cause is *the reason why* something happens. The effect is *what actually happens,* or results, from the cause. You'll often find an event in the subject's childhood (a cause) that explains why the subject believed or did something later in life (effects). Look for cause and effect in these other passages from parts of Freedman's biography about Lincoln.

from *Lincoln: A Photobiography*

NOTE
Key event = Lincoln seeing slaves

New Orleans was the first real city [Lincoln and another boy] had ever seen. Their eyes must have popped as the great harbor came into view, jammed with the masts of sailing ships from distant ports all over the world. The city's cobblestone streets teemed with sailors, traders, and adventurers speaking strange languages. And there were gangs of slaves everywhere. Lincoln would never forget the sight of black men, women, and children being driven along in chains and auctioned off like cattle. In those days, New Orleans had more than two hundred slave dealers.

The passage above describes a key moment in Lincoln's early life. The phrase "Lincoln would never forget" is a clue to the importance of this experience. As you read two more passages from the biography, pay special attention to what else you learn about Lincoln's feelings about slavery.

from *Lincoln: A Photobiography*

NOTE
Lincoln is against slavery.

NOTE
But he doesn't do much about it.

Early in his career, Lincoln made few public statements about slavery. But he did take a stand. As a twenty-eight-year-old state legislator, he recorded his belief that slavery was "founded on both injustice and bad policy." Ten years later, as a congressman, he voted with his party to stop the spread of slavery, and he introduced his bill to outlaw slavery in the nation's capital. But he did not become an antislavery crusader. For the most part, he sat silently in the background as Congress rang with angry debates over slavery's future.

NOTE
Cause =
1854
act that
allowed
slavery

The issue came to a head in 1854, when Congress passed the bitterly debated Kansas-Nebraska Act. Under the Missouri Compromise, the region that included the territories of Kansas and Nebraska had been declared off-limits to slavery. Under the new Act, however, the future of slavery in those territories would be determined by the people who settled there. They would decide for themselves whether to enter the Union as free states or slave states.

NOTE
Effect =
Lincoln
more
interested
in politics

The Kansas-Nebraska Act had been introduced by Lincoln's old political rival, Stephen Douglas, now a U.S. Senator from Illinois. Douglas's policy of "popular sovereignty" caused a storm of protest in the North. By opening new territories to slavery, his measure overturned the Missouri Compromise, which had held slavery in check. With the passage of Douglas's Act, Lincoln ended his long political silence. "I was losing interest in politics," he said, "when the repeal of the Missouri Compromise aroused me again."

Lincoln's words in this last passage explain what caused him to become more involved in politics and the movement to end slavery. The Kansas–Nebraska Act caused these changes in Lincoln. After that, he became more interested in politics and began to speak out against slavery.

Cause-Effect Organizer

Looking for cause and effect helps you understand the "life-shaping" events in a biography. Use a Cause-Effect Organizer to help show the relationship between a cause and its effects. Here is an example of how one reader used a Cause-Effect Organizer to understand the relationship between events in Lincoln's life and his strong beliefs against slavery.

CAUSE-EFFECT ORGANIZER

Nonfiction

CAUSES	EFFECTS
Lincoln visits New Orleans and sees slave trading for the first time. He would never forget the sight of black people being auctioned.	He believed slavery was a horrible injustice.
	As a congressman, he introduced a law to outlaw slavery in the capital but said little.
The Kansas-Nebraska Act introduced by Stephen Douglas opens new territories to slavery.	Lincoln got interested in politics again and wanted to fight the spread of slavery.

After Reading

After reading a biography, pause and think about what you've learned. Can you name several key events in the person's life and describe the sort of person he or she was? Do you have new questions about the person's life and times? Now is the perfect time to look back, think about what you've read, and sort out causes and effects.

If you need more information on something or if you have further questions, go back to key parts. Answer the questions you still have by going back and rereading here and there in the biography. You'll find that it helps you understand more from your reading.

Summing Up

- As you read a biography, look for key events in the subject's life. Try to form a portrait of the subject and learn what kind of person he or she was.

- Focus on cause and effect. Decide which events in the subject's life may have caused important beliefs or decisions later on.

- Use reading tools such as a Timeline, a Thinking Tree, and a Cause-Effect Organizer to record what you learned.

Focus on Real-world Writing

On any day of the week, you might read a bus schedule, a telephone book, a computer help screen, a TV guide, or directions for microwaving a snack. This is "informational," or "real-world," reading. You probably do a lot more of it every day than you think.

You don't need to remember what you read on a shampoo bottle, but some of your everyday reading is important. If you're reading school rules, a practice schedule, a map, or directions for using a new camera, you've got to get the information right.

Nonfiction

Goals

Here you'll learn how to:

✔ **understand different purposes for reading real-world writing**

✔ **recognize how real-world writing is organized**

✔ **skim to find the information you need**

Before Reading

Here are four tips that will speed you through your real-world reading:

1. Know what you're after—your purpose in reading.

2. Figure out how the material is organized.

3. Skim for the information you need.

4. Remember and use the information.

1. Know What You're After

Before starting to read, be sure you know exactly what you need to find out. Ask yourself, "What do I need to know?" Remember that your purpose in reading will change for different situations.

Here you'll read a school menu, a train system map, and a soccer schedule. Notice your specific purpose for reading each one.

PURPOSE NOTES

SCHOOL MENU
Question: What's for lunch on Wednesday the 23rd?

TRAIN SYSTEM MAP
Question: I'm at Powell Street. Which train line do I take to Orinda?

SOCCER SCHEDULE
Question: What was the final score of the game against Mexia?

2. Figure Out How the Material Is Organized

Now that you know your reading purpose, look at the reading. Preview it quickly to find out how it's organized. This will help you to find your information fast.

In real-world writing, information is organized in many ways. Computer help screens usually list topics and then show information in paragraphs or lists. Timetables and schedules set up information in tables with rows and columns. Directions for putting something together use diagrams and numbered lists of steps. Maps use graphics, symbols, and keys.

To understand how a real-world reading is organized, look for features like these:

- tables of contents
- main headings and titles
- words in large, boldface, or unusual type
- lists (1, 2, 3) or outlines (I., A., 1.)
- charts and tables
- pictures or diagrams

Now try previewing the three samples of real-world writing that appear on the next few pages. Figure out how each of them is organized.

Nonfiction

School Menu

PREVIEW

Title

PREVIEW

Headings in bold

LUNCH

Monday	Tuesday	Wednesday	Thursday	Friday
	1 Ham & Turkey Croissants, Potatoes, Tomatoes, Fruit Milk or OJ	**2** Wiener Winks Baked Beans Applesauce Muffins or Fruit, Milk or OJ	**3** Turkey, Peas, Potatoes, Rolls, Fruit, Milk or OJ	**4** Tuna or Turkey Salad, Chips, Tomatoes, Fruit Milk or OJ
7 NO SCHOOL	**8** Hot Ham & Cheese, Potato Wedges Applesauce Fruit Milk or OJ	**9** Spaghetti Tossed Salad Cornbread Fruit Milk or OJ	**10** Hamburgers, Onion, Pickles, Tomatoes, French Fries Fruit, Milk or OJ	**11** Ribs Macaroni & Cheese, Applesauce, Fruit Milk or OJ
14 Crispitos, Salsa, Cheese, Tossed Salad Cheesecake Milk or OJ	**15** Chicken Patties Green Beans Applesauce Fruit Milk or OJ	**16** Ham Dinner Mashed & Sweet Potatoes, Peas, Rolls, Fruit Milk or OJ	**17** Sloppy Joes Potato Wedges Cole Slaw Fruit Milk or OJ	**18** Chili, Peanut Butter & Jelly or Turkey Salad Sandwich Fruit Milk or OJ
21 Mini Hoagie Hashbrowns Applesauce Fruit Milk or OJ	**22** Taco Salad, Cheese, Lettuce, Salsa, Corn Fruit Milk or OJ	**23** Pot Luck Mashed Potatoes Vegetables Fruit Milk or OJ	**24** Pizza, Cheese Sticks, Baked Beans, Fruit Milk or OJ	**25** Chicken Nuggets Tater Tots Applesauce Fruit Milk or OJ
28 NO SCHOOL	**29** POT LUCK	**30** POT LUCK	**31** Last Day for Teachers - NO SCHOOL for Students	

A quick preview tells you this menu is organized like a calendar. That means you should read the menu as you would read a calendar, across and down.

188

Map

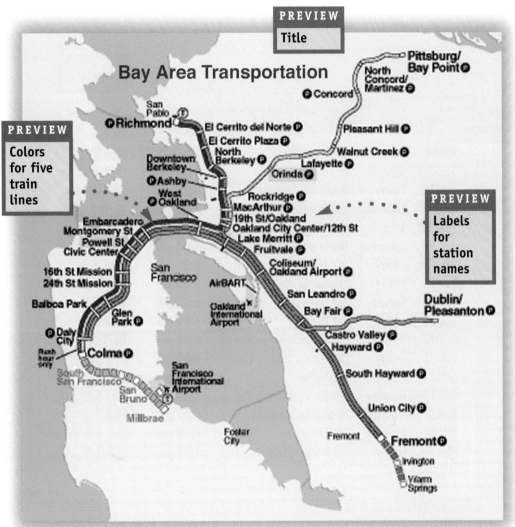

A map organizes information in a picture. Your quick preview of the train map shows you the title, five train lines drawn in different colors, and many labels for train station names. You need to skim the labels on the map for the names of the locations you want to find.

Schedule

PREVIEW

Title

PREVIEW

Column
headings

2001 Varsity Boys Soccer Schedule

DATE	DAY	OPPONENT	TIME	RESULT
Jan 6	Saturday	at Lorena	11:00 am	Lost 0-5
Jan 12	Friday	Home vs. LaVega	5:30 pm	Won 4-1
Jan 13	Saturday	Home vs. Robinson	2:00 pm	Tie 0-0
Jan 20	Saturday	at LaVega	1:00 pm	Won 3-2
Jan 25	Thursday	Home vs. Lorena	6:00 pm	Tie 3-3
Jan 26	Friday	at Mexia	6:00 pm	Won 4-3
Feb 2	Friday	*Home vs. Belton	6:00 pm	Lost 4-2
Feb 6	Tuesday	*at University	6:00 pm	Won 5-1
Feb 9	Friday	*at Midway	6:00 pm	Lost 5-0
Feb 13	Tuesday	*Home vs. Shoemaker	6:00 pm	Tie 1-1
Feb 16	Friday	*Home vs. Harker Heights	6:00 pm	Lost 6-1
Feb 23	Friday	*at Belton	6:00 pm	Tie 0-0
Feb 27	Tuesday	*Home vs. University	6:00 pm	Lost 5-2
Mar 2	Friday	*Home vs. Midway	6:00 pm	Won 1-0
Mar 6	Tuesday	*at Shoemaker	6:30 pm	Lost 3-0
Mar 9	Friday	*at Harker Heights	7:30 pm	Lost 2-1

*DISTRICT

How is this Soccer Schedule organized? In a quick preview, you probably noticed the title and the column headings with topics such as *date, day, opponent,* and so on. You probably also saw that each row gives you information about one game.

To read this schedule, you need to skim for the information you want to find. First, go to the column you need. Then look down the column and across the row for the specific information you want to find.

During Reading

Now that you know what information you need and how the readings are organized, you're ready for the next step.

3. Skim for the Information You Need

Real-world materials usually are written so that readers of all levels can understand. They give a lot of information, trying to answer all of the questions that readers might have.

When you're searching for specific facts, you don't have to read everything. Look only for what you need, and ignore the rest.

Nonfiction

Reading Strategy: **Skimming**

That's why **skimming** is a great reading strategy for real-world reading. When you skim, you glance over a piece of writing, looking for a fast path to the information you want. You hunt for headings, labels, and other organizational guides that will speed you to your goal.

Now give it a try. Use skimming to find answers to your specific questions about the school lunch menu, the train system map, and the soccer match. Look for fast paths to the information.

School Menu

Focus on the information you want. Remember your reading purpose was to find out about the lunch for Wednesday the 23rd. Now go back and look at the menu on page 188. Skim to find the information you need. Then think aloud about your path to the information, as shown below.

THINK ALOUD

LUNCH MENU

Question: What's for lunch on Wednesday the 23rd?

Answer: pot luck, mashed potatoes, vegetables, fruit, milk or OJ.

Path to Information: Read across the top to find the column marked Wednesday. Skim down the column until I find the menu for the 23rd. (I also can just skim for the 23rd.)

Train System Map

When you first look at the map on page 189, be sure you are clear about the information you want. You're starting at Powell Street and going to Orinda. Which train line should you take? Skim the map, looking for the names of the stops you need to find. Below is one reader's explanation of how to find the information that's needed.

THINK ALOUD

TRAIN SYSTEM MAP

Question: I'm at Powell Street. Which train line do I take to Orinda?

Answer: the yellow train

Path to Information: Skim the station names to find Powell Street. Then find the Orinda station. Note the yellow train line that goes between them.

Schedule

You've got the idea now. First, focus on your reading purpose question about the schedule. What was the final score of the match against Mexia? Skim the Soccer Schedule on page 190 for the name *Mexia*. Then trace your path across to the right to the score.

THINK ALOUD

SOCCER TEAM SCHEDULE
Question: What was the final score against Mexia?
Answer: We won, 4–3.
Path to Information: Look in column headings for Opponent. Skim down the opponent names to find Mexia. At the entry for Mexia, read across the row over to the result. It's 4–3.

Nonfiction

Sometimes it'll be fairly easy to find the information you're looking for. Other times it'll be more difficult. Real-world writing can be confusing. So, after you find the information you need, be sure to double-check it. If you're still not sure, ask a friend or someone nearby for help. Otherwise, you might get on a train at Powell Street and wind up in the wrong place!

If you didn't find what you need, go back and skim it again. Maybe you weren't looking in the right place the first time. After you've gotten the information you wanted, then decide whether you need to remember it.

4. Remember and Use the Information

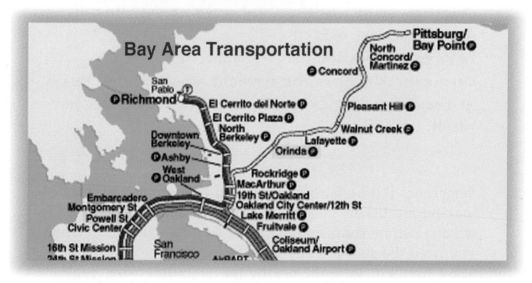

Jot down a few quick directions or highlight the route on the map. That information might be useful in the future.

Follow this process with real-world writing:

- ■ Know what you're after—your purpose in reading.
- ■ Figure out how the material is organized.
- ■ Skim for the information you need.
- ■ Remember to save the information if you need to use it again.

Elements of Nonfiction

As you read nonfiction—magazine articles, news stories, essays, biographies, and more—you'll need a way to talk about them. Here are the terms used to describe a number of key elements of nonfiction.

Check here for examples, descriptions, and definitions of these elements of nonfiction.

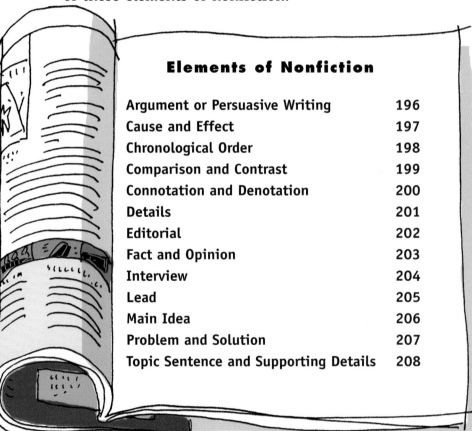

Elements of Nonfiction

Nonfiction

Argument or Persuasive Writing

Arguments are at the heart of persuasive writing. Writers often take a stand on an issue or offer an opinion.

EXAMPLE

from "Sacajawea" by Judy Alter

Supporting detail

Sacajawea had been kidnapped five years earlier by a party of Hidatsa raiders and she was later traded or sold to Charbonneau [her husband]. She knew both the language and the land of the Shoshoni—or the Snakes as they were often

Viewpoint

called—and she proved to be much more important to the expedition than her husband was.

The expedition left Fort Mandan on the Missouri River in April 1805. One of Sacajawea's earliest contributions was to keep the company supplied with roots and berries, an important

Supporting details

addition to their diet. When one of the pirogues (a native canoe, usually hollowed from a trunk of a tree) overturned, it was Sacajawea who kept her head and saved many irreplaceable supplies.

DESCRIPTION

In **argument** or **persuasive writing,** authors express a viewpoint or an opinion and then support it. A good persuasive argument may require two or three supporting pieces of evidence—or even more. Before you adopt an author's viewpoint, make sure that you understand it, have examined the evidence, and have considered opposing arguments.

DEFINITION

In **persuasive writing,** an author tries to convince readers to do something or to adopt his or her viewpoint.

Cause and Effect

The cause is the reason that an event happens. The effect is what happens as a result of the cause.

from *Jane Goodall's Animal World: Chimps* by Jane Goodall

Then two other scientists had another idea and this one worked. They taught the sign language that deaf people use to a young chimp named Washoe. She learned over 300 signs. She even invented signs of her own. She called a fizzing soda a "listen drink" (two signs she knew), a piece of celery "pipe food," a duck on a pond "water bird," and so on.

Cause

Effects

Nonfiction

DESCRIPTION

The **cause** is that scientists taught a chimp named Washoe sign language. The **effects** are that the chimp learned over 300 signs and invented signs of her own. The cause comes first—it is *the reason why* something happens. The effect comes second—it is *what results from* the cause.

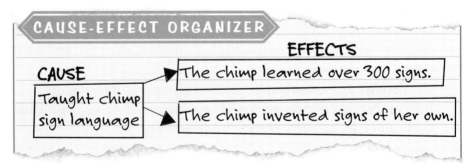

CAUSE-EFFECT ORGANIZER

EFFECTS

CAUSE

Taught chimp sign language

The chimp learned over 300 signs.

The chimp invented signs of her own.

Key words such as *because*, *so*, and *as a result* often, but not always, signal cause and effect.

DEFINITION

Cause and effect is a relationship that occurs between two or more events, in which one event—the cause—triggers another event—the effect.

197

Chronological Order

Writers often describe events or experiences in the order in which they happened in time. Here is an example from the biography of a well-known African-American doctor.

EXAMPLE — from *Charles Richard Drew, M.D.* by Rinna Evelyn Wolfe

Order of events

(1) In February 1941, the United States Armed Forces asked the Red Cross to organize American blood banks. (2) Dr. Drew was appointed assistant director of this national program. He immediately established the highest standards as he trained many staffs and volunteers. (3) Using mobile units, he directed the openings of blood collection centers nationwide. (4) When Japan bombed Pearl Harbor on December 7, 1941, the United States had an ample supply of plasma on hand.

DESCRIPTION

Every experience or event happens at a specific point in time. If an author describes a series of events in the order in which they happened, he or she is using **chronological,** or time, **order.** Key words such as *before, during,* and *after* signal chronological order. So do words and phrases such as *yesterday, immediately, suddenly,* and *in ten years.* Pay special attention to dates and words that express time, such as *year, month, decade,* and *century.*

DEFINITION

Chronological order means organizing events in time order, or the order in which they actually happened.

Comparison and Contrast

Comparing and contrasting two things helps you understand them better. Notice what is compared in the example below.

EXAMPLE   from an encyclopedia article

> The North (Union), made up of 23 states, had more men, more money, and more industry than the South. The North also controlled the navy and started a naval blockade that prevented the South from receiving help or supplies from abroad. The 11 states of the South (the Confederacy) were much weaker, but they had the benefit of good generals and a great fighting spirit.

Two sides in the Civil War

Nonfiction

DESCRIPTION

In a **comparison,** you examine two or more things by looking for similarities. In a **contrast,** you point out differences between two things. This chart sums up the comparisons in the example above.

COMPARISON AND CONTRAST

NORTH (UNION)	SOUTH (CONFEDERACY)
23 states	11 states
more men and money	much weaker
more industry	good generals
started blockade	fighting spirit

DEFINITION

A **comparison** points out how two or more things are alike. A **contrast** highlights differences between two or more things.

Connotation and Denotation

Nonfiction writers sometimes use emotional language to stir the feelings of their readers. They try to choose words that have strong, colorful meanings (words with connotations) rather than plain, ordinary words.

EXAMPLE

from "The Ingalls Wilder Women" by Judy Alter

. . . Laura Ingalls Wilder was a farmer, an early advocate of women's rights, a writer, and, in her sixties, a novelist. Her daughter, Rose Wilder Lane, was a journalist and prolific author who encouraged Laura to write and publish the "Little House" series.

Caroline Quiner [Laura's mother] was raised in Milwaukee County, Wisconsin, one of seven children in a family of Scottish ancestry. Laura later wrote that her mother's Scottish thrift helped the family survive during hard times.

Words with positive connotations

DESCRIPTION

A word's **denotation** is its dictionary meaning. Its **connotation** includes emotional feelings most people have about the word. The denotation of *prolific* is "producing numerous works" and of *thrift* is "using money carefully and wisely." These words send a much different message than saying Rose was *longwinded* or Caroline was *cheap*, which have negative connotations.

DEFINITION

The connotation of a word is the emotional feeling that a word carries. The denotation of a word is its exact dictionary meaning.

Details

Details are short facts or descriptions that add life and realism to writing. Writers use details to describe something exactly as it is.

EXAMPLE — from *John Glenn: A Memoir* by John Glenn with Nick Taylor

A boy could not have had a more idyllic [perfect] early childhood than I did. Sometimes it seems to me that Norman Rockwell must have taken all his inspiration from New Concord, Ohio. My playmates were freckle-faced boys and girls with pigtails. We played without fear in backyards and streams and endless green fields, and climbed trees to learn the limits of our daring. The adults— most of them—were concerned and reliably caring, and we respected them.

Specific details

Nonfiction

DESCRIPTION

Specific **details** explain a general idea, support an argument, or make it easy to imagine how a scene looks and feels. In the example above, details help you to picture the kinds of friends and places that the famous astronaut John Glenn used to play with and around as a boy. Even the smallest details can say a lot about a person, place, experience, or idea.

DEFINITION

Details are the words, facts, figures, or phrases that support an idea or describe a person, place, or thing.

Editorial

An editorial is a short, persuasive essay that offers an opinion about current topics or issues.

EXAMPLE · from "Is the Iditarod Fair to Dogs?" by Diana Maydosz

Viewpoint

The Iditarod may have been founded to commemorate a great event, but there is nothing great about the way it is run now. In the famous 1925 medicine delivery to Nome that the race honors, **1** a railway was used for part of the journey, and the rest was covered by a relay team of dogsleds, so that each team traveled only about 100 miles. Dogs in today's race run over 1,000 miles to the finish line.

Supporting details

2 These animals suffer back strain, injured paws, pneumonia, heart failure, and other stress-related injuries. Dogs also die of strangulation or are run over by sleds if they are not able to stay on their feet. **3** Veterinary care during the race is largely inadequate. There simply aren't enough vets present to give each sled dog a thorough exam at the checkpoints.

DESCRIPTION

A convincing **editorial** states a viewpoint clearly and then supports it with reliable facts and details. This editorial argues that the Iditarod sled-dog race doesn't treat dogs well and supports it with three details. You need to read persuasive writing critically and be sure the writer supports his or her opinions.

DEFINITION

An editorial is a brief but carefully organized essay that expresses an opinion and supports it.

Fact and Opinion

Can you tell the difference between the facts and opinions in this magazine article about homes for wildlife?

EXAMPLE

from *Habitats* by Dorothy Hinshaw Patent

Opinion

Facts

Unfortunately, homes for wild things are disappearing at a very fast rate in our crowded modern world. The human population keeps growing at a rate of about 2 percent each year. That means there are around 100,000,000 new people each year who need food, shelter, and water. Trees are cut down to build houses and to open up land for growing crops. Rivers are dammed to provide electricity, irrigation and drinking water. Marshes are filled to make land for shopping centers and new homes. Every time a piece of wild land is converted to human use, some plants and animals lose their habitat.

DESCRIPTION

A **fact** can be proved true or false. An **opinion** is a personal judgment that someone thinks is true, but that may be true or false. When reading, watch out for the difference between facts and opinions.

Be sure facts and opinions are supported by reliable evidence. The example above states that the population grows at a rate of about 2 percent a year. That fact can probably be checked and proved. But the idea that "homes for wild things are disappearing at a very fast rate" is an opinion.

DEFINITION

A **fact** is something that can be proved true or real.
An **opinion** is a personal judgment or belief.

Interview

Interviews can give you all kinds of information—from facts and statistics about issues or events to details about someone's personal life or opinions. What do you learn about school violence in the interview below?

EXAMPLE

from an interview with Dr. Bruce Perry

Questions

Question: What is the most common form of violence teens face in schools? Is it bullying? Fistfights?

Answers

Dr. Perry: The most common physical violence teens face is being shoved and pushed.

Question: What can we do to keep everyone safe, and at the same time not overreact to aggression that may be part of normal teenage life?

Dr. Perry: We shouldn't overreact, but we do need to act. We need to be more respectful of each other. . . .

We should create an environment in school in which everyone feels included.

DESCRIPTION

An **interview** is a special type of conversation. An interviewer asks prepared questions of one or more people called *interviewees*. They talk about their personal lives or topics they have special knowledge about. The goal of an interview is to get detailed information. You'll often find interviews in newspapers and magazines.

DEFINITION

An **interview** is a planned conversation in which an interviewer records information from one or more people.

Lead

The lead of a news story or magazine article occurs in the first few paragraphs. Sometimes it occurs in the very first sentence. A good news lead answers most (if not all) of the questions *who, what, where, when, why,* and *how.*

EXAMPLE from "When the Red Fox Comes to Town" by Peter Taylor

When
Who
What
Where

During the spring of 1998, Don Miller discovered that a red fox family with eight kits had taken up residence in his suburban backyard near Chicago. The retired heavy-machinery salesman was delighted. "The kits romp out back and are very enjoyable to watch," he said. "The mother is friendly and will come lie on our deck in the sun." So charmed were Miller and his wife that they practically stopped watching television to view the fox family's nearly nonstop antics.

DESCRIPTION

After the headline, the most important part of an article is the **lead.** It leads you into the story by presenting the subject and answering most of the *who, what, when, where, why,* and *how* questions. Leads give readers key information right away, at the beginning of a news story or article. They help readers decide whether they want to continue reading or not.

DEFINITION

The lead is the opening paragraph or paragraphs of a news story or magazine article. It establishes the topic and presents key information.

Nonfiction

Main Idea

The main idea is the key idea or message of a paragraph or work. What do you think is the main idea below?

EXAMPLE

from *The Life and Death of Crazy Horse* by Russell Freedman

Main idea

[Crazy Horse's] own people knew him as "Our Strange One," and at times, he seemed very strange indeed.① He wore no war paint, took no scalps, and

Details

refused to boast about his brave deeds.② A quiet loner, he would walk through the village lost in thought or ride out on the plains to be by himself. ③His fellow Sioux loved to dance and sing, but Crazy Horse never joined a dance, not even the sun dance, and they say that nobody ever heard him sing.

DESCRIPTION

To understand the author's purpose, you need to find the **main idea**. Main ideas can come at the beginning, middle, or end of a paragraph or work. Sometimes the main idea is stated clearly. Other times it is not, and then you have to infer it. To find the main idea, ask yourself as you read, "What is the most important point here?" Then look for the details that support the main idea.

In the example above, the main idea begins the paragraph and is followed immediately by three supporting details. Remember that the main idea is different from the subject or topic. The subject in the example above is Crazy Horse. The main idea is that Crazy Horse was strange.

DEFINITION

The **main idea** is the most important idea of a paragraph or work. It is the main point the author wishes to make.

Problem and Solution

Authors often organize their writing by first describing a problem and then explaining its solution.

EXAMPLE

from *George Washington* by Mary Pope Osborne

Washington wanted to force the British out of Boston, but first he needed more weapons. So he sent one of his officers, Colonel Henry Knox, to bring cannons back from two American forts in northern New York. Knox and his men secured about fifty cannons and loaded them onto sledges pulled by eighty pairs of oxen. As they crossed the Berkshire mountains heading back to Washington's camp near Boston, the oxen dragged the sledges over miles of snow and ice.

Problem

Solution

Nonfiction

DESCRIPTION

The **problem and solution** approach is one way of organizing detailed information. First, the writer describes a problem. Then, he or she describes either a proposed solution or how the problem was solved.

PARAGRAPH ORGANIZATION

PROBLEM needed more weapons

▼

SOLUTION   1. Col. Knox finds 50 cannons.
2. They pulled cannons on sledges to camp.

DEFINITION

The **problem and solution** organization first describes a problem and then gives one or more solutions.

207

Topic Sentence and Supporting Details

The topic sentence is the main idea or thought of a paragraph. It often comes at the beginning of a paragraph.

EXAMPLE

from "Harriet Tubman" by Jim Haskins

By 1851, [Harriet] had become a legend as a conductor on the Underground Railroad, the **Topic sentence** network of people, black and white, who aided slaves escaping from the South to the North and freedom. She established a pattern that she kept to for six years, until 1857. Each year she made two trips to the South, one in the spring and one in the fall. She spent the winters in St. Catherine's, **Supporting details** Ontario, where many fugitive slaves had settled, and the summers working in hotels in places such as Cape May, New Jersey, to earn money for her trips. In the spring of 1857, she managed to rescue her aged parents.

DESCRIPTION

Paragraphs often begin with a **topic sentence,** followed by sentences that give details about the topic. Sometimes the **supporting details** come first, followed by the topic sentence. At other times, the entire paragraph is made up of supporting details. In a tightly organized paragraph, all sentences relate to the topic. They support the topic sentence, just as a table's legs support its top.

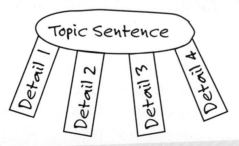

Topic Sentence

Detail 1   Detail 2   Detail 3   Detail 4

Topic Sentence and Supporting Details, continued

ORGANIZATION OF EXAMPLE PARAGRAPH

TOPIC SENTENCE Harriet Tubman was a legend as a conductor on the Underground Railroad.

DETAIL 1	DETAIL 2	DETAIL 3	DETAIL 4
She made regular trips to the South.	Harriet made two trips each year in the spring and the fall.	Harriet spent the rest of the year helping slaves in the North and earning money for trips.	She rescued her own parents in 1857.

All of the sentences in the example paragraph relate to Harriet Tubman and her work on the Underground Railroad. The writer states the subject and what he thinks about it in the first sentence. The rest of the paragraph is made up of details that explain what made Harriet Tubman so important.

DEFINITION

A **topic sentence** states the main idea or thought of a paragraph. The **supporting details** are in the surrounding sentences that relate to or support the topic sentence.

Nonfiction

Reading
Fiction

Fiction

Reading a Folktale

Remember "The Three Little Pigs"? It is a folktale, which is one of the oldest kinds of stories in the world. A **folktale** is a story handed down from parents to their children, and from the children to their children. Folktales are different from country to country, but people all around the world tell them.

Folktales are made-up stories, even if they have elements from the real world. Even though they are imaginary, not real, they are often told because they contain a lesson.

Goals

Here you'll learn how to:

✔ **recognize the common features of a folktale**

✔ **try the reading strategy of using graphic organizers**

✔ **understand how folktales are organized**

Before Reading

You read a folktale as you would any story. Before reading, set a purpose, preview, and choose a plan for reaching your reading purpose.

Set a Purpose

Because folktales often tell lessons, use finding the lesson as a purpose for reading. Here are some other elements to watch for when you read a folktale.

COMMON ELEMENTS OF A FOLKTALE

Element	Definition	In a Folktale . . .
Characters	people or figures in a story	Characters usually are either good or bad.
Setting	time and location of a story	The time usually is "long, long ago."
Plot	action or events of a story	Plots or story events are simple. Problems are often solved in surprising ways.
Theme	a story's statement about life	The main character often learns a lesson.

Setting a Purpose

■ What is the subject of the folktale?
■ What is the main lesson to be learned?

B Preview

Now preview "The Best Teacher." As you preview, look for:

Preview Checklist

✔ the title
✔ any repeated words or phrases
✔ any background information
✔ the first and last several paragraphs

Fiction

213

The Best Teacher

Romania, in eastern Europe, has beautiful mountains and forests. In the old days, gypsies roamed the countryside and dashing noblemen rode their fine horses into battle. The Romanian people have a great sense of fun and many of their folktales are full of laughter.

Once upon a time, long ago, a man was blessed with a fine house, healthy animals and fertile land. This man was also fortunate enough to have a handsome, loving son. But the boy had never known anything but good times and had never had to deal with any sort of problem.

"The lad must have some experience of dealing with ill luck," said his father.

From then on he gave his son all the awkward and difficult jobs to do. However, luck was with the young man until the day his father sent him into the forest to bring back timber. Only a rickety old cart was free for the work and the father watched his son harness two oxen to it.

If that cart breaks down today, then it will be a good experience for the boy, he thought. The father smiled at his son. "If that cart breaks up when you are alone in the forest, necessity will teach you what to do," he said.

"Right you are, Father," replied the lad, who was good and loyal, but not the cleverest young man in the world. He thought that Necessity must be some handyman who lived in the forest and helped travellers in trouble.

The son drove the oxen far into the forest where there were good trees suitable for felling. He worked hard, cutting down the trees, sawing them up and loading them on to the cart. When the cart was full, he collected the oxen from where they had been munching at the patches of forest grass, re-harnessed them and set off for home. However, as he drove over a patch of rough ground, the cart lurched and one of the axles broke.

PREVIEW

Repeated words

"I hope that Necessity fellow is nearby," thought the son. He stood up and shouted, "Necessity! NECESSITY!! NE-CESS-ITY!!!"

No one answered.

Then the young man ran up first one path, then another, always shouting at the top of his voice, "NECESSITY! NE-CESS-ITY!!"

Still there was no reply.

The son became worn out. "I will not bother searching for Father's clever friend any more," he said. "I will do the job myself. Father gave me useless advice."

NOTE

Climax

The young man went back to the cart, took off his coat, and unharnessed the oxen. He took some wood from the cart and mended the axle. Then he re-harnessed the oxen and drove home, having made a fine job of both the repair and of collecting good timber.

Fiction

His father was pleased with him, but the boy was not pleased with his father.

"I could not find that fellow, Necessity, anywhere," said the son. "He did not teach me anything. All I learned was that if a job needs doing, it is best to do it myself, then it is done quickly and well. If I go looking for help from other people, I can look forever."

"There you are," smiled the father. "Necessity did teach you a good lesson. I told you he would."

C Plan

In previewing "The Best Teacher," you probably learned a number of things.

- The characters are a father and his son.
- The father is concerned that his son doesn't know how to deal with bad luck.
- "Necessity" is important in the story.
- The son learns a lesson.

Now you need a plan for fulfilling your reading purpose.

Reading Strategy: Using Graphic Organizers

Graphic organizers are "word pictures." They shape information in a way that is easy to "see" to help you understand. As you read "The Best Teacher," **using graphic organizers** can help you keep track of what's happening in the folktale.

A Story String, for example, can organize the events in the plot by linking what happens first to what happens next, and so on. Story Strings are good organizers to use when a story has a long, winding plot with many events.

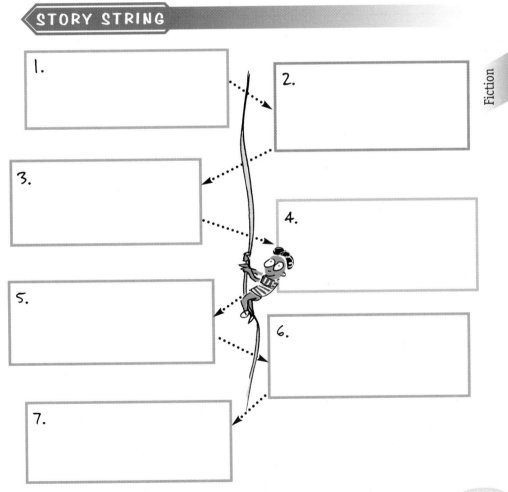

STORY STRING

1.

2.

3.

4.

5.

6.

7.

Fiction

During Reading

Now you are ready to read "The Best Teacher" carefully.

D Read with a Purpose

As you read, take notes and use a graphic organizer to record what happens. Remember, your purpose is to find out what the folktale is about and its main lesson.

1. Story String

Here is an example of the way to take detailed notes on the plot in a folktale. This Story String helps you keep track of what happens event by event.

STORY STRING

1. A father wants his son to have some experience dealing with bad luck.

2. He gives his son hard jobs to do. The son handles them well.

3. The father sends his son to the forest to cut wood. He gives him an old cart and tells him that "Necessity" will teach him what to do.

4. The son does his work well and starts home, but his cart breaks.

5. The son calls for Necessity, but no one answers.

6. The son gives up and fixes the cart himself. At home, he tells his father he's learned that if a job needs doing, he should do it himself.

7. The father is glad that his son has learned this lesson.

2. Story Organizer

Another kind of graphic organizer you might try looks at the beginning, middle, and end of the story. It simplifies a story into three parts to make it easier to see what happened. It helps you to see what changes during the story.

STORY ORGANIZER

BEGINNING	MIDDLE	END
The father thinks his son needs some experience of bad luck.	The father sends his son to the forest for wood. He tells him to rely on Necessity for help. The son calls for help when the cart breaks. But when no one answers, he solves the problem himself.	The son tells his father he learned that if a job needs doing, he should do it himself.

Fiction

How Folktales Are Organized

Most folktales follow a pattern like this one.

2. Rising Action
A problem or conflict arises which the characters try to solve. Tension builds.

3. Climax
Action reaches a critical point. The tension reaches a peak.

4. Falling Action
The conflict begins to be settled, and tension decreases.

1. Exposition
Background about the characters and their situation is given.

5. Resolution
The problem or conflict is solved, and the story ends.

PLOT DIAGRAM

2. RISING ACTION
Father sends son to forest to get wood. He tells son to rely on Necessity to solve any problems that arise. The cart breaks. Son calls again and again for Necessity but gets no answer.

3. CLIMAX
Son decides that his father gave him bad advice. He fixes the cart himself.

4. FALLING ACTION
After fixing the cart himself, he goes home with the wood.

1. EXPOSITION
A father worries that his son has little experience in solving problems.

5. RESOLUTION
The son learns a lesson: to handle problems by himself.

E Connect

As you read, imagine the scene and listen to your own thoughts. Try to connect with the reading. How do you feel about the father and the son? Does this folktale remind you of anything in your experience? Take notes on your reactions.

Here are one reader's responses to part of "The Best Teacher."

from "The Best Teacher"

Then the young man ran up first one path, then another, always shouting at the top of his voice, "NECESSITY! NE-CESS-ITY!!"

Still there was no reply.

The son became worn out. "I will not bother searching for Father's clever friend any more," he said. "I will do the job myself. Father gave me useless advice."

The young man went back to the cart, took off his coat, and unharnessed the oxen. He took some wood from the cart and mended the axle. Then he re-harnessed the oxen and drove home, having made a fine job of both the repair and of collecting good timber.

This is funny. But he must have been mad.

He starts to think for himself.

Good for him!

After Reading

After you finish reading, your job is to pull together all of what you have read.

F Pause and Reflect

Think for a minute about your reading purpose when you started. Consider those questions again.

Looking Back

- ■ **Do I know what the subject of the folktale is?**
- ■ **Do I know what main lesson is to be learned?**

You may not be sure about the lesson of the folktale, or you may have new questions.

G Reread

To answer any remaining questions, go back and reread parts of the folktale again. Try the strategy of close reading.

Rereading Strategy: Close Reading

Close reading means looking slowly and carefully at parts of a reading. To do close reading, you read line by line. Jot down your ideas about key quotes in a Double-entry Journal. Ask yourself questions like these:

What is this supposed to mean?

Why did the author describe it that way?

Why is this detail important?

DOUBLE-ENTRY JOURNAL

TEXT	MY THOUGHTS
" 'The lad must have some experience of dealing with ill luck,' said his father."	The father wants to teach his son a lesson. Maybe the father is the "best teacher" in the title.
"If that cart breaks up when you are alone in the forest, necessity will teach you what to do."	The father says "necessity will teach you." Maybe that means "the best teacher" is necessity.
"All I learned was that if a job needs doing, it is best to do it myself, then it is done quickly and well."	Here's what the son learned. I think the father was smart to send the son into the forest like he did.

Fiction

The Double-entry Journal above shows one reader's ideas about the title and lesson of the folktale. As a close reader, you focus on certain parts you want to study further. Look for sentences that sum up key parts of the story. Read them closely and decide what *you* think they mean.

H Remember

The key to learning is remembering what you have read. It's easy to remember something when it has meaning in your life. After reading, take a moment to make what you've read your own.

Because folktales are about what happened long ago, you might want to update this one and imagine what it would be like if it happened now. In your journal, "translate" the story of the folktale into the modern day. Here's the beginning of a modern version:

JOURNAL ENTRY

Everyone thinks I'm a softie. They think I never seem to work very hard—to get good grades, make the soccer team, or get picked for the solo in the concert. So my parents send me off to camp and say, "Maybe you'll learn how good you have it." We go camping in the woods, but to me it's like heaven. I love hiking and sleeping under the stars, but then it starts to rain and we get lost.

Summing Up

When you read a folktale, remember to use the reading process. After you preview and set a purpose, try the strategy of **using graphic organizers.** Use reading tools such as:

- Story String
- Plot Diagram
- Story Organizer
- Double-entry Journal

Note, too, the **five parts of the plot** of folktales. As you look back and reread, try using the strategy of **close reading.** It will help you focus on key passages.

Reading a Novel

Some readers gobble up one novel after another. Others look at a novel and think, "Yikes! How can I read all that?" No matter which group you fall into, you can make novel-reading easier if you use the reading process and apply the right strategies and tools.

Novels are works of fiction, imaginary rather than real. They can be based on real events and real characters, but they don't have to be. Novels are longer than stories or folktales. They allow writers more space for developing their stories and characters. In a novel, a writer can create new worlds that you can lose yourself in as a reader.

Goals

Here you'll learn how to:

✔ recognize the **basic elements of a novel:** character, setting, plot, and theme
✔ use the reading strategy of **synthesizing**
✔ understand the **organization of novels**

Fiction

Before Reading

Before reading a novel, set a purpose, preview, and plan.

A Set a Purpose

How do you set a purpose for reading a novel? You might be reading it only for fun. Or, you might be reading the novel for an assignment. Where do you start?

With long works like novels, focus your reading with a few good questions. Try to answer questions like these.

Setting a Purpose

- **Who are the main characters in the novel?**
- **When and where does the novel take place?**
- **What is the plot of the novel?**
- **What is its theme?**

B Preview

Novels can sometimes be hard to preview. But one of the keys to previewing well is knowing *where* to look. Use the Preview Checklist below to help you know where to look.

Preview Checklist

✔ the title and author

✔ the front and back covers

✔ any information on the inside front and back covers

✔ the table of contents and any chapter titles or illustrations

✔ the first paragraph

cover

LAURENCE YEP

The Magic Paintbrush

PREVIEW Author

PREVIEW Title

PREVIEW Illustration

back cover

PREVIEW Paragraph

When Steve grasped the painting, it tingled against his fingertips. He felt as if he had rubbed his shoes fast over a carpet. And the tingling spread through his whole hand. "What's going on?" he asked, scared.

PREVIEW Information about characters and plot

From the moment Grandfather gives Steve a magic paintbrush that grants wishes, life in Chinatown will never be the same.

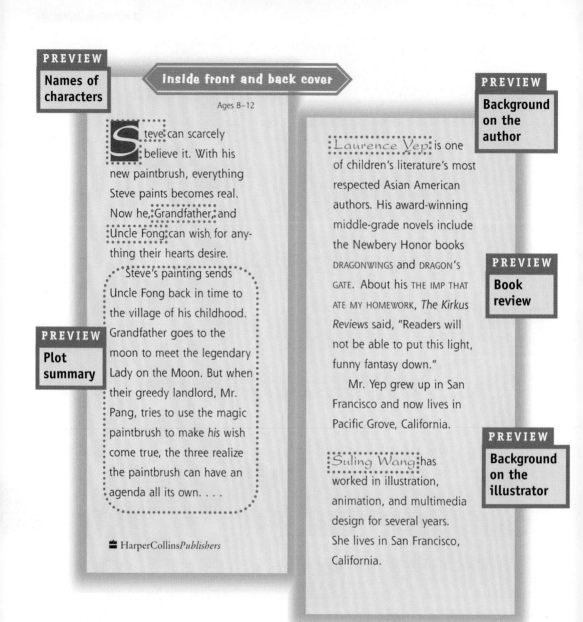

PREVIEW
Names of characters

inside front and back cover

Ages 8–12

PREVIEW
Background on the author

PREVIEW
Plot summary

Steve can scarcely believe it. With his new paintbrush, everything Steve paints becomes real. Now he, Grandfather, and Uncle Fong can wish for anything their hearts desire.

Steve's painting sends Uncle Fong back in time to the village of his childhood. Grandfather goes to the moon to meet the legendary Lady on the Moon. But when their greedy landlord, Mr. Pang, tries to use the magic paintbrush to make *his* wish come true, the three realize the paintbrush can have an agenda all its own. . . .

HarperCollins*Publishers*

Laurence Yep is one of children's literature's most respected Asian American authors. His award-winning middle-grade novels include the Newbery Honor books DRAGONWINGS and DRAGON'S GATE. About his THE IMP THAT ATE MY HOMEWORK, *The Kirkus Reviews* said, "Readers will not be able to put this light, funny fantasy down."

Mr. Yep grew up in San Francisco and now lives in Pacific Grove, California.

PREVIEW
Book review

Suling Wang has worked in illustration, animation, and multimedia design for several years. She lives in San Francisco, California.

PREVIEW
Background on the illustrator

The front and back covers on the previous page and the inside covers above give you a lot of information. They help you know what to expect in *The Magic Paintbrush*. Now preview the table of contents and the beginning of the first chapter. What do they tell you?

Table of Contents

PREVIEW

Table of Contents

Contents

PREVIEW

Chapter titles

Fiction

Chapter One

PREVIEW

Title of first chapter

Failure

PREVIEW

Beginning of story

Steve sat in the school yard long after school was over. He was really scared. What would his grandfather say when Steve went home? He preferred shivering outside to facing his grandfather.

C Plan

In your preview, you probably learned things like this:

- Laurence Yep is an award-winning Asian-American author.
- The novel is about a magic paintbrush that grants wishes.
- Characters include Steve, Grandfather, and Uncle Fong.

As you read, you have a lot to keep track of. You want to learn about characters, setting, plot, and theme:

- A **character** is a person or figure in a novel.
- The **setting** is where and when the novel takes place.
- The **plot** is the action or events of the novel.
- The **theme** is the author's statement about life.

You need a plan that will help you achieve your reading purposes.

Reading Strategy: Synthesizing

Synthesizing means "pulling together." It means looking at different elements of the novel—characters, setting, plot, and theme—and then pulling them all together.

A Fiction Organizer like the one below can help you record information that you find about the main elements of the novel.

FICTION ORGANIZER

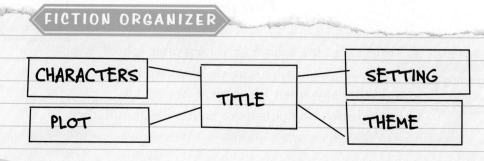

CHARACTERS

PLOT

TITLE

SETTING

THEME

During Reading

Now you are ready to read parts of *The Magic Paintbrush*.

D Read with a Purpose

As you read, think about your reading purposes. You want to learn about the novel's characters, setting, plot, and theme. You also want to know how the magic paintbrush affects the lives of the characters.

1. Characters

The **characters** are the people, creatures, or animals in the novel. In most novels, characters are the most important element. You learn about a novel's characters in the same way that you learn about real people. You note how they look, act, speak, think, and feel. You watch the way other characters react to them.

READING A NOVEL

✔ Fiction Organizer
✔ Character Map
✔ Setting Chart
✔ Summary Notes
✔ Plot Diagram
✔ Theme Diagram

Fiction

See what you learn about the character Steve in this passage. As Steve sits in the schoolyard, he thinks about his dead parents.

> from *The Magic Paintbrush* by Laurence Yep
>
> He tried to remember what they looked like, but all he could see were flames. He screwed his eyebrows together as he fought to recall them. No matter how hard he struggled, they were always hidden by fire.

NOTE
What he does

231

NOTE

How he feels

He was all alone now—except for his grandfather. And that was the same thing as being alone.

Grandfather was mean. Steve knew his grandfather didn't want him. After the fire he had to go live in Chinatown. Grandfather had told Steve he could bring only one box with him to Chinatown. How do you put your whole life into just one box? Not that he had much left after the fire. He had lost everything . . . his parents, his toys, his books, his clothes.

NOTE

What others think

And everything Steve did just made his grandfather meaner. He never spoke to Steve except to scold him. And now Steve was sure his grandfather was going to blow his top.

CHARACTER MAP

Use a Character Map to take notes on what a character is like. You might start an organizer like this one for Steve.

CHARACTER MAP

WHAT HE SAYS AND DOES	WHAT OTHERS THINK
Steve tries to please Grandfather. He wants to remember his parents.	Grandfather is mean to him and scolds him.

STEVE

HOW HE LOOKS AND FEELS	HOW I FEEL ABOUT HIM
• misses his parents • feels all alone • afraid of grandfather	I feel sorry for him.

2. Setting

The **setting** is the time and place of the novel. Novels usually have a general setting—one place and time period—for the whole book. Then events happen at specific times and places. Sometimes setting creates a mood for the story and helps you learn about the characters. What do you learn here?

> **from** *The Magic Paintbrush*
>
> [Steve] opened his eyes now. He was still caught in a nightmare, and it was getting worse. The Chinatown shadows were growing longer. All around him the doorways started to look like mouths. They stretched wide to swallow him.
>
> Finally he got more scared of the Chinatown streets than of his grandfather. Slowly he walked through the narrow alleys until he reached his grandfather's apartment building. Steve couldn't think of the ugly building as his home.
>
> The tenement house was all of dark-red brick. Dirt made the bricks look even darker. It had a narrow front that rose for three stories.

NOTE
Time of day

NOTE
General place

NOTE
How the character feels

NOTE
Exact place

Now read what Steve finds inside the apartment.

> **from** *The Magic Paintbrush*
>
> The bare bulb dangling from the ceiling cast a harsh light over the tiny, cramped room. The paint on the old walls was peeling or stained orange and brown where the rain had leaked or pipes had burst. It was tiny compared to his old bedroom. The room was barely ten by ten feet. A small table stood near the doorway as he entered. On the table were their hot plates, glasses, dishes, and chopsticks. None of the dishes matched. Most of them came from restaurants where Grandfather had washed dishes.

NOTE
What the room looks like

Fiction

233

SETTING CHART

As you read a novel, record what you learn about times and places in a Setting Chart like the one below. Use a Setting Chart to help you summarize settings for the entire novel.

SETTING CHART

CLUES ABOUT TIME	CLUES ABOUT PLACE
Time of Day	**General place**
afternoon or	Chinatown
evening	**Exact place**
Historical Period	• tiny, crowded apartment
now	in rundown tenement
	building
	• not very fancy things

3. Plot

A **plot** is the series of events that make up a piece of fiction. These might be exciting events like rocket launches or forest fires. Or they might be quieter events like changes in the ways that characters feel, think, act, or relate to each other.

What are the plot events of *The Magic Paintbrush*? You already know that Steve's parents have died and that he feels lonely living with Grandfather. When the novel opens, Steve is afraid to go home and tell Grandfather that he got an F and needs a new paintbrush for school. Grandfather is not mad. Instead, he starts looking for something in an old suitcase when Steve finally tells him about the F.

from *The Magic Paintbrush*

As Grandfather continued to sift through the contents of the suitcase, Steve heard mysterious clinkings and clackings. They sounded like music, and Grandfather looked as if he were far away. Steve wondered what Grandfather was remembering.

NOTE
Plot events

"Ah," Grandfather finally said when he found what he wanted. "Here. You can use this, Steve."

When he turned around, Grandfather had a brush in his hands.

SUMMARY NOTES

As you read a novel, you can keep track of plot events like these by using a number of different organizers. One way to do it is with chapter-by-chapter Summary Notes like those below. These notes will help you remember what happened in the novel. Write down events as you read about them.

SUMMARY NOTES

Fiction

CHAPTER 1
- Steve's parents died in a fire, and he now lives in Chinatown with his grandfather and Uncle Fong.
- Steve feels lonely and afraid.
- His teacher gave him an F in art class, and he shows Grandfather the picture with an F.

CHAPTER 2
- Grandfather doesn't get mad.
- He gives Steve a paintbrush he finds in an old suitcase.

How Novels Are Organized

The plots of novels usually follow a pattern like this one.

PLOT STRUCTURE

2. Rising Action
*The characters try
to solve the problem.
It usually gets worse.*

3. Climax
*Action, conflict, and tension
reach a critical point.*

4. Falling Action
*The conflict gets
worked out.*

1. Exposition
*The characters,
setting, and conflict,
or problem, are
introduced.*

5. Resolution
*The ending tells
the outcome.*

As you read a novel, look for these five parts of the plot.
Try making a Plot Diagram.

PLOT DIAGRAM OF *THE MAGIC PAINTBRUSH*

Climax
Steve, Grandfather, and Uncle Fong rescue
Mr. Pang, who is trapped in a painting.

Rising Action
Mr. Pang, the mean landlord,
tricks them into giving him
the paintbrush.

Falling Action
Mr. Pang fixes up the
building.

Exposition
Steve feels sad and alone
living with his Grandfather
and Uncle Fong.

Resolution
Steve, Grandfather,
and Uncle Fong are
happy together.

E Connect

As you read, read actively. Make personal connections between what you're reading and your own life. How do you feel about the characters? What do you think about the events of the story? What can you learn about yourself and about your life from this novel? If you read actively, you'll learn much more from your reading.

Here are one reader's reactions to a scene in the novel. Steve has just discovered that whatever he paints becomes real.

from *The Magic Paintbrush*

When they had cleaned up everything, they sat down on their beds. As Steve picked up the brush again in his right hand, he felt it tremble in his fingers. "So what do I paint next?"

"I would like a peach from home." Uncle Fong closed his eyes. "One with a lovely scent that fills the room. And when you bite into it, the juice runs into your mouth. And it's as sweet as summer. And the scent is like perfume."

"That's a tall order," Grandfather said, glancing uncertainly at Steve.

Uncle Fong folded his arms. "That's what I want."

"And anyway, who said you could go first?" Grandfather demanded.

Steve thought he saw a way to please both old men. In his hand he felt the brush twitching eagerly. He had to use two hands to keep it still. "Do you still want a window, Grandfather?"

I can almost taste it.

He sounds like my grandfather.

Fiction

After Reading

After you finish a novel, you may want to move on right away
to another one, especially if it's as much fun as *The Magic
Paintbrush*. But you'll also want to think about some
of the novel's "big ideas." To understand the novel, your
job is to pull all of its parts together.

F Pause and Reflect

After reading, think for a moment about your reading
purpose. Can you answer all of these questions?

Looking Back

■ **Who are the main characters in the novel?**
■ **When and where does the novel take place?**
■ **What is the plot of the novel?**
■ **What is its theme?**

If you can't answer these questions—or if you don't
understand parts of the novel—rereading can help you.

G Reread

Novels are long and full of details. To find any details or
information you might have missed, you'll need to reread
key parts or chapters.

Rereading Strategy: Using Graphic Organizers

Using graphic organizers can help you to focus on a specific
part of the novel. Organizers allow you to pull together all of
the elements—characters, setting, plot, and theme.

4. Theme

A novel's **theme** is a statement that the author makes about life. In novels, themes often are statements about such topics as courage, love, childhood, justice, family, prejudice, war, or friendship.

Sometimes an author states the theme directly. Other times, you need to find the theme. When you look for theme, ask yourself three questions:

1. What topics or "big ideas" is the novel about?

2. What do characters say or do that relates to that topic?

3. What do these things tell you is important to learn about life?

As a first step, try finding the topics or "big ideas" in this passage. Then see how one reader completed a Theme Diagram.

---

from The Magic Paintbrush

Grandfather cleared his throat. "In other words, what would make you happy?"

"Well, I . . ." Uncle Fong said, and then scratched his head. "You know, I'm not sure. I never thought about that part."

Grandfather wagged one leg up and down. "Just so. None of us have. We don't want money. We want what money can buy. We want our hearts' desire, as the poets say."

Steve looked at his grandfather, impressed. He hadn't thought Grandfather was such a wise man.

Grandfather awkwardly patted Steve on the back. "Steve can give us our dreams."

Uncle Fong shook his head. "I gave up dreaming a long time ago."

"Then start again, old man," Grandfather said.

NOTE
Wishes

Fiction

NOTE
Dreams

Step 1: What topic or "big idea" is the novel about?

WISHES AND DREAMS

Step 2: What do the characters say or do that relates to this topic?

The magic paintbrush can make wishes come true.	Uncle Fong and Grandfather get to live their dreams by visiting Fong's home in China and meeting the Lady on the Moon.	Grandfather wants others to dream.

Step 3: What do these things tell you that is important to learn about life?

Following your dreams can lead to happiness.

H Remember

The key to learning is remembering what you have read. In your reading journal, create a summary of the novel by taking notes or creating an organizer. Look at how one reader used a Fiction Organizer to gather important information.

FICTION ORGANIZER

CHARACTERS: Steve, Grandfather, Uncle Fong, and Mr. Pang

SETTING: Time: today
Places: Chinatown in San Francisco, schoolyard, apartment, Uncle Fong's village in China, the moon, a mansion

TITLE AND AUTHOR:
The Magic Paintbrush
by Laurence Yep

PLOT: Steve lost his parents in a fire and now lives with Grandfather and Uncle Fong. He feels sad and lonely. Grandfather gives him a magic paintbrush that makes things real. Steve and the two old men have adventures. By the end, Steve feels happy and loved.

THEME: Following your dreams can lead to happiness.

Fiction

Summing Up

When you read a novel, remember to use the reading process and apply the reading strategy of **synthesizing.** Pay attention to the **plot structure of a novel** and use tools such as:

- Fiction Organizer
- Character Map
- Setting Chart
- Summary Notes
- Plot Diagram
- Theme Diagram

As you reread, remember that the strategy of **using graphic organizers** can be helpful in pulling together all the main elements of a novel.

Focus on Characters

Think about your favorite books and stories. What do you like best about them? If you are like most readers, your favorite thing is the **characters**—the people or animals created by the author. Characters usually are the central point of interest in fiction.

Goals

Here you'll learn how to:

✔ **identify major and minor characters**

✔ **find out how to understand characters in fiction**

✔ **recognize the ways characters change or develop through a story**

Before Reading

As you preview fiction, look for names of important characters on the back and inside book covers. You'll also find characters' names in the first few paragraphs and repeated throughout the story.

Identify Major and Minor Characters

In fiction, the major characters are central to what you read. Minor characters play smaller roles.

To identify major characters, ask yourself these questions:

Who is most involved in the main conflict of the story?

Whose name appears most often?

Which character do I learn the most about?

In this passage, who do you think the main character is?

from *The Midnight Fox* by Betsy Byars

The first three days on the farm were the longest, slowest days of my life. It seemed to me in those days that nothing was moving at all, not air, not time. Even the bees, the biggest, fattest bees that I had ever seen, just seemed to hang in the air. The problem, or one of them, was that I was not an enormously adaptable person and I did not fit into new situations well.

I did a lot of just standing around those first days. I would be standing in the kitchen and Aunt Millie would turn around, stirring something, and bump into me and say, "Oh, my goodness! You gave me a scare. I didn't even hear you come in. When *did* you come in?"

"Just a minute ago."

"Well, I didn't hear you. You are so *quiet.*"

Or Uncle Fred would come out of the barn wiping his hands on a rag and there I'd be, just standing, and he'd say, "Well, boy, how's it going?"

"Fine, Uncle Fred."

> **NOTE**
> Narrator of story

> **NOTE**
> New character

> **NOTE**
> New character

Fiction

How many characters did you spot? You probably saw names of two characters—Aunt Millie and Uncle Fred. But the passage is mostly about the main character, who is the narrator, a boy named Tom. You can tell by the pronouns *I, me,* and *my.* That's the narrator talking about himself. In this story, you see all of the other characters through his eyes.

To find and keep track of the characters in a story, look for:

- names of people
- words that show relationships, such as *mother, father, sister, aunt,* and *uncle*
- pronouns such as *I, me, he, she, him,* and *her*

243

During Reading

As you begin to read a story, watch the characters as if they were real people. Notice details about them. Writers give you details about characters little by little throughout the story.

Learn about Characters

Look for details about characters by paying attention to:

■ how they look and what they say, think, and feel

■ how they act and react to others

■ what the author says about them

Note all of the details about characters sprinkled through this passage.

---

from *The Midnight Fox*

[Aunt Millie] looked at me and nodded. "I think it got one of the hens sometime last week too."

Uncle Fred turned his iced-tea glass up and drained the contents.

NOTE
How Aunt Millie acts

"Well?" Aunt Millie said to him. She had been very irritable with all of us for a week. The heat was unbearable and with each passing day, as the ground got drier and the sun hotter, she had grown more

NOTE
How the narrator feels about her

fussy. She had been saying for days, "I don't know what I'll do if it doesn't rain," and now it was as if she had made up her mind, and what she had decided to do was take out all her ill feelings on my fox.

"I'm not going to put up with it," she continued. "I mean it, Fred. Once a fox gets started, he'll clean

NOTE
How Aunt Millie feels

out the whole henhouse. I have worked too hard on those hens to just stand by and watch some fox walk off with them one by one."

from *The Midnight Fox*, continued

"I know that, Millie."

"Well, you are certainly acting mighty unconcerned about the whole thing," she snapped. She pressed her napkin to her face. "If the fox had made off with one of your precious pigs, I'd like to see what you'd do."

"I'll take care of it," Uncle Fred said.

> **NOTE**
> What Aunt Millie says

> **NOTE**
> What Uncle Fred says

Using a Character Map

To learn about characters, pay attention to the details that authors give you throughout a story. A Character Map helps you take notes about the details of a character. It is a good tool to use when you want to look at a character from several angles. The Character Map helps you collect details about how the character looks, thinks, and feels. It also records what the character says and what other characters think about him or her.

Fiction

CHARACTER MAP

WHAT CHARACTER SAYS AND DOES	WHAT OTHERS THINK ABOUT THE CHARACTER
• acts crabby and fussy • seems only to care about her hens	• Uncle Fred seems nervous or afraid. • Tom is afraid of her and what she'll do.

(AUNT MILLIE)

HOW THE CHARACTER LOOKS AND FEELS	HOW I FEEL ABOUT THE CHARACTER
• She feels hot. • She thinks Uncle Fred doesn't care. • She doesn't care about Tom's fox.	• I don't like her. • She seems mad.

Watch How Characters Develop

Characters often change in the course of a story. Little by little, you learn about them. The more you read, the more you learn. As a reader, part of your job is to note the ways that characters change and develop.

Now read one of the dramatic moments in *The Midnight Fox*. First, find out what happens. Then, reflect on what you learn about Tom, the narrator, from this passage.

NOTE
What character says

NOTE
How the character feels

NOTE
What character does

from *The Midnight Fox*

I got up and ran to the rabbit hutch. The baby fox was huddled in one corner of the pen where there was some shelter from the rain. The lightning flashed and I saw him watching me.

"I'm going to get you out," I said.

He crouched back farther in the hutch. In the next flash of lightning I looked on the ground for a rock and I saw at my feet a small dead frog. I knew that the black fox in all this rain had brought that frog here to her baby. She was right now watching me somewhere.

There were bricks stacked in a neat pile under the hutch and I took one and began to bang it against the lock. I was prepared to do this all night if necessary, but the lock was an old one and it opened right away.

The noise had scared the baby fox and he was now making a whimpering sound. I unhooked the broken lock, opened the cage, and stepped back against the tree.

The baby fox did not move for a moment. I could barely see him, a small dark ball in the back of the cage. He waited, alert and suspicious, and then, after

from *The Midnight Fox*, continued

a moment he moved in a crouch to the door of the cage. He cried sharply. From the bushes there was an answering bark.

It took a lot of courage for Tom to set the fox free. Then you learn he's not the only character who changes.

from *The Midnight Fox*

"Tom," she said again.

"Tom?"

"Yes, he was just standing out there on the porch."

They both turned and looked at me, waiting for an explanation, and I cleared my throat and said, "Uncle Fred and Aunt Millie, I am awfully sorry but I have let the baby fox out of the rabbit hutch." I sounded very stiff and formal and I thought the voice was a terrible thing to have to depend on, because I really did want them to know I was sorry, and I didn't sound it the least bit. I knew how much Uncle Fred had looked forward to the hunt and how important getting rid of the fox was to Aunt Millie, and I hated for them to be disappointed now.

There was a moment of silence. Then Aunt Millie said, "Why, that's perfectly all right, isn't it, Fred? Don't you think another thing about that. You just come to bed."

NOTE
Change in Tom

Fiction

NOTE
Change in Aunt Millie

Watch for how characters change in a story. Changes in character are often shown by what they feel or think. By tracking what happens to characters during a story, you often understand the theme, or author's statement about life.

After Reading

At the end of the story, it's time to review what you've learned about the characters. One good way to see how characters have changed is with a Character Development Chart. To make one, note how a character acts or what a character does at the beginning, middle, and end of a story. Then, if you can, tell what lesson about life (or theme) the change in the character suggests.

CHARACTER DEVELOPMENT CHART

BEGINNING	MIDDLE	END
Tom—afraid to speak his mind	Tom—afraid to defend the foxes	Tom—sets the baby fox free and tells aunt and uncle
POSSIBLE THEME:		
It's important to stand up for what you believe.		

Often at the end of a story, you will want to go back and reread parts to see exactly what one character says or does at a specific point. By doing that, you will see how characters develop. If you reread the passages in this lesson, you would see that Tom doesn't say anything to his aunt at first. But, by the last passage, he gains the courage to tell her he set the fox free.

Summing Up

- Fictional characters can be major or minor.
- You learn about characters by watching what they say, think, feel, and do and how other characters react to them.
- Seeing how characters develop during a story helps you understand the theme.

Focus on Setting

Do you like action in stories? Do you like to find out what happens? If so, you might skip over details about setting in a rush to find out how things turn out. But those details about the **setting**—the time and place—aren't just fluff that you can skip over.

Good readers know that the details of the setting can tell you a lot about what's really going on in a story. In fiction, the time and place of the story often have a great effect on the characters and on the story's overall feeling, or mood.

Fiction

Goals

Here you'll learn how to:

✔ **find clues about the setting**

✔ **see, or visualize, a setting**

✔ **read the setting to learn more about the mood and characters**

Before Reading

To find information about the setting, start looking for words about time and place. You can do this during a preview. Many writers describe the setting in the first few paragraphs or pages.

Find Clues about the Setting

When your focus is setting, look for words that tell about:

- time of day, day of the week, month, or season
- specific dates or historical details
- place names, such as city, state, or country
- physical surroundings, such as weather, buildings, and landscape

Read this paragraph from the beginning of a novel. Note how much you can learn from a few carefully placed details.

from *Song of the Trees* by Mildred D. Taylor

NOTE
Time of day is morning.

NOTE
Place is a farm.

NOTE
Place: Mississippi

NOTE
Season is just before corn is ripe.

I opened the window and looked outside. The earth was draped in a cloak of gray mist as the sun chased the night away. The cotton stalks, which in another hour would glisten greenly toward the sun, were gray. The ripening corn, wrapped in jackets of emerald and gold, was gray. Even the rich brown Mississippi earth was gray.

Record the details in a Setting Chart. It gives you a way to organize information about the time and place of the story.

SETTING CHART

CLUES ABOUT TIME	CLUES ABOUT PLACE
Time of Day	**Place Name**
morning	Mississippi
Season	**Surroundings**
just before corn is ripe	a farm with cotton and corn
(late summer)	and rich, brown earth

During Reading

As you read, note details about the time and place. Start by creating a picture of the setting in your mind. Then make inferences about what the setting tells you about the characters and mood of the story. Remember that writers will often signal that something is about to happen through changes in the setting.

Picture the Setting

Maybe you have noticed that authors choose words very carefully when they're describing a setting. They give specific details to help you picture the scene in your mind. Read the passage below and "see" the scene that's described.

from *Song of the Trees*

After breakfast when the sun was streaking red across the sky, my brothers and I ambled into the coolness of the forest leading our three cows and their calves down the narrow cow path to the pond. The morning was already muggy, but the trees closed out the heat as their leaves waved restlessly, high above our heads.

"Good morning, Mr. Trees," I shouted. They answered me with a soft, swooshing sound. "Hear 'em, Stacey? Hear 'em singing?"

"Ah, cut that out, Cassie. Them trees ain't singing. How many times I gotta tell you that's just the wind?"

NOTE
Beautiful scene

NOTE
Lots of sensory details

Fiction

As you picture the scene in your mind, you might even try to sketch it. Besides being fun, the act of drawing the scene will help you "see" the details more clearly as well as remember them better.

"Read" the Setting

After you picture a setting, you need to "read" it. That is, you need to read between the lines and make inferences about what it tells you. Usually the setting tells you:

■ about the feeling, or mood, of the moment

■ about how characters feel or what they are like

■ about something new that is about to happen in the plot

A reading tool called a Double-entry Journal gives you a good way to make inferences about specific details you've noticed about the setting.

DOUBLE-ENTRY JOURNAL

QUOTES	MY THOUGHTS
"...my brothers and I ambled into the coolness of the forest...."	The mood is slow, relaxed, and happy.
"'Good morning, Mr. Trees,' I shouted. They answered me...."	Cassie sees the trees as her friends. She's fun and playful.

After Reading

To understand the setting in a story or novel, you often have to look back and think about it. Try to remember where the action of the story takes place. Ask yourself questions like these:

Where did the important parts of the story take place?

How would I describe the setting?

How was the setting important to what happened there?

What else would change if the setting had been different?

In *Song of the Trees*, for example, you might ask yourself why the farm setting in Mississippi is important. Why is it important that the story is set there in Mississippi and not, say, in Alaska?

Fiction

Summing Up

- Authors usually give you clues about the time and place at the beginning of the story.
- Look for details about time, place, location, weather, and physical surroundings.
- Try to picture the setting in your mind as you read and, if possible, sketch it.
- Read between the lines of the setting to see what you can learn about the mood and the characters of the story.

Focus on Dialogue

Dialogue means "talking together" or "conversation." It refers to the conversation that characters have with one another in fiction and in other writing. As a reader, you'll probably find the dialogue among characters to be some of the most interesting and important parts of your reading.

Goals

Here you'll learn how to:

✔ **recognize the form of dialogue**

✔ **understand how dialogue gives you clues about character, plot, and mood**

✔ **look at ways of analyzing dialogue**

"Can we stop and

Mama Rosa laughed.

I begged.

she let me go.

Before Reading

You know what dialogue sounds like. You hear people talking all day long. Can you recognize it in written works?

As you preview most readings, you can find the dialogue by looking for two things:

- quotation marks at the beginning and end of words
- speech tags (information about who's speaking and how the speaker is feeling or acting)

Use these clues to find the dialogue in this passage.

NOTE
Quotation marks

NOTE
New paragraph for new speaker

from "Birthday Piñata" by Lulu Delacre

NOTE
Speech tag

Fiction

"Can we stop and look at the *piñatas*— PLEASE—Mama Rosa?" I begged.

"How many times have you seen them?" Mama Rosa laughed. But of course, she let me go.

You could probably tell there are two speakers in this passage. Did you notice the short, indented lines? Usually a writer starts a new paragraph when beginning dialogue. Then, when the next speaker starts, another new paragraph starts. Quotation marks are used to signal the beginning and end of the exact words of a speaker.

Reading Strategy: Close Reading

Dialogue can sometimes be tough to read, so you need to read it slowly and carefully. Imagine what the conversations would sound like. Sometimes you have to examine key parts line by line and word by word, as you do in **close reading**.

During Reading

As you read, dialogue gives you clues about what characters are like, how the plot will change, and what the mood of the story is.

Dialogue and Character

In real life, you learn a lot about a person by listening to him or her talk. It works the same for stories. When you read dialogue, pay close attention to what the different characters say to one another. Look for details about who the characters are, what they believe, and what they think of themselves and others.

You can learn about characters by watching for:

■ what characters say

■ how characters feel

■ what characters do

Now read another part of "Birthday Piñata." What do you learn about Mami? She has just returned to her home in Mexico after a day of working for a woman in the United States.

from "Birthday Piñata"

"You won't believe the day I had!" [Mami] exclaimed. She was out of breath. "This morning they stopped me at the border. They held me for hours, asking all kinds of questions. They asked what was I going to buy . . . how much was I going to spend . . . what stores was I going to. . . I was so nervous, I couldn't even answer. By the time they let me go, it was very late, and I thought I might lose my job. I was lucky Señora Smith didn't get mad. Then I worked late to make up for the time I lost." Mami collapsed next to me on the small couch where I sat, and her head sunk into her hands. "I was careful to return after the change of border patrols," she said.

> **NOTE**
> Mami is excited.

> **NOTE**
> Mami worries about keeping her job.

> **NOTE**
> Mami plans ahead to avoid trouble.

Fiction

Sometimes you might want to use a Double-entry Journal like the one below to record your thoughts about dialogue. Choose a few key sentences and record your thoughts about them. Here's how one reader reacted to what Mami said about working late.

DOUBLE-ENTRY JOURNAL

DIALOGUE	MY THOUGHTS
"I was lucky Señora Smith didn't get mad. Then I worked late to make up for the time I lost."	Mami must have needed to work to make money. She really doesn't want to lose her job. After this bad experience, she still went to work and even worked late. She seems very hard-working and responsible.

Dialogue and Plot

The plot of a story is what happens—the series of events that the author describes. So, when characters talk, they often give you clues about the plot.

Think of all that you learned about what happened to Mami.

- Mami's probably not supposed to work across the border. She was held and questioned for hours.

- She got to work late and then stayed late.

- Mami and her family need the job with Señora Smith.

- Mami's nervous about crossing the border.

One short bit of dialogue can give you a lot of background.

Dialogue and Mood

What the characters say and how they say it can affect the mood, or feeling, that the story gives you. In the passage below, note the speech tags and clues the dialogue gives about the characters' emotions and the overall mood.

from "Birthday Piñata"

NOTE
Tension and sadness

   "I don't like it," Mama Rosa complained. "What if the guards filed a report? You could end up in jail. Can't you quit?"

   "No," said Mami, weeping. "We need the money I bring home."

NOTE
Speech tags

   "It is true that with the money you bring we can buy many things we need," Papa said. "But it is not worth it if you get into trouble. We can do without some things."

The questions and doubts here create an overall mood. The feeling you get is that things are tense.

After Reading

After reading, reflect on what you learned from the dialogue. One way to do that is with a Thinking Tree that looks at dialogue three ways:

- clues it gives about characters
- information it gives about the plot
- what it tells about the mood

THINKING TREE

DIALOGUE

gives character clues

what they say and how

Example: "I was so nervous. . . ."

gives plot information

what will happen

Example: "You could end up in jail."

tells about mood

can add tension

Example: "No," said Mami, weeping.

Fiction

A Thinking Tree helps you organize details you learned from dialogue. Make your Thinking Tree as detailed or as simple as you want and need.

Summing Up

- **Speech tags and quotation marks signal dialogue in a written work.**
- **Usually a new paragraph begins whenever there's a new speaker.**
- **Dialogue and speech tags provide many clues about the characters, plot, and mood.**

Focus on Plot

After seeing a terrific movie, you call up your best friend and report what happened from beginning to end. You may not know it, but you've just summarized the plot of the movie.

A **plot** is the action or series of events in a work of fiction. Sometimes important events in a plot are changes in a character's feelings or attitudes.

Other times they are action-packed events, such as earthquakes, space journeys, or shipwrecks.

Goals

Here you'll learn how to:

✔ understand what the plot of a story is

✔ recognize parts of a plot

✔ understand subplots and how they relate to the main plot

Before Reading

In most stories, the plot concerns one or more problems or conflicts. To keep you reading, authors set up interesting characters and situations. Then, they give their characters big problems or conflicts to deal with. As a reader, you get interested in watching how the characters struggle to overcome their problems.

As you preview this passage from the beginning of the novel *Matilda*, look for the conflict. What problem faces young Matilda Wormwood?

Fiction

from *Matilda* by Roald Dahl

By the time she was *three*, Matilda had taught herself to read by studying newspapers and magazines that lay around the house. At the age of *four*, she could read fast and well and she naturally began hankering after books. The only book in the whole of this enlightened household was something called *Easy Cooking* belonging to her mother, and when she had read this from cover to cover and had learnt all of the recipes by heart, she decided she wanted something more interesting.

> NOTE
> **Problem for Matilda**

"Daddy," she said, "do you think you could buy me a book?"

"A *book*?" he said. "What d'you want a flaming book for?"

"To read, Daddy."

"What's wrong with the telly, for heaven's sake? We've got a lovely telly with a twelve-inch screen and now you come asking for a book! You're getting spoiled, my girl."

> NOTE
> **Conflict with her father**

During Reading

Once you find a problem or conflict in a story, you'll want to pay attention to how it develops. For instance, as you read *Matilda*, you'll follow the problems Matilda has with her parents, who make her life miserable. You will also discover that she has problems at school with the mean headmistress, Miss Trunchbull. Some plots can be complicated. Several kinds of organizers can help you keep track of the plot.

Note Beginning, Middle, and End

For example, one easy way to think about the plot is to note what happens in the beginning, middle, and end. A Story Organizer gives you a clear, simple way to keep track of important events and changes in a story. Here is how one reader summarized the plot of *Matilda*.

STORY ORGANIZER

BEGINNING	MIDDLE	END
Matilda is brilliant and wants to read and learn. But she's unhappy at home with parents who don't understand her.	Matilda goes to school, but she has problems with Miss Trunchbull, who's mean to everybody.	Matilda is finally happy. Miss Trunchbull and Matilda's family leave, and Matilda goes to live with her teacher Miss Honey, who loves her.

Look for Parts of the Plot

Once you have read a number of stories, you begin to see similarities in how plots are organized. A character and situation begin a story. Then, a problem develops, gets a little worse, builds to a climax, and finally comes to an end. A Plot Diagram gives you a way to keep track of the five parts of a plot.

Here is a Plot Diagram one reader made for *Matilda*.

⟨ PLOT DIAGRAM ⟩

3. CLIMAX
Matilda uses her magical powers to defeat Miss Trunchbull and help Miss Honey.

2. RISING ACTION
Matilda becomes more upset at her family and mean Miss Trunchbull.

4. FALLING ACTION
Miss Honey moves to a bigger house, and Miss Trunchbull leaves the school.

1. EXPOSITION
Matilda is upset by her parents, who don't understand her.

5. RESOLUTION
Matilda moves in with Miss Honey when Matilda's family leaves town.

Fiction

As you read fiction, be on the lookout for these parts of the plot. Not all stories will have all five parts. But pay attention to how action builds to a climax and how a problem is solved.

Find Plots and Subplots

A *subplot* is a brief story within the larger story. This plot is less important than the main plot. It might involve different problems, characters, or settings.

In *Matilda*, most of the action in the main plot centers around young Matilda. But, a subplot about her father develops, too. It comes to a climax in the final pages as Matilda learns her family is suddenly moving to Spain.

> **from *Matilda***
>
> "Why?" Matilda cried. "Please tell me why." She was still out of breath from the running and from the shock of it all.
>
> "Because your father," Miss Honey said, "is in with a bunch of crooks. Everyone in the village knows that. My guess is that he is a receiver of stolen cars from all over the country. He's in it deep."
>
> Matilda stared at her open-mouthed.
>
> Miss Honey went on, "People brought stolen cars to your father's workshop where he changed the number-plates and resprayed the bodies a different color and all the rest of it. And now somebody's probably tipped him off that the police are on to him and he's doing what they all do, running off to Spain where they can't get him. He'll have been sending his money out there for years, all ready and waiting for him to arrive."

NOTE
What Matilda's father has done

NOTE
What Matilda's father will do

Writers add subplots to increase readers' interest, to develop some characters further, and to add a second or third theme to the story. The subplot about Mr. Wormwood's illegal business activities makes readers like him less and like Matilda even more.

After Reading

When you finish a story or novel, stop to think about it. See whether you can summarize the key events. Can you describe the conflicts and how they're resolved? Try also to identify what *changed* in the story. Important events and changes are the keys to understanding plot.

Track Key Events

Use a Storyboard to track the key events and changes in a story. Draw a picture of each main event or change, with a note for each one. The Storyboard below, for instance, shows four events that make Matilda happy.

STORYBOARD

1. Matilda reads by herself at the library.

2. She goes to school and gets away from her parents.

3. She meets mean Miss Trunchbull, but defeats her.

4. Matilda goes to live with her teacher Miss Honey.

Fiction

Talk about the Plot

Another way to remember the plot is to tell a friend what you think of the events of a story. Share your questions about what happened and your ideas about what the plot means. For instance, you might have enjoyed the scenes of Matilda at home with her mean family, but your friend might have liked the times when Matilda uses her magical powers. Here's a Venn Diagram you could use to compare and contrast the plot and the subplot.

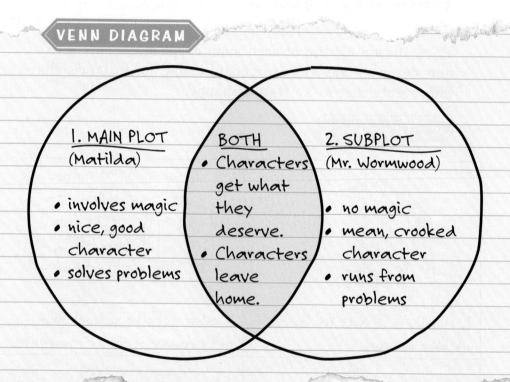

VENN DIAGRAM

1. MAIN PLOT (Matilda)
- involves magic
- nice, good character
- solves problems

BOTH
- Characters get what they deserve.
- Characters leave home.

2. SUBPLOT (Mr. Wormwood)
- no magic
- mean, crooked character
- runs from problems

Summing Up

- The plot usually revolves around a problem or conflict that a character faces.
- Most plots have five parts: exposition, rising action, climax, falling action, and resolution.
- A subplot is a smaller story within the main plot.

Focus on Theme

When you read, you can learn a lot about life. In fact, one reason to read is to learn what writers say through their work. A writer's message in a folktale, story, novel, or play is called a **theme.**

Part of your job as a reader is to understand what a writer is trying to say. How do you figure that out? Writers seldom come right out and tell you, "Hey, reader, this is what I want you to know." You need to make inferences and draw conclusions about what a writer is trying to express. Here you will read a folktale and learn to use an easy, three-step plan to find the theme.

Goals

Here you'll learn how to:

✔ **find the topic, or big idea**

✔ **look at what the characters say and do relating to the topic**

✔ **decide what the theme is**

Fiction

Before Reading

Looking for the theme begins when you start the reading process and begin to preview. As you read, you think about what the theme might be. Then, after reading, you decide what statement about life the writer is making.

Here's an easy, three-step plan for finding a theme.

FINDING A THEME

1. *What is the topic, or "big idea," of the work?*

2. *What do the characters say or do that relates to each topic?*

3. *What do these things tell you that is important to learn about life?*

1. Find the General Topic

First, find the general topic, or "big idea," of a work. When you first preview the work, try to spot any big, general ideas that are introduced. Themes are usually about big ideas like freedom, trust, friendship, family, and so on. Here is a list of some common topics for themes.

COMMON TOPICS FOR THEMES

courage	dreams	family	prejudice
equality	imagination	loneliness	friendship
revenge	suffering	understanding	growing up
desire	faith	fears	love

Now preview a folktale called "The Pedlar of Swaffham." As you preview, look for the clues to the general topic in the title, in the first and last paragraphs, and in any repeated words or ideas.

"The Pedlar of Swaffham"

NOTE
Title

Legend has it that hundreds of years ago, in the village of Swaffham in the county of Norfolk in England, there lived a pedlar who was constantly having a certain dream. A voice told the pedlar that, if he went and stood on London Bridge, he would hear joyful news.

NOTE
First paragraph

At first the pedlar took no notice. A journey to London would not be easy. It was nearly one hundred miles to London, so it would take him two or three days to walk there. And he would have to sleep in barns or hedges along the way.

NOTE
Repeated word

But the dreams persisted, and the voice was so insistent that the pedlar became upset and worried. He began to dread going upstairs to bed.

At last he said to his wife, "It is no use. I shall have to go to London and stand on London Bridge or I shall have no peace for the rest of my life."

He packed a few belongings, some food, and a little money. He whistled up his dog, and they walked the long road to London.

NOTE
What character does

In those days London Bridge was a bustling place with houses and shops on either side of the roadway. It was the only way across the Thames [River] unless you went by boat. For several days the pedlar stood on the bridge, first in one spot and then another, but no one spoke to him and no one gave him joyful news.

I was a fool to come, he told himself, but still he waited.

NOTE
What character thinks and does

Finally, when he had nothing but a crust of bread in his pocket and knew that he must leave for Norfolk within the hour, a shopkeeper stepped out of his shop and came and spoke to him.

Fiction

269

"Satisfy my curiosity," said the shopkeeper. "I have seen you here for several days. You do not beg, you do not pick pockets, you are not selling anything. Why are you standing here?"

NOTE
Repeated word

The pedlar replied honestly that he had dreamed that if he stood on London Bridge, he would hear joyful news.

The shopkeeper burst out laughing. "You don't want to take any notice of foolish dreams," he said. "I keep having this dream that if I go to Swaffham in Norfolk—a place I know nothing of—and ask for

NOTE
What character says

the pedlar's house and go into the orchard at the back and dig under a great oak tree, then I will find a hoard of treasure. What nonsense! I am sure that if I took any notice of that dream, I would make a long journey to Swaffham and find nothing when I got there. You be off home, my friend, and take no notice of your dreams."

NOTE
Last paragraph

The pedlar hurried home to Swaffham. He went into the orchard at the back of his house and dug under the great oak tree. He found a chest of treasure and was wealthy for the rest of his life.

In your preview, you may have noticed the word *dream*. This "big idea" appears in the first paragraph and a few more times later in the folktale. Look for it now as you go back and read the folktale more carefully.

During Reading

Now read the folktale straight through. Look for the general topics, or big ideas, that come up again and again.

2. Look at What Characters Say and Do

Notice, too, what the main characters say and do that relates to those topics.

■ What actions do the main characters take?

■ What are some important things they say?

■ How do the characters change during the story?

Answering these questions can help you find the theme. Once you know what "big idea" the work is about, look for what the characters say or do related to that idea. That will help point to possible themes.

Two easy ways to keep track of what happens are to use a Character Development Chart or a Story String.

CHARACTER DEVELOPMENT CHART

BEGINNING	MIDDLE	END
Pedlar's dream says to stand on London Bridge. It's about hearing joyful news.	Pedlar goes to the bridge. A shopkeeper tells him his own dream about buried treasure.	Pedlar returns home, finds the buried treasure, and is rich.
POSSIBLE THEME: Dreams can sometimes come true.		

A Character Development Chart makes it easy to focus on how a character changes.

Fiction

271

1. Pedlar's dream tells him to go to stand on London Bridge.

2. The pedlar tries to ignore his dream, but finally he gives in and goes to London.

3. He waits on the bridge. Nothing happens.

4. Finally, a shopkeeper asks him what he's doing. The pedlar tells him.

5. The shopkeeper tells him to forget his dreams. He has been dreaming he could find treasure behind a pedlar's house in Swaffham.

6. The pedlar goes home and finds treasure that makes him rich.

A Story String focuses more on the events of the plot. As you read, record your notes in Story String boxes like the ones above. A Story String gives you a way to keep track of each event that happens in a story.

After Reading

After you finish reading, you're ready to pull together your ideas about the story and decide on the theme.

3. Decide What the Theme Is

Remember, the theme is not the topic of the work but a point made *about* the topic. It is a statement about life. The theme of "The Pedlar of Swaffham" isn't dreams. That's just the topic. A good theme statement is not just about one set of characters. It's about people and life in general.

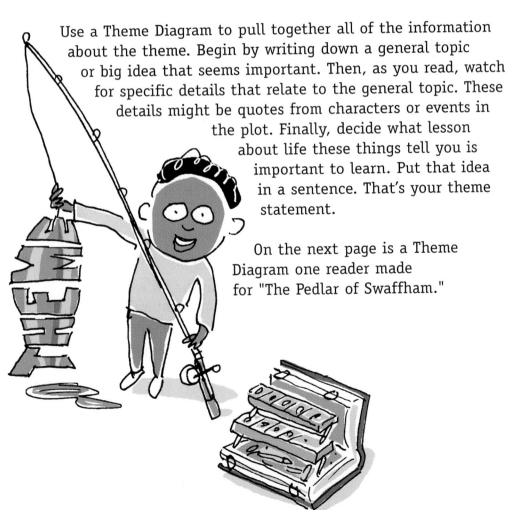

Use a Theme Diagram to pull together all of the information about the theme. Begin by writing down a general topic or big idea that seems important. Then, as you read, watch for specific details that relate to the general topic. These details might be quotes from characters or events in the plot. Finally, decide what lesson about life these things tell you is important to learn. Put that idea in a sentence. That's your theme statement.

On the next page is a Theme Diagram one reader made for "The Pedlar of Swaffham."

Fiction

Step 1: What is the topic or big idea of the work?
(dreams)

Step 2: What do the characters say or do that relates to the topic?

| One person, the pedlar, follows his dreams. | Another person, a shopkeeper, pays no attention to his dreams. | The pedlar's dream comes true. |

Step 3: What do these things tell you that is important to learn about life?

Pay attention to your dreams.

Summing **Up**

Remember this about finding a theme:

■ It's important not to confuse theme with topic. The theme is an author's statement *about* a topic.

■ To find a theme, follow a three-step plan:
  1. Find the general topic, or "big idea."
  2. Find what characters say or do relating to it.
  3. Decide what these things say that's an important lesson about life.

Focus on Authors

If you're like most people, once you like something, you stick with it. Once you read one good book by an author, you try another . . . and another . . . until you've read them all.

It's fun to become an "expert" on an author, just like it's fun to know a lot about an athlete or other famous person.

Goals

Here you'll learn how to:

✔ **compare important elements of works by one author**

✔ **read an author's books for character, plot, setting, and theme**

Fiction

Before Reading

After you've read one or two books by one author, you may want to study them in depth for a report or because you are curious. Where's the best place to start?

Collect Information

The first thing to do is read, read, read, and enjoy! But, as you read, you'll want to look for several ways to compare the author's books. Start by setting a purpose, previewing the works, and planning a strategy.

For your reading purpose, it makes sense to think about the main elements of any type of fiction:

ELEMENTS OF FICTION

- characters
- plot
- setting
- theme

In reading several books by the same author, your purpose might be to collect information about characters, plots, settings, and themes. That way, you can see how they compare with each other. When you preview each book, you can begin to look for this information.

During Reading

As you read books by an author, collect information about characters, plots, settings, and themes. Be an active reader. Jot notes on index cards or sticky notes. Use organizers to keep track of important details. Below are some examples based on books written by the author Jane Yolen.

Read for Character

As you read each of the author's books, try to get a good description and sense of the main character. Here's an example of a way to look at Jess, a character from Jane Yolen's book *The Mermaid's Three Wisdoms*.

Character Map

A Character Map gives you a way to record notes about fictional characters.

Fiction

CHARACTER MAP

WHAT SHE SAYS AND DOES	WHAT OTHERS THINK ABOUT HER
She doesn't speak well or often because she is deaf. After the mermaid leaves, Jess talks more.	Her mother tries to help her. The captain is her friend. The mermaid also becomes her friend.

JESS

HOW SHE LOOKS AND FEELS	HOW I FEEL ABOUT HER
Before the mermaid comes, she is ashamed of her speech and hearing problem. After saving the mermaid, Jess becomes more confident.	I understand better what it must feel like to be deaf or to be different from others.

Read for Plot

A plot is a series of events or actions. An author's plots will differ from book to book. After reading many books, you also may find that an author's plots may be somewhat similar. Start your focus on plot by identifying what conflict or problem the characters face.

Story Organizer

Here is an example of how a Story Organizer can briefly describe the main action of the plot in Jane Yolen's book *The Acorn Quest*. A Story Organizer is especially helpful for describing the plot of stories in a simple, clear way. Notice how the main problem in the plot is summarized at the beginning.

STORY ORGANIZER

BEGINNING	MIDDLE	END
The animals in the Woodland are running out of food. Five animals, called the fellowship, go to search for the Golden Acorn.	The fellowship has three adventures. One is dangerous, one is sad, and one is very weird.	The fellowship returns home with the magical Golden Acorn. It will grow and feed all of the Woodland.

Read for Setting

In fiction, the setting means the time and place—when and where the action takes place. The general setting is the overall time and place for the work. Within the general setting, the times and places for various events change.

Setting Chart

A Setting Chart is a useful organizer for recording clues about times and places in a story or novel. Here are some of the main times and places in Jane Yolen's book *And Twelve Chinese Acrobats*.

Fiction

SETTING CHART

TITLE: And Twelve Chinese Acrobats

CLUES ABOUT TIME:
- 1910
- when Lou was a little boy
- when Lou was almost a man
- various times during the year when Lou is away at school
- one day after he is expelled

CLUES ABOUT PLACE:
- Ukraine [Russia]
- village near Kiev

Read for Theme

A theme is an author's statement about life. An author's themes may differ from book to book, or they may be very similar. Jane Yolen uses what seem like simple fables or fairy tales to illustrate some very big ideas. Here is an example from her book *The Sultan's Perfect Tree*.

Theme Diagram

A Theme Diagram asks the key questions that help you find the theme of a work. Read the book carefully and answer the three questions in the Theme Diagram. Go back to the text and reread if necessary.

THEME DIAGRAM

Step 1: WHAT IS THE SUBJECT OR "BIG IDEA" OF THE WORK?

perfection

Step 2: WHAT DO THE CHARACTERS DO OR SAY RELATED TO THIS SUBJECT?

The sultan says that he wants everything to be perfect.	The sultan orders his servants to make everything perfect.	By the end, he changes his mind.

Step 3: WHAT DO THESE THINGS TELL YOU THAT IS IMPORTANT TO LEARN ABOUT LIFE?

It's a mistake to want only perfection. Instead, value things that live, grow, and change.

After Reading

After reading, pause and think about what you've read. Stop and look a little more closely at the characters, plots, settings, or themes of books that you have read.
You don't need to compare everything in all of the books.
Pick one element to compare.

Compare Several Works

For example, here's a way to use Summary Notes to summarize the plots of several books by Jane Yolen.

Fiction

SUMMARY NOTES

TITLE	PLOT
1. The Mermaid's Three Wisdoms	A deaf girl saves a mermaid, who becomes her friend.
2. The Acorn Quest	A group of animals searches for a magic acorn to help others in the Woodland.
3. And Twelve Chinese Acrobats	A boy who always gets in trouble joins the circus and goes to America.
4. The Sultan's Perfect Tree	A sultan who tries to make everything in life perfect finds that he cannot.

Draw Conclusions

Now that you've finished reading, it's time to draw conclusions. What similarities, for instance, do you see in the plots Jane Yolen uses? Use your notes and organizers to help you plan a good comparison.

WAY TO COMPARE WORKS

1. Opening
Begin with a sentence that names what's being compared and whether the works are similar or different for at least two reasons.

2. Body
Explain each reason with several details or quotes from each work.

3. Conclusion
End with a sentence that restates how the works are alike or different.

Summing Up

- As you read, take notes and collect information about characters, plots, settings, and themes of an author's works.

- To compare works by one author, summarize and draw conclusions about one element of several works.

Elements of Fiction

You may know a good story or book when you read one, but can you explain *why* you liked it?

Here you can read about the different elements of a work of fiction. These elements can help you to understand and discuss what you read.

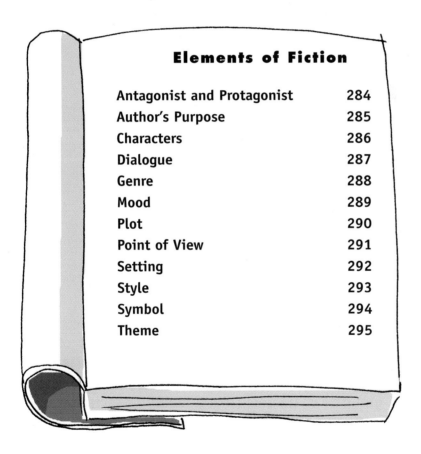

Elements of Fiction

Fiction

Antagonist and Protagonist

Stories usually center on conflicts between two main characters. Read the beginning of the story below and look for the main characters.

from *The Imp That Ate My Homework* by Laurence Yep

Protagonist   My teacher, Ms. Mason, told my class to write about our grandparents. I put up my hand. "My grandmother is dead," I said.

"Is your grandfather alive, Jim?" she asked me. Reluctantly I nodded my head. "Then you could interview him," she suggested.

I was afraid she would say that. Half of the class lived in Chinatown. They looked at me **Antagonist** sympathetically. They knew my grandfather. They knew it would be hard to write about him.

Nobody liked Grandpop much. He spoke his mind and had a sharp tongue too. So he was always getting into a fight with someone. On any given day, he feuded with half of Chinatown.

DESCRIPTION

The boy Jim is the **protagonist,** or the main character of the story. His grandfather is the **antagonist,** because he has a conflict with Jim. In fiction, the antagonist might be another character, a group of characters (like a family or society), a force of nature (like a flood or storm), or even a character fault (such as pride, jealousy, or greed).

DEFINITION

The **protagonist** is the main character in a piece of fiction. The **antagonist** is the person or thing working against him or her.

Author's Purpose

Author Julius Lester describes in the preface of his book *To Be a Slave* his reason for writing it.

EXAMPLE

> from *To Be a Slave* by Julius Lester

> My object in writing the book was to enable the reader to experience slaves as human beings. "To be a slave was to be a human being under conditions in which that humanity was denied. They were not slaves. They were people. Their condition was slavery." Those words are from the one-page description I wrote for [my editor] Phyllis Fogelman, and that description became the opening pages of the first chapter.
>
> Of course, my underlying and hidden purpose was simply this: If a child could experience slaves as human beings, then it might be possible for that same child to look at the descendants of slaves and also see another human being, no more, no less.

Author states purpose.

Fiction

DESCRIPTION

Authors write for many reasons. Sometimes authors want to persuade or convince you. Sometimes they feel like being funny and want to entertain. Sometimes they want to explain something, as in *To Be a Slave*. Authors often have several purposes for writing—say, to entertain and persuade you to believe a certain point of view. An author will not always state his or her **purpose** for writing, so you often have to infer the purpose.

DEFINITION

The **author's purpose** is his or her reason for creating a work.

Characters

The people, animals, and make-believe things that an author writes about are called characters. To learn about characters, watch what they do, what they say, and how they interact with other characters.

EXAMPLE

from *The Imp That Ate My Homework* by Laurence Yep

Three characters

Dad said there were ten thousand ways to pick a fight, and Grandpop knew them all. By now people knew to find Dad or Mom and they would calm Grandpop down.

Last month a tourist's car had almost run over him in the crosswalk as he tried to cross Grant Avenue, the busiest street in Chinatown. Grandpop hammered on the car hood with his cane. Then he started smashing the headlights. When he got tired, he stood in front of the car so it could not drive away. He halted cars for half an hour. The big traffic jam spread into downtown San Francisco.

What a character does

DESCRIPTION

Some stories have many **characters**, and some have only a few. You may learn a lot about the *main character* but very little about a *minor character*. The more you know about how characters look and what they say and do, the better you'll understand who they are and what their roles in the story might be.

DEFINITION

A **character** is a person, animal, or make-believe creature that takes part in the action of a story.

Dialogue

In fiction, as in real life, you can learn a lot about people by listening to them talk.

EXAMPLE

from *Boys at Work* by Gary Soto

Quotes around exact words of a speaker

"Dad," Rudy asked as he plopped on the couch. "You ever get in any trouble when you were little?"

"Trouble?" his father teased. He ran his fingers down his chin, pulling on an invisible beard. He became reflective. He shook his head and answered, "Nah, I don't think so. I was a saint."

Speech tag tells who's speaking.

New paragraph for new speaker

"Dad, come on. Level with me," Rudy pleaded.

His dad put down the newspaper and told Rudy that he had gotten into more trouble than a fox in a chicken coop. He had played with matches, gotten in fights, jumped from rooftops, squirted his grandfather with a hose, chased girls with a *moco* on his finger, eaten crayons and paste, burped in church, and stolen fruit from trees — all by the time he was six years old!

Fiction

DESCRIPTION

Dialogue is one of an author's most important tools. Good dialogue draws you into the action. You see and hear the characters. You learn not only *what* they say and do but *why*. Written dialogue is set off with quotation marks. A *speech tag* such as "he said" or "Rudy pleaded" tells who's speaking. Sometimes dialogue goes on for several paragraphs. Whenever a new character begins to speak, the author starts a new paragraph.

DEFINITION

Dialogue is the talking that characters do in fiction.

Genre

There are many different types, or **genres**, of literature. The chart below will help you understand eight common genres. Each genre has its own characteristics.

DESCRIPTION

GENRE	DESCRIPTION
Drama	*A written story meant to be acted out on a stage*
Fable	*A story meant to teach a useful lesson that often has animals who speak and act like humans*
Folktale	*A traditional story with a moral or lesson handed down by people of a region from one generation to the next*
Myth	*An old story, handed down through time, that might tell about gods and heroes or explain events in nature*
Novel	*A fictional story that is long enough to fill up a book*
Short story	*A short work of fiction with a limited number of characters and usually a single plot*
Poetry	*A short piece of writing, often with rhyme and a particular rhythm*
Essay	*A short piece of writing that gives information or the author's opinion on a subject*

DEFINITION

A **genre** is a certain kind or type of literature.

Mood

What feeling do you get when you read the first two paragraphs of this folktale?

EXAMPLE from "East of the Sun and West of the Moon" by Joanna Cole

Once upon a time there was a poor husbandman who had so many children that he hadn't much of either food or clothing to give them. Pretty children they all were, but the prettiest was the youngest daughter, who was so lovely there was no end to her loveliness.

So one day, 'twas on a Thursday evening late at the fall of the year, the weather was so wild and rough outside, and it was so cruelly dark, and rain fell and wind blew, till the walls of the cottage shook again. There they all sat round the fire busy with this thing and that. But just then, all at once something gave three taps on the windowpane. Then the father went out to see what was the matter; and, when he got out of doors, what should he see but a great big White Bear.

Fearful, scary mood

Fiction

DESCRIPTION

In the second paragraph, the wild storm creates suspense and a sense of danger. The tapping on the window and the appearance of the White Bear seem frightening. Authors use setting, dialogue, and images to help create a mood. The mood may change many times in a story or novel. For example, a cheery mood might be replaced by sudden terror. Pay attention to the **mood**, or feeling you get, as you read.

DEFINITION

Mood is the feeling that a literary work gives to readers.

Plot

The action of a story is called its plot. In this passage from early in the novel, the characters, setting, and beginning of the plot all are established.

EXAMPLE

from *The Great Gilly Hopkins* by Katherine Paterson

William Ernest scrambled off the couch after the two women, and Gilly was left alone with the dust, the out-of-tune piano, and the satisfaction that she had indeed started off on the right foot in her new foster home. She could stand anything, she thought—a gross guardian, a freaky kid, an ugly, dirty house—as long as she was in charge.

She was well on the way.

Main character

Setting

Opening situation

DESCRIPTION

Gilly Hopkins is moving into her third foster home in three years. After she meets her new foster mother, the **plot** of the novel gets under way. A plot is usually made up of five parts:

1. Exposition Introduction of the setting, the main characters, and the opening situation

2. Rising Action Growing tension as characters face and try to solve a conflict or problem

3. Climax Turning point of the story when the action reaches a critical point

4. Falling Action The events in which the conflict or problem begins to work out

5. Resolution Description of how things turn out

DEFINITION

In fiction, the **plot** is the action, or what happens.

Point of View

Who is telling each of the two stories below?

EXAMPLE — from "Bear" by Betsy Byars and others

I looked at our big Newfoundland, and it struck me. The boy was right. Our new dog looked exactly like a bear. I had been trying to think of a name ever since we got the dog. I've never been very good at that. Now I had my name.

Bear!

First-person narrator

EXAMPLE — from *The Summer of the Swans* by Betsy Byars

Sara Godfrey was lying on the bed tying a kerchief on the dog, Boysie. "Hold your chin up, Boysie, will you?" she said as she braced herself on one elbow. The dog was old, slept all the time, and he was lying on his side with his eyes closed while she lifted his head and tied the scarf.

Third-person narrator

Fiction

DESCRIPTION

A story's **point of view** depends on who's telling it. In the first example, one of the characters tells the story. This means that it is told from the *first-person point of view*. When a narrator who isn't part of the story tells it, this is called *third-person point of view*. Then, the narrator tells about events as an observer who is watching them happen, as in the second example.

DEFINITION

Point of view is the way a story is told. That is, point of view is who is telling the story—one of the characters or a narrator.

Setting

What can you tell about the setting—the time and place—
in the opening paragraph of this novel?

EXAMPLE

from *Julie of the Wolves* by Jean Craighead George

Time

Place

Miyax pushed back the hood of her sealskin
parka and looked at the Arctic sun. It was a yellow
disc in a lime-green sky, the colors of six o'clock in
the evening and the time when the wolves awoke.
Quietly she put down her cooking pot and crept to
the top of a dome-shaped frost heave, one of the
many earth buckles that rise and fall in the crackling
cold of the Arctic winter. Lying on her stomach, she
looked across a vast lawn of grass and moss and
focused her attention on the wolves she had come
upon two sleeps ago. They were wagging their tails
as they awoke and saw each other.

DESCRIPTION

A single paragraph can tell you a great deal about where and
when a story is taking place. The author usually gives you
clues about the **setting** in the first few paragraphs of a story
or novel. To identify the setting, look for words that tell
something about the time or place, such as *Arctic, winter, six
o'clock, evening,* and so on. Setting can be a very important
factor in creating a mood and developing the characters and
plot of a story.

DEFINITION

The setting is the time and place of a fictional work.

Style

A writer's style is his or her unique way of putting words together. What do you notice about this writer's style?

EXAMPLE
from "At the Beach—Abuelito's Story" by Lulu Delacre

When we were ready to leave, Papi, the only one in the family who owned a car, packed his Ford woody wagon with the nine of us. No one cared that we children had to squeeze into the back along with the clutter of pots and plates, food and bags, towels and blankets and hammocks. Soon the engine turned, and the car rumbled down the road into the rising sun.

Along the way, we drove past sugarcane fields and roadside markets. My cousins and I shouted warnings to the barking dogs and laughed at the frightened hens that scurried in every direction at the sight of our car. It seemed like a long time until the cool morning breeze that blew into the windows turned warm. And the growing heat made the aroma of Mami's tortilla all the more tempting.

Long sentence

Sensory details

Fiction

DESCRIPTION

The kinds of sentences and words a writer includes make up his or her writing **style.** The children "squeeze into the back" and feel the "growing heat." You see what the children see— "rising sun," "sugarcane fields," "frightened hens." You hear what they hear—"rumbled," "shouted," "barking dogs."

DEFINITION

The style is the way a writer puts words, phrases, and sentences together to express his or her ideas.

Symbol

In fiction, authors often use symbols. That is, authors sometimes choose a person or thing to represent something else. In the example below, Melusina the mermaid has gone back to the sea, leaving Jess, her deaf human friend, alone. Note the use of an object to stand for something more in this example.

EXAMPLE

> from *The Mermaid's Three Wisdoms* by Jane Yolen

> The captain opened one of her fists and dropped something into it. "You didn't dream this," he said. "I found it there on the blanket. She left it for you, to show how much she cared, I be thinking. Friend to friend."
>
> Jess looked and saw the crystal tear, gathering sunlight and showering her hand with rainbows.

Object and what it represents

DESCRIPTION

The crystal tear is a symbol of love and friendship that Melusina left for Jess. There are many common **symbols** with which you're familiar. A dove symbolizes peace. To most Americans, an American flag symbolizes freedom. A heart symbolizes love. Authors use symbols to give another level of meaning to their works. As a reader, look for the suggestions the author gives to help you figure out what a symbol means.

DEFINITION

A **symbol** is a person, place, thing, or event used to represent something else.

Theme

Sometimes a fictional character tells you what the theme of a work is. Other times, you have to dig for it. See if you can find clues about the theme in this example.

EXAMPLE

from *The Midnight Fox* by Betsy Byars

Theme statement

One time my mom and dad had me sit down and make a list of all the things I was afraid of, because they thought that if I wrote all these fears down on paper—things like being afraid of high places and being afraid of dogs—I would see how foolish my fears were.

DESCRIPTION

A **theme** is an author's statement about life. Pay attention when you see statements about life made by the writer or a character in a story. These can be a clue about the story or novel's theme. The importance of overcoming fears is one of this novel's themes.

To find a work's theme, first look for the subject or "big idea." Then, see what characters say and do that relates to that idea. Finally, use your own words to come up with a general statement or lesson about life that sums up the author's message.

DEFINITION

The **theme** is the main idea or message of a work, an author's statement about life.

Fiction

Reading
Poetry

Reading a Poem

Ways of Reading Poetry

Focus on Language
Focus on Meaning
Focus on Sound and Shape

Elements of Poetry

FREE VERSE IMAGERY

STANZA

Poetry

Reading a Poem

Reading poetry is different from the usual reading you do. Poetry looks different. It says a lot in only a few words. Poetry also says things in special ways that please the ear, and poetry often stirs your feelings.

Poets often write in short lines and use patterns of rhythm and rhyme. They choose words for sound and beauty as well as for their meanings. But some poets also feel free from following any rules. They experiment with words, shapes, language, and subjects. Poets write about anything and everything—from the silly to the serious.

Goals

Here you'll learn how to:

✔ discover the meanings of the **poems** you read
✔ use the strategy of **close reading** to understand poetry
✔ understand **how poems are organized**

Before Reading

Before reading a poem, set your reading purpose. Then, preview the poem and make a plan for reading.

A Set a Purpose

Think about why you are reading the poem. You might read poetry for pleasure or to learn something new. Or, you may read poetry only because of an assignment. In either case, you need to set a clear purpose.

Setting a Purpose

■ **What is the poem saying?**

■ **What makes this poem special or memorable?**

Choose one of those purpose questions and make it your reason for reading.

B Preview

Use the Preview Checklist below to get an overview of the poem "Whatif" by Shel Silverstein. As you preview, look for:

Preview Checklist

✔ the poem's title and author
✔ its overall shape and organization
✔ the first and last lines
✔ any rhymes and where they occur
✔ any repeated or key words

Poetry

"Whatif" by Shel Silverstein

Last night, while I lay thinking here,
Some Whatifs crawled inside my ear

And pranced and partied all night long
And sang their same old Whatif song:
Whatif I'm dumb in school?

Whatif they've closed the swimming pool?
Whatif I get beat up?
Whatif there's poison in my cup?
Whatif I start to cry?
Whatif I get sick and die?

Whatif I flunk that test?
Whatif green hair grows on my chest?
Whatif nobody likes me?
Whatif a bolt of lightning strikes me?
Whatif I don't grow taller?
Whatif my head starts getting smaller?
Whatif the fish won't bite?
Whatif the wind tears up my kite?
Whatif they start a war?
Whatif my parents get divorced?
Whatif the bus is late?
Whatif my teeth don't grow in straight?
Whatif I tear my pants?
Whatif I never learn to dance?
Everything seems swell, and then
The nighttime Whatifs strike again!

C Plan

You probably learned several things from your preview:

- The poem is about nighttime fears.
- *Whatif* is a repeated word. It looks made-up.
- Most of the poem is made up of "Whatif" questions.

You should probably plan to read a poem several times, looking for different things each time.

1. On the first time, read for fun.
2. On the second time, read for meaning.
3. On the third time, read to appreciate the poem's organization and sounds.

The strategy of close reading can help you explore the rich layers of meaning in a poem.

Reading Strategy: Close Reading

Poetry

Close reading means thinking about each word and phrase in the poem. Why did the poet use this word? What does that phrase mean? Why state the idea that way? By asking such questions, you can examine a poem in detail and consider why the poet chose to write it in that particular way.

A Double-entry Journal gives you one way to do close reading. In the first column, write lines from the poem you want to look at more closely. In the second column, write your thoughts about these lines and what you think they mean.

DOUBLE-ENTRY JOURNAL

QUOTES	MY THOUGHTS

During Reading

Now go back and read "Whatif" carefully, using your reading plan.

D Read with a Purpose

While reading, remember your reading purpose question. Look for what the poem is saying or what makes it special.

First Reading

The first time you read "Whatif," read for fun. Write down phrases or lines that you enjoy in a Double-entry Journal. Then, explain what you enjoy about them.

READING A POEM
✔ Double-entry Journal
✔ Two Per Line
✔ Paraphrase Chart

This completed Double-entry Journal shows what one reader thought about "Whatif."

DOUBLE-ENTRY JOURNAL

QUOTES	MY THOUGHTS
"Some Whatifs crawled inside my ear"	These Whatifs seem real, like insects.
"Whatif I'm dumb in school?"	That sounds like a real worry.
"Whatif a bolt of lightning strikes me?"	This one isn't serious.
"Whatif I flunk that test?"	Everybody worries about this.
"Whatif green hair grows on my chest?"	This one is just silly.

Second Reading

Now read the poem again, and this time look for the poem's meaning. What do you think the poet is trying to say?

Try a reading tool called a Two Per Line to focus on a poem's meaning. First, make a copy of the poem you can write on or copy the poem in your writing journal. Then, circle or highlight the two words in each line that you think are most important. In the second column, write your thoughts about the meaning of the words you circled.

Here is part of one reader's completed Two Per Line chart.

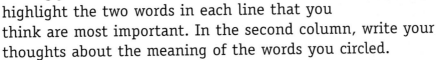

Poetry

TEXT	MY IDEAS
"Last night while I lay thinking here,	Speaker is probably in bed at night, about to go to sleep.
Some Whatifs crawled inside my ear	The Whatifs creep up on him. They are his worries.
And pranced and partied all night long	"Pranced" and "partied" means he can't stop them.
And sang their same old Whatif song:"	"Same old" means this has happened before. The speaker probably isn't surprised by what they say.

Doing a Two Per Line helped this reader see that the poem is describing things that many kids worry about right before they go to sleep.

303

How Poems Are Organized

Poets are free to experiment and play with language—its sounds, its meanings, its appearance. They shape poems to create and build meaning. For example, Silverstein combined the words *What* and *if* and made up *Whatif*. Because poets are so free to do what they want, you will find it helpful to look at the choices they do make as they write. Here are some examples of ways poets can organize their work.

1. With or without rhyme
2. With shape and structure or without

1. With or Without Rhyme

When words **rhyme,** they sound alike. Look at the rhymes in Silverstein's "Whatif" questions. Silverstein uses rhyme to group pairs of lines.

from "Whatif"

Whatif the bus is late?
Whatif my teeth don't grow in straight?

Sometimes rhyme helps to emphasize a poem's meaning or helps set a mood. But poems don't have to rhyme.

2. With Shape and Structure or Without

Sometimes the look of the poem on the page is important. Poets may use extra white space between words or lines to make some words stand out, or they may arrange the lines in unusual ways. Poets can shape their poems as they wish. Some poems are organized into groups of lines called **stanzas.**

Did you notice that "Whatif" is only a single stanza? The lines do not follow any set pattern or length.

Third Reading

Now go back and read "Whatif" for a third time. This time focus on the poem's organization and sound. Did you notice the way the poem follows a simple, familiar pattern?

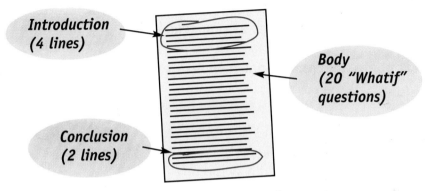

Introduction (4 lines)

Body (20 "Whatif" questions)

Conclusion (2 lines)

Note, too, how the lines rhyme most of the time. How would the poem be different if there were no rhyme?

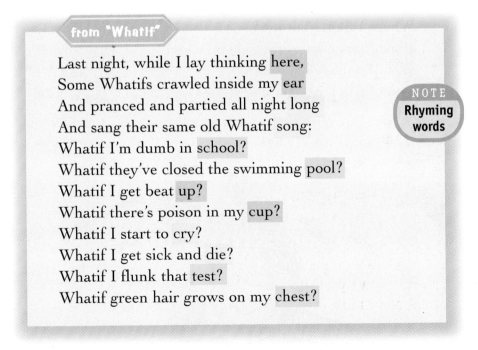

from "Whatif"

Last night, while I lay thinking here,
Some Whatifs crawled inside my ear
And pranced and partied all night long
And sang their same old Whatif song:
Whatif I'm dumb in school?
Whatif they've closed the swimming pool?
Whatif I get beat up?
Whatif there's poison in my cup?
Whatif I start to cry?
Whatif I get sick and die?
Whatif I flunk that test?
Whatif green hair grows on my chest?

NOTE
Rhyming words

Poetry

Even in a poem like "Whatif" that looks like a jumble of lines, the poet follows an order. Be sure to look for the way poets organize their poems when you read.

E Connect

Poetry touches both your mind and your heart. So, when you read a poem, read actively. Tune in with your thoughts *and* feelings. Think about how the poem connects with your own experience. Does it remind you of anything else you've read? Take note of your reactions as you read.

Here is one reader's personal response to part of "Whatif."

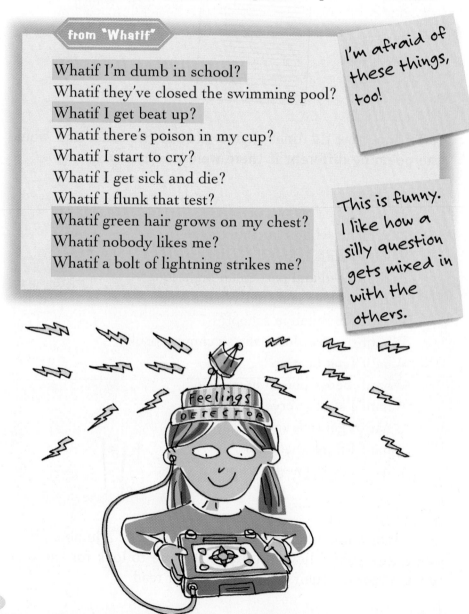

from "Whatif"

Whatif I'm dumb in school?
Whatif they've closed the swimming pool?
Whatif I get beat up?
Whatif there's poison in my cup?
Whatif I start to cry?
Whatif I get sick and die?
Whatif I flunk that test?
Whatif green hair grows on my chest?
Whatif nobody likes me?
Whatif a bolt of lightning strikes me?

I'm afraid of these things, too!

This is funny. I like how a silly question gets mixed in with the others.

After Reading

After reading, take a moment to think about the poem you just read. Collect your thoughts about it. You might even want to discuss it with your friends.

F Pause and Reflect

As you collect your thoughts about the poem, first decide whether you've answered your reading purpose questions.

Looking Back

- **Do I know what the poem is saying?**
- **Can I explain how this poem is organized?**
- **Can I say what makes this poem special?**

If you're not sure about these questions or if you have other questions, go back to reread the poem again. Rereading is perfectly normal, especially with poetry.

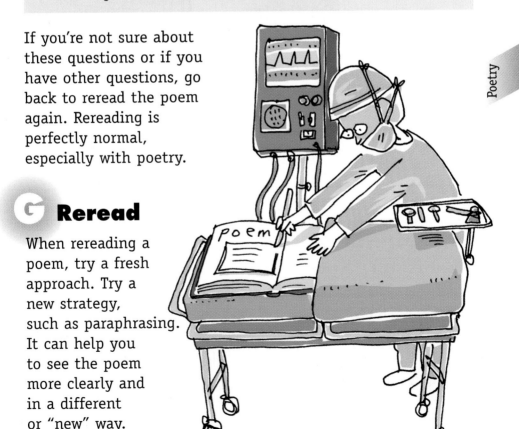

G Reread

When rereading a poem, try a fresh approach. Try a new strategy, such as paraphrasing. It can help you to see the poem more clearly and in a different or "new" way.

Rereading Strategy: Paraphrasing

Paraphrasing means restating key parts of a poem in your own words. The process of explaining poetry in your own words helps you to put it in terms you understand.

<u>Use a Paraphrase Chart to help you "translate" key parts of a poem into your own words.</u> To do that, first write a quotation from the poem on the left. Then, write your paraphrase of the quotation on the right and any other thoughts that you have below.

Here is one reader's Paraphrase Chart for "Whatif."

PARAPHRASE CHART

LINES	MY PARAPHRASE
"Everything seems swell, and then / The nighttime Whatifs strike again!"	I feel fine during the day, but I worry a lot at night.

MY THOUGHTS
The kid in the poem says that everything seems scarier at night. I agree. I often imagine things and feel afraid when I'm alone in the dark.

Remember

You usually remember something when it has meaning in your own life. To help you make this poem your own and remember it, try the activity below.

Write a Poem Like "Whatif"

Use "Whatif" as a model for your own poem. Try to use some of the same rhyme or organization. Here's an example from one reader.

STUDENT JOURNAL

How Come?

How come I'm not tall?
How come I'm not strong?
How come my family lives way out here,
Where driving takes so long?

Poetry

Summing Up

When you read a poem, use the reading strategy of **close reading.** Try to read the poem three times. As you read, remember to use reading tools, such as:

- **Double-entry Journal**
- **Two Per Line**
- **Paraphrase Chart**

On one reading, note **how the poem is organized.** Then, use the rereading strategy of **paraphrasing** to think through key parts of the poem and put them in your own words.

Focus on Language

When a poem touches your feelings, it's often because of its language. The special language of poetry can make a poem come alive. It's as if you can almost see, hear, or even touch whatever the poet is describing.

When you first read a poem, you read for fun and to get a general idea of what the poem is saying. As you read it more closely, look at how the poet uses words.

Before Reading

Even when you first preview a poem you can begin to focus on the language. Read the poem "For Forest" by Grace Nichols on the next page. Notice what one reader wrote about certain words and phrases.

"For Forest" by Grace Nichols

Forest could keep secrets
Forest could keep secrets

Forest tune in every day
to watersound and birdsound
Forest letting her hair down
to the teeming creeping of her forest-ground

But Forest don't broadcast her business
no Forest cover her business down
from sky and fast-eye sun
and when night come
and darkness wrap her like a gown
Forest is a bad dream woman

Forest dreaming about mountain
and when earth was young
Forest dreaming of the caress of gold
Forest roosting with mysterious eldorado

and when howler monkey
wake her up with howl
Forest just stretch and stir
to a new day of sound

but coming back to secrets
Forest could keep secrets
Forest could keep secrets
        And we must keep Forest

I like how the forest seems like a person.

These are unusual descriptions.

What do these words mean?

There are no punctuation marks.

Why does the poet repeat these lines?

Poetry

During Reading

In your preview, you probably noticed that the subject of this poem is the forest. The poem experiments with language, using some unusual words and leaving out normal punctuation. What else about the poem's language caught your eye?

The first step with any poem is to look up words you don't know. Keep a dictionary handy and write definitions in your own words.

VOCABULARY JOURNAL

caress—gentle touch
eldorado—place of fabulous wealth

These two words are used in the fourth stanza. The first part of the poem describes the forest in the morning and at night. Knowing what these words mean gives you a clearer picture of what the forest is like—a special place full of treasures and sweet dreams.

Recognize Figurative Language

Besides using unfamiliar words, poets often use language in special ways. For example, a poem might describe two different things by comparing them. As you read poems, watch for:

- words that describe something or someone in an unusual way
- words that create a picture in your mind

The special language poets use is called *figurative language*. Three important types of figurative language are simile, metaphor, and personification.

1. Simile

A **simile** compares two things by using the words *like* or *as*. For example, you might say, "He ran as fast as a cheetah." Look back at "For Forest" again and find the simile in the third stanza: "darkness wrapped her *like a gown*." The idea that night is like a dark gown wrapped around the forest puts a surprising picture in your mind's eye. Similes like that can help you experience something familiar in a new way.

2. Metaphor

A **metaphor** describes a thing or person as if it were something or someone else. For example, in "For Forest" saying the forest is "a bad dream woman" is a metaphor.

3. Personification

Another kind of figure of speech is called **personification**. It happens when a poet gives human qualities to an animal or something else that isn't human. Did you notice the forest does many things a human being does— from keeping secrets and letting her hair down to dreaming and stretching? All of these are examples of personification in "For Forest."

Note the Images in the Poem

An image is a mental picture, or what you "see" in your mind. Poets use **imagery** to appeal to your senses—sight, hearing, smell, touch, and taste. Images, or "word pictures," make it easy for you to "see" what the poet is trying to show you as a reader. What images come to mind as you read these lines again?

313

Forest tune in every day
to watersound and birdsound
Forest letting her hair down
to the teeming creeping of her forest-ground

The sounds of the water and birds and the creatures that live under the trees paint a vivid picture of a forest scene. One way to appreciate the images in a poem is to make a sketch of what you "see" as you read. Here is an example of how one reader pictured this description of the forest.

VISUALIZING

Remember that not all images are designed to appeal to your eyes. In this same stanza, the poet wants your ears to "hear" images, too.

After Reading

After reading a poem, stop to think about it. You may not fully understand a poem on your first reading. For most poems, two or three readings are needed.

As a reader, you'll find it easier to go back and read a poem with different purposes in mind.

- Read it once just to get a feeling of the poem.
- Read it a second time to look at what it means.
- Read it a third time to look at the language and organization of the poem.

Note How a Poem Affects You

How did you react to the language in "For Forest"? Ask yourself questions like these:

What feelings did I have when I read the poem?

Which of the images stirred me the most?

What was the overall feeling, or mood, of this poem?

Share your feelings about the poem and its language. Write one or two sentences that sum up your reactions or talk about the poem with a friend.

Poetry

> ### JOURNAL ENTRY
>
> "For Forest"
>   I thought the poem was kind of hard to understand, but it had a spooky, mysterious feeling. The idea of Forest being a woman who keeps secrets is really mysterious and kind of scary, too.

Write Your Own Poem

Sometimes it can be fun to play with language by writing a poem of your own. Be creative. Start out with one of the unusual words or images you notice in the poem you read. Or, create a poem with some of the same language, but make it about a completely different subject. The example below shows how one reader used the beginning of "For Forest" as a model for a poem about a house.

> ### POEM MODELED ON "FOR FOREST"
>
> House could tell secrets
> House could tell secrets
>
> House hears every day
> the TV sound and people sounds
> House filling its walls and floors
> with the voices of the family

Summing Up

- As you read a poem, look up any unfamiliar words in a dictionary.
- When reading poetry, look for similes, metaphors, personification, and imagery.
- Think about how a poem's language affects you and make sketches of what you "see" in your mind.

Focus on Meaning

Poets usually want you to focus not only on *how* they say things, but also on *what* they say. When you read a poem, you often want to know what it means.

Sometimes the meaning of a poem is easy to figure out. Other times a poem can be like a puzzle that's almost impossible to solve. To understand a poem's meaning, you need to understand all of its words and what it says line by line.

Goals

Here you'll learn how to:

✔ **read a poem word by word and line by line**

✔ **understand a poem's overall meaning**

✔ **explore your own feelings about the meaning of a poem**

Poetry

Before Reading

When your focus is on the meaning of a poem, you'll need to read the poem several times. The first time you read, you'll preview the poem to get a "feel" for it. When you want to focus on meaning, pay special attention to the title, the first and last few lines, and any words that are repeated or seem important.

Now preview "Mother's Day" by Janet S. Wong. Note how one reader began to focus on meaning.

Mother's Day morning
and I have no present.
No money.
I walk outside.

about a child finding a present for Mother's Day

Kicking the dirt,
my toe hits a rock.
A smooth speckled oval,
it could be a gargoyle egg.
Or a paperweight.
Stuck in a box,
wrapped in the gold paper
Mother saved from Christmas,
the old tape peeled off,
it looks like a good gift.

repeated words

She shakes the box, smiling,
while I stare at her hands
untying the ribbon,
tearing the paper,
lifting the lid.
She holds the rock with flat fingers,
like some rotten egg.

Mother walks into the kitchen,
puzzling. She puts a clove of garlic
on her thick round cutting board
and brings the rock down hard.

ends with mother liking the present

"A garlic rock," she says,
pulling chunks of garlic
from the broken skin.
"Just what I needed."

During Reading

You've learned a lot from your first reading. The poem is about a Mother's Day present. You probably noticed that the words *I, Mother, rock,* and *she* are repeated. These words tell you about the speaker and main people in the poem.

Now read through the poem again quietly to yourself.

Read Each Word and Each Line

Poets choose words carefully. They try to find strong and unusual ways of saying things. That's why it helps to look closely at the key words and phrases of a poem.

Two Per Line

When you're having trouble figuring out the meaning of a poem, use a reading tool called a Two Per Line. In the first column, write key lines from the poem that you're trying to understand. Then circle or highlight what you think are the two key words in each line. Think about what those words mean—their dictionary meanings (denotations) and the feelings you have about them (connotations). In the second column, write your thoughts about the words you marked.

Poetry

TWO PER LINE

TEXT	MY IDEAS
"Stuck in a box, wrapped in the gold paper"	The word "stuck" makes me think the present got wrapped in a hurry. Using gold paper might make the present seem fancy.
"it looks like a good gift."	I don't think a rock is such a good gift.

Explore the Poem's Meaning

Now consider the poem's meaning. Remember that the meaning is not the same thing as the subject. The poem's subject is what the poem is about. The meaning is the poet's feeling about the subject. A poem's overall meaning is not always obvious. Often it is an insight, observation, or statement about life.

Go back to read the poem again. Focus on what the poem is saying about the subject—the Mother's Day present. Look for key words in each line. What do you think they mean?

Double-entry Journal

A Double-entry Journal gives you another good way to look closely at parts of a poem. A Double-entry Journal can help you to "read between the lines" and draw conclusions about what you've read. In the first column, write key quotations from the poem. In the second column, write your thoughts about them or what you think they mean.

DOUBLE-ENTRY JOURNAL

QUOTES	MY THOUGHTS
"She holds the rock with flat fingers, like some rotten egg."	The mother holds it in an odd way. Comparing it to a rotten egg makes me think that she doesn't like it.
"'A garlic rock,' she says, pulling chunks of garlic from the broken skin. 'Just what I needed.'"	The mother was smart to use the rock to break the garlic. She's found a use for the present. The kid was probably glad that she said she liked it.

Explore Your Feelings

As you think about a poem's meaning, pay attention to how the words make you feel. Listen to what you are thinking about as you read the poem. To record your thoughts, write some notes like the ones below. Or you can ask questions and then try to answer them. Your thoughts and feelings can help you decide what the poem means.

from "Mother's Day"

Mother's Day morning
and I have no present.
No money.
I walk outside.

Kicking the dirt,
my toe hits a rock.
A smooth speckled oval,
it could be a gargoyle egg.
Or a paperweight.
Stuck in a box,
wrapped in the gold paper
Mother saved from Christmas,
the old tape peeled off,
it looks like a good gift.

I feel terrible when I don't have a present.

I keep a rock I found at the beach last summer on my desk.

When I don't have money, I make presents, too.

Poetry

After Reading

Now that you've read the poem a few times, pause to think about what the poem means. Go back to the poem and review your notes, if you need to. Ask yourself questions like these:

> Do I understand how the speaker feels about the present?

> Do I understand what the speaker is saying about the subject (the Mother's Day present)?

> Can I put the meaning of the poem into a sentence of my own?

Write a Journal Entry

A great way to sum up your ideas about the meaning of a poem is to write a brief journal entry about it.

JOURNAL ENTRY

This situation has happened to me, too. If I can't buy a present, I usually make something. My mom and dad are just like this mother in the poem. They always make a big deal about what I give them. I think this poem means that parents usually try to show kids that the idea of giving is what matters.

Summing Up

- The overall meaning of the poem is what the poet says about the subject.
- To understand a poem's meaning, pay attention to the denotations and connotations of words.
- Explore your feelings about a poem in organizers, such as a Two Per Line and a Double-entry Journal, to help you figure out the meaning of a poem.

Focus on Sound and Shape

In poetry, the sounds of words usually are important. The words may rhyme or have a certain beat. Or they may repeat certain sounds or create a particular mood.

The words and lines of poetry usually are very carefully shaped. The way the lines are grouped and the words that end each line have been very carefully chosen. Poets use the sounds of words and the look of the poem on the page to speak to you as a reader.

Understanding more about the sounds and shapes of poems will help you to appreciate them more.

Poetry

Goals

Here you'll learn how to:

✔ **notice a poem's rhyme**
✔ **figure out a poem's rhythm**
✔ **note the shape and organization of a poem**

Before Reading

Get ready to focus on the sound and shape of Jack Prelutsky's poem "My Dragon Wasn't Feeling Good" by doing a quick preview.

Preview for Sound and Shape

As you read the poem, listen for words that rhyme. Listen, too, for a beat, or rhythm. Look also at the way the lines appear on the page.

PREVIEW
Title and author

PREVIEW
Rhymes

PREVIEW
Organized into two groups of lines

"My Dragon Wasn't Feeling Good" by Jack Prelutsky

My dragon wasn't feeling good,
He had a nasty chill
And couldn't keep from shivering,
I saw that he was ill.
His eyes were red and watery,
His nose was running too,
His flame was but a fizzle,
And his cheeks were pallid blue.

I took him to a doctor
Just as quickly as I could,
A specialist in dragons,
And she's in our neighborhood.
She took his pulse and temperature,
Then fed him turpentine
And phosphorus and gasoline—
My dragon's doing fine.

During Reading

In your preview, you probably noticed a few things about the poem. For example, you probably saw that some of the words rhyme and that the poem has two groups of lines. Why did Jack Prelutsky decide to make his poem look and sound this way? To answer that question, read through the poem carefully two or three times.

Read for Rhythm

Read the poem out loud so you can hear its **rhythm**, or beat.

If you play an instrument or listen to music, you know about rhythm. It's a pattern of beats. In a line of poetry, some syllables in words are stressed more than others. That's what gives a line of poetry or a song a rhythm.

Go back and look at the poem's first group of lines. Listen for the number of beats, or stressed syllables, in each line. Try clapping your hands for every stressed syllable. The stressed syllables are marked like this: *good*. The unstressed ones are marked like this: *My*

> **LISTENING FOR RHYTHM**
>
> My dragon wasn't feeling good,
> He has a nasty chill

Can you hear the pattern of beats as you read these lines? How would the poem be different if each line had a completely different rhythm? How does the rhythm help create the playful feeling of the poem?

Poetry

Notice Rhyme

When words **rhyme**, they sound alike. As you read the first stanza of "My Dragon Wasn't Feeling Good" again, note all of the words that rhyme.

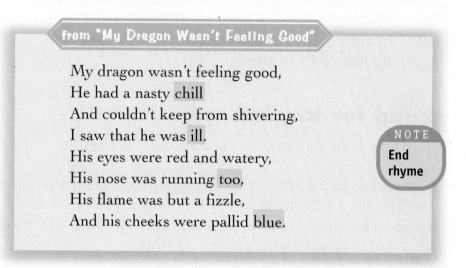

from "My Dragon Wasn't Feeling Good"

My dragon wasn't feeling good,
He had a nasty chill
And couldn't keep from shivering,
I saw that he was ill.
His eyes were red and watery,
His nose was running too,
His flame was but a fizzle,
And his cheeks were pallid blue.

NOTE
End rhyme

The rhyming words appear at the ends of lines. This is called *end rhyme*. But some lines rhyme, and others don't.

You can see a pattern. It's called a *rhyme scheme*. Every other line rhymes, beginning with the second line of each group. Poets use rhyme to give their poems pleasing sounds. Do you like the rhymes? What do they add to the poem?

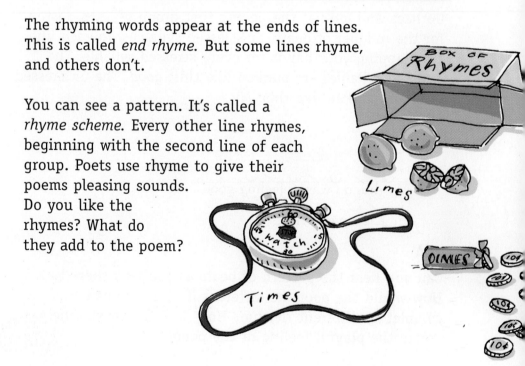

Look for a Poem's Shape and Organization

As you read a poem, ask yourself these questions.

> **What is the poem's shape on the page?**

> **How does the poet arrange the lines?**

As you look again at the poem, you will see that it's divided into two groups of eight lines. Most of the lines are about the same length. In poems, groups of lines are called **stanzas.** Poets use stanzas as a way of organizing their ideas. Often each stanza takes up a different idea or image.

To understand a poem's shape and organization, try turning it into a picture. Read the notes one reader connected to the two stanzas of "My Dragon Wasn't Feeling Good."

"My Dragon Wasn't Feeling Good"

My dragon wasn't feeling good,
He had a nasty chill
And couldn't keep from shivering,
I saw that he was ill.
His eyes were red and watery,
His nose was running too,
His flame was but a fizzle,
And his cheeks were pallid blue.

Stanza 1: the sick dragon

I took him to a doctor
Just as quickly as I could,
A specialist in dragons,
And she's in our neighborhood.
She took his pulse and temperature,
Then fed him turpentine
And phosphorus and gasoline—
My dragon's doing fine.

Stanza 2: dragon feeling well

Poetry

After Reading

After you've read the poem a few times and have studied it, think about what you've read.

- What did I learn about its rhythm, rhyme, and shape?
- Why did the poet make the poem look and sound the way it does?
- What questions do I have about the poem's sound and shape?

To help you remember the poem, try to *do* something with it. For example, try this activity.

Write a Dragon Poem

Write your own poem about dragons or something else. If you can, use rhythm and rhyme. Model your poem on "My Dragon Wasn't Feeling Good."

> **JOURNAL ENTRY**
>
> **My Dragon Poem**
> My dragon wasn't very smart,
> He had a tiny brain
> And couldn't keep from goofing off,
> I saw he was a pain.

Summing Up

- When you read poems, remember to listen to the sounds of the words.
- Notice the rhythms (or beats) and rhyme of a poem. Note how they add to the poem's overall feeling and meaning.
- Think about why the poem is organized the way it is.

Elements of Poetry

Poets have many tools that they can use. These tools can add to the poem's sound, meaning, and emotional effect on the reader.

This part of the handbook describes these elements of poetry. They will help you understand what to look for in the poems you read.

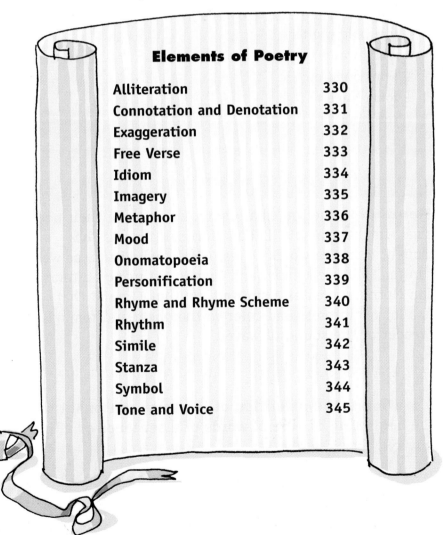

Poetry

Alliteration

What repeated consonant sounds do you hear in the poem below?

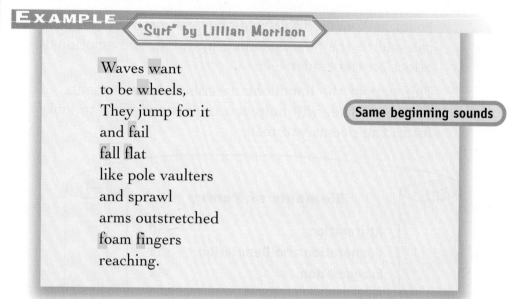

"Surf" by Lillian Morrison

Waves want
to be wheels,
They jump for it
and fail
fall flat
like pole vaulters
and sprawl
arms outstretched
foam fingers
reaching.

Same beginning sounds

DESCRIPTION

Alliteration is one tool that poets use to make their poetry musical. In the example, Lillian Morrison repeats the consonant *w* in the words *waves, want,* and *wheels,* as well as *f* in *fail, fall, flat, foam,* and *fingers.* By using alliteration, Lillian Morrison creates a spirited, rhythmic sound that adds a lot of interest and color to the poem and reminds the reader of the sound of waves.

DEFINITION

Alliteration is the repetition of the same consonant sound at the beginning of several words of a sentence or a line of poetry.

Connotation and Denotation

Poets try to choose words that have strong and colorful feelings (connotations) in addition to their usual dictionary meanings (denotations).

EXAMPLE

"Octopus" by X. J. Kennedy

The octopus is one tough cuss
With muscles built like truckers'—
It lifts great weights in several arms,
Each lined with sticky suckers.

If you should meet an octopus
That greets you, "Hi—let's shake!"
You'll stand a long while wondering
Which tentacle to take.

Phrases with connotation

DESCRIPTION

Cuss means "an odd or annoying person." That's the **denotation** of the word, but the phrase "one tough cuss" is often used informally to suggest someone old and a little cranky. The meanings or feelings a word creates are called **connotations.** The poet might have used the phrase "a harsh creature." But, by using "one tough cuss," the poet makes the octopus sound odd but more lovable than frightening. A few lines later, the poet uses another informal phrase. The connotation of the phrase "sticky suckers" describes the octopus's arms as unpleasant without making them sound dangerous or without sounding too scientific.

DEFINITION

The **connotation** of a word reflects its emotional qualities or meanings. The **denotation** of a word is its exact dictionary meaning.

Poetry

331

Exaggeration

Poets sometimes "go beyond the truth." That's what *exaggeration* means—to describe something as larger or wildly different than it actually is.

EXAMPLE

"Beetles" by Monica Shannon

Beetles must use polish,
  They look so new and shiny,   **Exaggeration**
Just like a freshly painted car,
  Except for being tiny.

DESCRIPTION

In everyday conversation, people often **exaggerate,** or stretch the truth. This helps you to make a point forcefully or to make listeners laugh. Poets use exaggeration, too. In this example, the poet stretches the truth about how beetles become shiny to make readers smile and to create greater interest in these insects. The exaggeration creates a mental picture and sparks a reader's imagination.

DEFINITION

Exaggeration is going beyond, or stretching, the truth.

Free Verse

Free verse is a type of poetry that doesn't use rhyme or regular rhythms. It's "free" and sounds natural, just like everyday conversation.

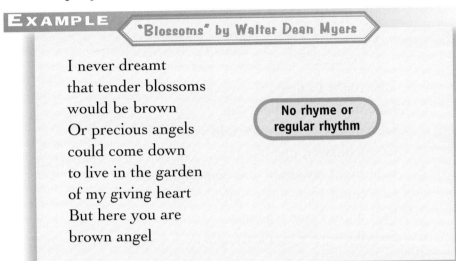

EXAMPLE   "Blossoms" by Walter Dean Myers

I never dreamt
that tender blossoms
would be brown
Or precious angels
could come down
to live in the garden
of my giving heart
But here you are
brown angel

No rhyme or regular rhythm

DESCRIPTION

A poem written in **free verse** is "free" of rhymes and set rhythms. Poets use free verse because it allows them to experiment with the shapes and sounds of their poetry.

Note in the example above that different lines have different numbers of words. The lines are not grouped in sets of three or four. The poem stands as one single group of lines. Nor does the poem have rhyme or regular rhythm. All of these are signs the poet is using free verse.

DEFINITION

Free verse is poetry written without a regular rhyme, rhythm, and form.

Poetry

Idiom

The phrase "hanging in there" is an idiom. It doesn't mean that somebody is physically hanging somewhere. It means "going on" or "not giving up." What do the highlighted idioms below mean?

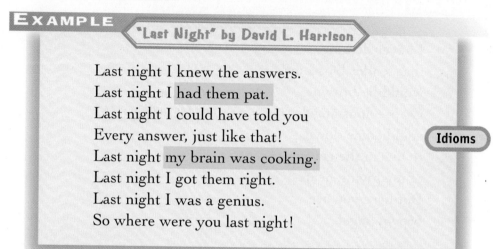

"Last Night" by David L. Harrison

Last night I knew the answers.
Last night I had them pat.
Last night I could have told you
Every answer, just like that!
Last night my brain was cooking.
Last night I got them right.
Last night I was a genius.
So where were you last night!

Idioms

DESCRIPTION

An **idiom** is an everyday saying that doesn't exactly mean what the words say. For example, "my brain was cooking" doesn't actually mean that the brain was cooking on a stove! It means that it was working fast, bubbling over with ideas. "I had them [answers] pat" has nothing to do with patting or tapping one's hands. It means knowing something perfectly. Poets use idioms because that's the way people talk to each other.

Here are a few other examples of idioms:

easy as pie—able to be done without difficulty

break a leg—good luck (in a performance)

pay one's dues—earn through hard work

DEFINITION

An **idiom** is a common phrase made up of words that can't be understood by their literal, or ordinary, meanings.

Imagery

Poets use imagery to draw you into a scene or experience. What pictures do you see in your mind as you read this poem?

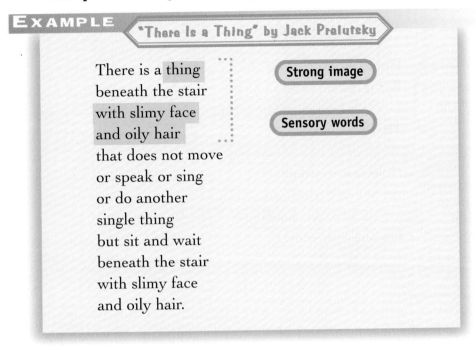

EXAMPLE "There Is a Thing" by Jack Prelutsky

There is a thing
beneath the stair
with slimy face
and oily hair
that does not move
or speak or sing
or do another
single thing
but sit and wait
beneath the stair
with slimy face
and oily hair.

Strong image

Sensory words

Poetry

DESCRIPTION

Poets use words that appeal to your five senses. Poets' images might describe feelings, scenes, or objects. Images help you to picture things and imagine how things sound, smell, taste, and feel. Those "word pictures" in poems are called **imagery.** Imagery can help you experience familiar things in a fresh way.

DEFINITION

Imagery is language that appeals to the five senses—sight, hearing, smell, taste, and touch.

Metaphor

In a metaphor, two unlike things are compared. One thing is spoken of as if it actually *were* something else.

"Dreams" by Langston Hughes

Comparison of life to a bird

Hold fast to dreams
For if dreams die
Life is a broken-winged bird
That cannot fly.

Comparison of life to a field

Hold fast to dreams
For when dreams go
Life is a barren field
Frozen with snow.

DESCRIPTION

A **metaphor** is a kind of figurative language that compares two things. In a metaphor, a poet doesn't use the words *like* or *as*. Instead, the poet describes a thing or person as if it actually *were* the other thing or person. In "Dreams," Langston Hughes first says that a life without dreams "is a broken-winged bird" and later that it "is a barren field." A good metaphor creates a clear, memorable picture and inspires you to see the original subject in a new way.

DEFINITION

A **metaphor** is a direct comparison between two things. It does not use the words *like* or *as*. It states that one thing *is* another.

Mood

Poetry touches your emotions. What feeling do you get from the poem below?

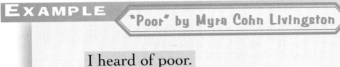
"Poor" by Myra Cohn Livingston

I heard of poor.
It means hungry, no food.
No shoes, no place to live.
Nothing good.

> Short words and lines create a serious mood.

It means winter nights
And being cold.
It is lonely, alone.
Feeling old.

Poor is a tired face.
Poor is thin.
Poor is standing outside
Looking in.

> Words create a feeling of sadness.

DESCRIPTION

A poem's mood may be dark and mysterious (a scary poem) or bright and cheerful (a happy poem). The **mood** colors the whole poem and creates a feeling in the reader. The length of the sentences, the words that are chosen, and the sounds of the words all work to create the mood of a poem. Words such as *poor, lonely, old, alone,* and *tired* in the example above create a mood and make the reader feel sad.

DEFINITION

The feeling that a poem creates in the reader is called mood.

Poetry

337

Onomatopoeia

Poets use language to its fullest. They choose words not only for what they mean but also for how they sound. Note how language is used in this poem.

EXAMPLE

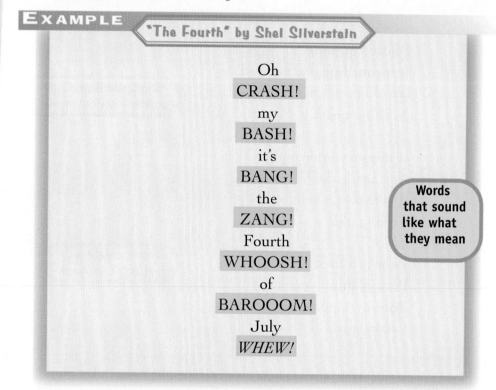

"The Fourth" by Shel Silverstein

Oh
CRASH!
my
BASH!
it's
BANG!
the
ZANG!
Fourth
WHOOSH!
of
BAROOOM!
July
WHEW!

> Words that sound like what they mean

DESCRIPTION

On the Fourth of July, you hear many *crashes*, *bangs*, and *barooms* in fireworks. In this poem, the words that are in capital letters all sound like the thing they name. That means that they all are examples of **onomatopoeia.** Writers use onomatopoeia to liven up their writing and add fun sounds to it.

DEFINITION

Onomatopoeia is the use of words that sound like the noises they describe.

Personification

Poets often create strong images by making nonhuman things seem human. That way you can understand them in a fresh and unusual way.

"Snowy Benches" by Aileen Fisher

Do parks get lonely
in winter, perhaps,
when benches have only
snow on their laps?

Giving nonhuman things human qualities

Poetry

DESCRIPTION

Personification is a type of figure of speech that gives human qualities to animals, objects, or ideas—just as in the example above. Parks have feelings, and benches have laps. Use of personification adds life to a poem and helps you view a familiar thing from a new point of view. In the example above, the poet asks whether parks feel lonely in winter, like people sometimes do. By using personification, the poet makes you as a reader look differently at parks and benches after reading the poem.

DEFINITION

Personification is a figure of speech in which poets give an animal, object, or idea human qualities, such as the ability to cry, feel, talk, and make decisions.

Rhyme and Rhyme Scheme

When two words rhyme, they sound the same at the end.
Listen for the words that rhyme as you read this funny poem.

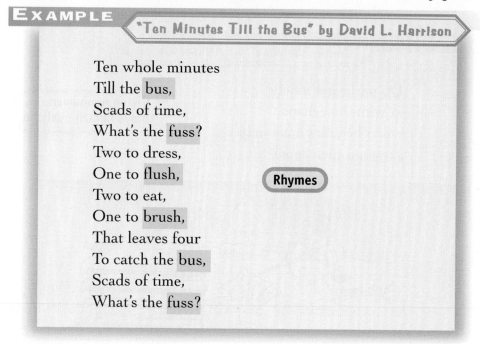

EXAMPLE

"Ten Minutes Till the Bus" by David L. Harrison

Ten whole minutes
Till the bus,
Scads of time,
What's the fuss?
Two to dress,
One to flush,   **Rhymes**
Two to eat,
One to brush,
That leaves four
To catch the bus,
Scads of time,
What's the fuss?

DESCRIPTION

In the example, the words *bus* and *fuss* **rhyme,** and so do
flush and *brush*. A pattern of rhymes is called a **rhyme
scheme.** In this stanza (group of lines), the rhyme scheme
is regular. Every other line ends with a rhyme. Poets use
rhyme to add a musical sound to their poems.

DEFINITION

When words **rhyme,** they have the same sound. Poems
often use rhyme, usually at the ends of lines. A **rhyme
scheme** is a pattern of rhymes in a poem.

Rhythm

As you read the lines below listen for the pattern of beats, or stressed and unstressed syllables. Can you hear hoof beats?

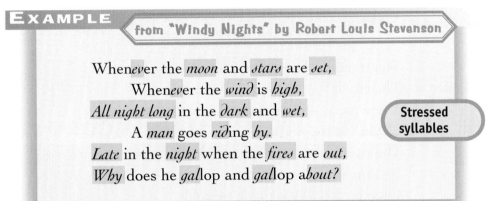

EXAMPLE

from "Windy Nights" by Robert Louis Stevenson

Whenever the *moon* and *stars* are *set*,
Whenever the *wind* is *high*,
All night long in the *dark* and *wet*,
A *man* goes *riding* by.
Late in the *night* when the *fires* are *out*,
Why does he *gallop* and *gallop* a*bout*?

Stressed syllables

DESCRIPTION

Try reading the lines softly to yourself. Can you hear the beat? That's what poets call **rhythm.** Poets create rhythm by using words in which parts are emphasized (stressed syllables) and some parts are not emphasized (unstressed syllables). In the example, the italics show what's stressed and what isn't. Look at how this line is marked.

Poetry

Listening for Rhythm

∪ / ∪ ∪ / ∪ /
Whenever the wind is high

The stressed syllables are marked like this: wínd. The unstressed ones are marked like this: thĕ. The rhythm creates a rocking or bouncing beat in this poem, like the galloping of a horse.

DEFINITION

Rhythm is the pattern of beats or a series of stressed and unstressed syllables in a poem.

Simile

Poets often make comparisons between things to make you think about them in a new way.

EXAMPLE

"The World" by Noel Berry

Similes

The trees are like the hair of the world.
The city is like the heart of the world.
The wind is a flute player
playing in the night.
The cars beeping horns are like buttons
beeping inside the earth.
Each bird is like a single piccolo
singing away
and the grass, just like me,
being buried under the snow.

DESCRIPTION

In a figure of speech called a **simile,** a poet uses the words *like* or *as* to compare two things. Similes help readers see things differently and experience them in a new way. In the example above, the poet strings together several similes. Have you ever thought of comparing trees to hair, a city to a heart, car horns beeping to buttons, a bird to a piccolo, or grass to a person? Poets use similes to surprise you as a reader and to create strong images that you can "see" as you read.

DEFINITION

A **simile** is a comparison between two things, using the words *like* or *as.*

Stanza

Notice the appearance of this poem on the page.

"First and Last" by David McCord

1. A tadpole hasn't a pole at all,
   And he *doesn't* live in a hole in the wall.

2. You've got it wrong: a polecat's not
   A cat on a pole. And I'll tell you what:

   Four stanzas

3. A bullfrog's never a bull; and how
   Could a cowbird possibly be a cow?

4. A kingbird, though, *is* a kind of king,
   And he chases a crow like anything.

DESCRIPTION

This poem has four groups of two lines. In poetry, groups of lines are called **stanzas.** Stanzas often have four, five, or six lines. Two-line stanzas like the ones in the example are called *couplets*.

Poets use stanzas to give their poems structure and to help emphasize the different ideas. Note that in this poem each stanza talks about a different animal. Often, by beginning a new stanza, the poet signals the beginning of a new image, thought, or idea.

DEFINITION

A stanza in a poem is a group of lines that usually develops one idea.

Symbol

We use symbols all the time. The American flag is a symbol of freedom. A policeman's badge is a symbol of justice. When something is used as a symbol, it suggests another, larger meaning. What symbol can you find in the poem below?

EXAMPLE

"The Farmer" by Carole Boston Weatherford

A plot of weeds,
an old grey mule.
Hot sun and sweat
on a bright Southern day.
Strong, stern papa
under a straw hat,
plowing and planting
his whole life away.
His backbone is forged
of African Iron
and red Georgia clay.

DESCRIPTION

A **symbol** is something that stands for more than just itself. In the example, one man, the farmer, is a symbol of the proud African culture and of the South. The ideas of "African Iron" and "red Georgia clay" describe the farmer, but they link him to his ancestors in Africa and his fellow southerners. In other words, the farmer stands for more than just himself. He stands for two whole groups of people.

DEFINITION

A **symbol** is something that stands for something more than just itself.

Tone and Voice

Read the beginning of this poem. How would you describe the speaker? How does the speaker feel about the subject?

EXAMPLE

"Commas" by Douglas Florian

Do commas have mommas
Who teach them to pause,
Who comfort and calm them,
And clean their sharp claws?
Who tell them short stories
Of uncommon commas
And send them to bed
In their comma pajamas?

Not a serious question

DESCRIPTION

A poet's attitude toward the subject of the poem is called the poem's **tone.** In the poem above, the poet asks a question that isn't serious or important. The question is fun and playful, and so is the overall feeling of the poem.

As a reader of poetry, you want to know who is speaking in a poem. The speaker in a poem or the speaker's feeling or attitude is called **voice.** How would you describe the speaker of this poem? Look for clues in the language the writer uses. The speaker in this poem must know at least a little about punctuation marks and has a good sense of humor—and a lot of imagination.

DEFINITION

Tone is the attitude a writer takes toward the audience or subject. **Voice** is the attitude or feeling of the speaker who tells the poem.

Poetry

345

Reading
Drama

Reading a Play

Ways of Reading Drama
Focus on Language
Focus on Theme

Elements of Drama

Drama

Reading a Play

Have you ever seen or acted in a school play? A **play** is a written story meant to be acted out on stage. Plays not only entertain you, but they can also help you learn more about yourself.

When you read a play, note how very different it looks from a novel or story. Most of the play is **dialogue**, or the conversation between two characters. The other text in plays is called **stage directions**. These are written instructions for the actors and actresses. Because plays are all dialogue and stage directions, they put special demands on you as a reader.

Goals

Here you'll learn how to:
- ✔ recognize the major parts of a play
- ✔ use the reading strategy of summarizing
- ✔ understand how plays are organized

Before Reading

When reading a play, you go through the same steps as for a folktale or novel. Before reading you set a reading purpose, preview parts of the play, and create a plan for reading. But first you need to learn a little about plays.

Plays begin with opening stage directions that may include:

■ the list of **characters**—the people or "human-like" animals who will be in the play

■ a list of **props**—things like blankets, dishes, or any other objects used in the play

■ information about **costumes**— what the actors will be wearing

■ information about **setting**—the time and place of the play

■ suggestions for **lighting, music,** and **sound effects**

Most plays are organized into main sections called **acts.** Each act is broken down into smaller **scenes** that establish different times or places in the story.

A Set a Purpose

Here are some key questions to consider while reading a play.

Setting a Purpose

■ **Who are the main characters? What are they like?**

■ **What are the settings?**

■ **What happens during the play?**

■ **What is the theme?**

Drama

B Preview

Take time to preview a play before you read it. Your preview will give you a head start in understanding and enjoying the play. As you skim the play, look for:

Preview Checklist

✔ the title, playwright (author), and introduction
✔ the cast of characters
✔ the setting, the number of acts (main parts) and scenes (smaller parts)
✔ any background information, photographs, or illustrations

Now preview the play *Star Sisters*, looking for the items in the Preview Checklist.

Star Sisters

Ojibway

by Joseph Bruchac

PREVIEW
Title and playwright

PREVIEW
Introduction

The Ojibway people, who are also known as the Chippewa, are one of the largest tribes in North America. The center of their homelands is the Great Lakes region of the present-day United States and Canada. Their lifestyle was much like that of their cousins, the Abenakis, who lived far to the east of them. The Ojibway people relied on their great knowledge of the forests and waters—not only hunting and fishing, but also making maple syrup, gathering berries, and traveling widely in their birchbark canoes.

Characters
Narrator
Red Star Sister
White Star Sister
Red Star
White Star
Star People (as many as the group size accommodates)
Star Grandmother
Little Star
Bear
Lynx
Wolverine
Trees (two or more)

PREVIEW
Cast of characters

Drama

PREVIEW

First Scene

Scene I: A Forest at Night

Red Star Sister and White Star Sister lie on blankets outdoors in the forest.

NARRATOR: One night, two sisters went outside to sleep under the stars.

RED STAR SISTER: Look up into the sky.

WHITE STAR SISTER: It is beautiful up there.

RED STAR SISTER: I would like to marry a star.

WHITE STAR SISTER: I, too, would like to marry a star.

RED STAR SISTER: Which one would you marry?

WHITE STAR SISTER: I would marry that big white star.

NOTE

Opening event

RED STAR SISTER: I would marry that bright red star.

WHITE STAR SISTER: I am feeling very tired.

RED STAR SISTER: I am tired too.

NOTE

Stage directions introduce new characters.

The two Sisters fall asleep. As soon as they do so, Red Star and White Star enter. Their entry should suggest that they come from above the stage area, by jumping down onto the stage from a box or coming down a ladder.

RED STAR: This is my wife-to-be.

WHITE STAR: This is the one who wants to marry me.

RED STAR: Let us take them to the Sky Land now!

PREVIEW

New scene and new setting

Scene II: The Sky Land

White Star Sister and Red Star Sister are asleep on the bare stage. They are surrounded by a crowd of Star People.

RED STAR SISTER (*waking*): Where are we? Sister, wake up!

Star Sisters, continued

WHITE STAR SISTER: I dreamt that a star came down from the sky. Ah, who are these people?

ALL OF THE STAR PEOPLE: We are the Star People.

WHITE STAR SISTER: Sister, I am still dreaming. I want to wake up now and go back home.

STAR GRANDMOTHER: You are not dreaming.

LITTLE STAR: You are in the sky.

Red Star Sister and White Star Sister stand up.

RED STAR SISTER: How did we get up into the sky?

RED STAR: Do you not remember? You said you wanted to marry me. I am Red Star.

WHITE STAR: And your sister said she wanted to marry me. I am White Star.

WHITE STAR SISTER: Where is our wigwam?

LITTLE STAR *(pointing to floor)*: It is way down there.

STAR GRANDMOTHER: Every night our job is to look down through the holes in the sky.

ALL OF THE STAR PEOPLE: When people look up, they see our faces looking at them.

WHITE STAR *(taking White Star Sister's hand)*: Come with me, my wife. I will show you your new home.

RED STAR *(taking Red Star Sister's hand)*: My wife, come with me. I will show you your new home too.

Scene III: Nighttime in Another Part of the Sky Land

White Star Sister and Red Star Sister are walking around the stage. The basket is on one side of the stage. All around

NOTE
Sisters are confused and homesick.

Drama

PREVIEW
New scene and another new setting

353

them Star People are kneeling or lying on the stage with their faces looking down through the holes in the sky. As White Star Sister and Red Star Sister walk around, the Star People look up at them and then look back down again.

WHITE STAR SISTER: We have been in the sky for a long time, Sister.

RED STAR SISTER: Has White Star been kind to you?

WHITE STAR SISTER: He has been very kind to me, but there is nothing to do here in the Sky Land.

RED STAR SISTER: Red Star has been kind to me too. But I miss my home.

LITTLE STAR: Are you sad?

RED STAR SISTER: Yes, we are, Little Star.

LITTLE STAR: Why?

WHITE STAR SISTER: I miss my mother and father.

RED STAR SISTER: I miss my home and my friends.

LITTLE STAR: Come with me. I will take you to my grandmother.

Little Star leads the Star Sisters across the stage to Star Grandmother. Red Star and White Star are nearby, looking through holes in the sky.

LITTLE STAR: Grandmother, they are sad. They miss their families and their friends.

STAR GRANDMOTHER: Look down through this hole. What do you see?

RED STAR SISTER *(looking)*: I see my family's wigwam.

WHITE STAR SISTER *(looking)*: I can hear my people singing.

NOTE

Sisters are still unhappy.

STAR GRANDMOTHER: You are ready to go
  home.
RED STAR *(standing up)*: If you are ready to go
  home, we will help you.
WHITE STAR *(also standing)*: We will miss you.
RED STAR: But you should be with your family.
STAR GRANDMOTHER: Get into this basket. We
  will tie a long rope to it.
The Star Sisters climb into the basket.
ALL OF THE STAR PEOPLE: We will lower you
  to the world below.

NOTE
Climax =
Sisters
leave sky.

Scene IV: Eagle's Nest in the Forest
*White Star Sister and Red Star Sister are standing in the
nest, peering upward. The Trees stand in the background.*
RED STAR SISTER: Wait, Star People! Do not
  take the basket away. We have not reached the
  ground yet. We are in an eagle's nest at the top of
  a tree.
WHITE STAR SISTER: They cannot hear you.
RED STAR SISTER: How can we get down from
  this treetop?
WHITE STAR SISTER: We will call for help.
  Look, there is Bear.
RED STAR SISTER: Come up here and help us get
  down.
BEAR: Who is asking for help?
WHITE STAR SISTER: We are! Up here, in the
  eagle's nest!
BEAR: I am too busy to help you. I am looking for
  berries and honey.
RED STAR SISTER: He is going away. Oh, how
  can we get down?

PREVIEW
Another
new
scene and
setting

Drama

NOTE
New
problem

WHITE STAR SISTER: Look, there is Lynx.

RED STAR SISTER: Please help us get down.

LYNX: Who wants help?

WHITE STAR SISTER: Here, up here.

LYNX: My claws are not sharp enough. That is too far to climb up.

RED STAR SISTER: He is going away too.

WHITE STAR SISTER: Who is that coming?

RED STAR SISTER: Oh no, it is Wolverine. If Wolverine helps us, he will make us live with him.

WOLVERINE: Did I hear someone speak my name? Ah, looook. Twoooo pretty sisters in a tree. I will help them get doooown.

RED STAR SISTER: Go away, we do not need any help.

WHITE STAR SISTER: Shh. Let him help us down. I have a plan.

Wolverine helps the Star Sisters climb out of the eagle's nest and down the tree.

WOLVERINE: There, I have helped you doooown. Now you can come and cooook my fooood and live with me.

WHITE STAR SISTER: Wait, I forgot my comb.

RED STAR SISTER: I forgot my comb too.

WHITE STAR SISTER: Please climb back up and get our combs.

WOLVERINE: The forest is thick here. Hooooow will I find yoooou when I come back doooown?

WHITE STAR SISTER: We will whistle to you.

WOLVERINE: Wait here for me. Don't forget toooo whistle when I get back.

NOTE

Sisters plan to trick Wolverine.

RED STAR SISTER: He's gone. Now let's run away. This is the path to our village.

WHITE STAR SISTER: Wait. I have to ask the trees for help. *(Takes the kinnikinnick from her pouch.)* Trees, I am placing this *kinnikinnick* (kih-NEE-kin-nik) here on the ground for you as a gift. Help us. When Wolverine comes down, whistle to him.

TREES: We will help you, little ones.

WHITE STAR SISTER: Now let's run away!

WOLVERINE: I am back noooow. I could not find your coooombs. Sisters, where are yoooou? Whistle toooo me. *(A Tree whistles.)* There yoooou are. *(Another Tree whistles.)* Or are yoooou there? *(Trees whistle all around him.)* Oh noooo, they have tricked me. Now I have noooo one to cooook for me.

NARRATOR: So White Star Sister and Red Star Sister tricked Wolverine and came home safely. And from then on, they never again slept out at night under the stars.

NOTE
The plan works.

NOTE
Happy ending

Drama

357

C Plan

From your preview, you probably learned a lot about the play:

- There are four scenes.
- The two main characters are Star Sisters.
- The Star People take the Star Sisters from the forest into the sky.
- The Star Sisters return home.

Think about the times you've looked into the sky and dreamed about things. Think, too, about how you feel when you are in a strange place away from home. Add this to the information you've learned from your preview. Now make a plan to find more specific information to answer your reading purpose questions.

Reading Strategy: Summarizing

Summarizing is a good way to make sure you understand what you've read. When you summarize, you explain the main events and the author's main ideas in your own words. It helps to include important information about the setting, characters, and events in the plot. To summarize a play, you need to tell what happens in the beginning, middle, and end. A Story Organizer can help you sum up the plot.

STORY ORGANIZER

BEGINNING	MIDDLE	END

During Reading

Now you are ready to go back and carefully read the play. Pay attention to key details about characters, setting, and plot events.

READING
A PLAY

✔ Story Organizer
✔ Summary Notes
✔ Web
✔ Plot Diagram
✔ Theme Diagram

D Read with a Purpose

When you read, take notes to keep track of information. There are many tools that will be useful as you summarize the play. Try different ones, depending on whether your focus is on plot, characters, setting, or theme.

1. Story Organizer

A Story Organizer helps you keep track of the major changes in a play. Here is a finished Story Organizer for *Star Sisters*. Would you add any other plot events?

> STORY ORGANIZER

BEGINNING	MIDDLE	END
• Star Sisters lie in the forest. • Sisters would like to marry stars.	• Red Star and White Star take Sisters to live in the sky. • Sisters are sad because they miss home. • Star People return the Sisters to earth, but the Sisters get stuck in an eagle's nest.	• Sisters trick Wolverine into helping them. • Trees help Sisters run from Wolverine. • Star Sisters return home.

Drama

2. Summary Notes

With another kind of summary, you take notes on each scene of the play. After you read each scene, stop to summarize what happened. Write only two or three sentences per scene. Summary Notes give you a complete record of the important plot events and give characters' feelings.

SUMMARY NOTES

TITLE: Star Sisters

SCENE I:
Star Sisters are sleeping in the forest at night.
They say they'd like to marry stars. Then, they fall asleep.
Red Star and White Star take them to Sky Land.

SCENE II:
Star Sisters wake up in Sky Land.
Red Star and White Star take them to their new homes.

SCENE III:
Star Sisters are lonely and miss home.
The Star People lower them to the world below.

SCENE IV:
Star Sisters are stuck in an eagle's nest in the forest.
Bear and Lynx won't help them down.
They trick Wolverine into helping them and then go home.

3. Web

<u>A Web lets you organize ideas around key events, characters, or ideas.</u> After you read one scene—or even all of a play—think of a "magnet word." It is something that attracts details. Once you have written details connected to the key word, you can write a brief summary, using all the details. Here is how a reader used the Star Sisters to create a Web.

WEB

- think the sky is beautiful
- feel homesick and bored in Sky Land
- talk about missing home a lot
- dream of marrying a star
- want help to get out of eagle's nest
- **Star Sisters**
- love their family and friends
- get home safely
- trick Wolverine

Drama

Once you have made a Web, use it to help you write about the play.

JOURNAL ENTRY

A lot of this play is about how much Red Star Sister and White Star Sister love their home. They start out thinking about marrying stars and how beautiful the sky is. But once they're taken to Sky Land, all they want is to go back home. They're sad and homesick. They were smart to think of tricking the wolverine to help them get home.

How Plays Are Organized

Star Sisters has only one act, which has four scenes. Many plays, however, have several acts and a number of scenes in each act. In most plays, a new scene reflects a change in time or place or both. Most plays have the same basic five parts as a novel or story. Make a Plot Diagram like the one below to help you follow the organization of a play.

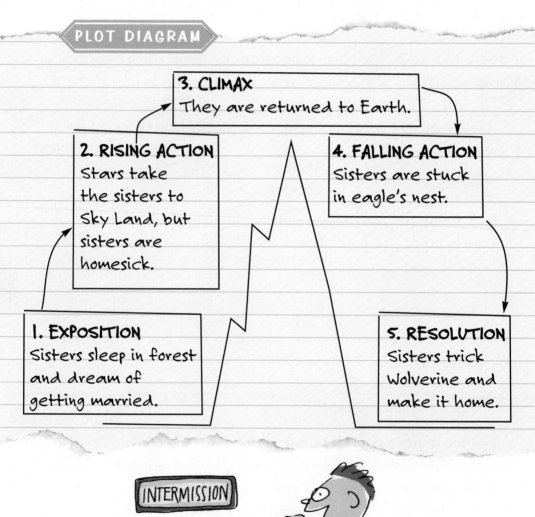

PLOT DIAGRAM

3. CLIMAX
They are returned to Earth.

2. RISING ACTION
Stars take the sisters to Sky Land, but sisters are homesick.

4. FALLING ACTION
Sisters are stuck in eagle's nest.

1. EXPOSITION
Sisters sleep in forest and dream of getting married.

5. RESOLUTION
Sisters trick Wolverine and make it home.

INTERMISSION

E Connect

As an active reader, remember to connect your own life with what you read. Sometimes that's not so easy. For example, how can you connect with two sisters who dream of being married to stars in the sky? Here's how one reader did it.

from *Star Sisters*

WHITE STAR SISTER: We have been in the sky for a long time, Sister.

RED STAR SISTER: Has White Star been kind to you?

WHITE STAR SISTER: He has been very kind to me, but there is nothing to do here in the Sky Land.

I get bored a lot, too.

RED STAR SISTER: Red Star has been kind to me too. But I miss my home.

LITTLE STAR: Are you sad?

RED STAR SISTER: Yes, we are, Little Star.

LITTLE STAR: Why?

WHITE STAR SISTER: I miss my mother and father.

RED STAR SISTER: I miss my home and my friends.

Drama

Remember these helpful ways to connect to plays.

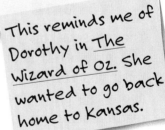

This reminds me of Dorothy in The Wizard of Oz. She wanted to go back home to Kansas.

- Connect the play to other things you've read.

- Connect with how others (like a friend) might react.

- Connect to what the writing makes you feel and think about.

After Reading

Plays sometimes take a long time to read, so it's important to think back on what you've read. Think about your original reading purpose and whether you found what you wanted to find.

F Pause and Reflect

Take a few minutes to think about the details of the play. Ask yourself questions to check your understanding.

Looking Back

■ **Do I know who the main characters are?**

■ **Can I name the settings?**

■ **Can I describe what happens during the play?**

■ **Can I state the theme?**

If you're not sure about the answers to any of these questions, return to the play to find them. As you go back to reread, try a new strategy.

G Reread

The message, or theme, of a play often isn't clear until you think back about the play. One reading strategy to help you do that is called questioning the author.

Rereading Strategy: Questioning the Author

Questioning the author can help you find the theme. You can't really ask an author questions, but you can ask questions of yourself. Then, you try to answer them as the author would if he or she were there.

- Why did they fall into an eagle's nest?
- Why did the sisters have to go up to Sky Land?
- What's the play supposed to mean?

Making a Theme Diagram can help you figure out the theme and state it in your own words. Here is how one reader made sense of the theme of *Star Sisters*.

THEME DIAGRAM

Step 1: What is the topic or "big idea" of the play?

home   or   family

Step 2: What do the characters say or do that relates to the topic?

The Sisters are taken from home and family to marry stars.	They are homesick and want to come home.	Red Star says that they should be with their families.	The Sisters trick Wolverine so they can get home.

Step 3: What do these things tell you that's important to learn about life?

Home is not in the sky or in nature, but where your family is.

Drama

365

H Remember

Often after you read a play, you'll need to remember the details so you can write about it. It's easy to remember something when it has meaning in your life. Here is a way to make the play your own.

In your reading journal, write down one or two lines that stand out for you. Then, tell what you like about them or what they make you think about.

JOURNAL ENTRY

"Every night our job is to look down through the holes in the sky." That's a neat way to think about stars. This reminds me of a planetarium show I saw last year. It was about how people long ago saw the shapes of people or things in the night sky.

Summing Up

When you read a play, remember to use the reading process and the strategy of **summarizing.** To help you summarize, use reading tools like:

- Story Organizer
- Summary Notes
- Web
- Plot Diagram
- Theme Diagram

Remember, too, to look for the **organization of a play.** Then, in looking back, use the strategy of **questioning the author** to help you make sense of the theme.

Focus on Language

When you first read a play, you might be surprised by its language. A play's language looks different because a play wasn't written to be read. It's written to be spoken by actors and actresses on a stage in front of an audience. One type of language in a play is called **stage directions.** They are instructions to the actors and actresses. A second type of language in a play is the conversations among characters, the **dialogue.**

Focusing on a play's language can teach you more about a play's characters, plot, and theme.

Goals

Here you'll learn how to:

✔ **recognize stage directions in a play**

✔ **note how dialogue is used in a play**

✔ **use the strategy of close reading to focus on key lines and speeches**

Drama

Before Reading

Looking at a play's language is one way to get a deeper understanding of a play. When you first read a play, you probably will read to find out what happens. But, by focusing a little on the language, you can understand the play a lot better.

Look at Stage Directions

The stage directions are the playwright's directions for performing the play. The audience never hears these stage directions, but they are very important for a reader. Stage directions are usually printed in italics and enclosed in parentheses.

Describe the Scene

Among the key jobs stage directions perform is giving information that helps readers "see" the scene. Notice how the stage directions below help you picture the scenery as you begin to read this play about Anansi, a spider.

---

from *How Anansi Got a Thin Waist* by Pamela Gerke

CHARACTERS:
NARRATOR
ANANSI
KUMA—Anansi's son
KWAKU—Anansi's son
VILLAGERS (2–6 or more)

NOTE
Description of the scene

(Setting: The forest near Anansi's village in West Africa. There may be a forest backdrop and/or tree and bush sets . . . Backstage on one side is a long rope. The middle of the rope is tied in a loop, big enough to fit around Anansi's waist; the loop will get smaller when both ends of the rope are pulled. LIGHTS UP.)

Describe the Action

Another job of the stage directions is to describe the action. A play is mostly dialogue. First one character speaks, and then another one speaks. But, the playwright still needs to describe what's happening. Stage directions do that. They give information about how actors should sound, how they should move, and how they should handle props.

from *How Anansi Got a Thin Waist*

(*KUMA & KWAKU simultaneously give a pull on the rope. ANANSI cries out in alarm and struggles to go one direction or another, but can't.*)

KUMA & KWAKU: (*Simultaneously.*) Why hasn't father come to the feast yet? I'd better pull harder!

(*They pull on the rope again while ANANSI jerks around, crying out in alarm while pulled this way and that.*)

NOTE
What characters do

NOTE
How characters sound

Drama

Notice in this example how "the action" of the play occurs in the stage directions. The stage directions describe the pulling on the rope, which is how Anansi gets a thin waist.

During Reading

As you read a play, notice what you can learn from the dialogue and the way language is used. Watch also for key lines and speeches.

Reading Strategy: Close Reading

When you read closely, you select a part of the text and look at it carefully, line by line and word by word. **Close reading** helps you to pay attention to an author's language and to interpret dialogue, key lines, and speeches.

See How Dialogue Is Used

You often judge your friends and learn about them by listening to what they say, and you do the same with characters in a play. Dialogue can also tell you who the characters are, what they think, how they react to each other, and what's happening.

NOTE
What Anansi says

NOTE
What characters are doing

from *How Anansi Got a Thin Waist*

ANANSI: (*Sniffing the air.*) FOOD!!! Why, I'd almost forgotten—today is the harvest festival and everyone in the villages is preparing for a feast!

(*VILLAGERS enter, talking to each other.*)

VILLAGER #1: I'm cooking yams and cassava, and chicken with peanut-flavored sauce!

VILLAGER #2: I'm preparing fish and peppers, and rice boiling in a great big pot over the fire.

from *How Anansi Got a Thin Waist,* continued

ANANSI: *(Eagerly.)* Can I come to the feast?

VILLAGER #3: No! You haven't done any work to prepare for it!

VILLAGER #4: You didn't plant yams or potatoes or rice!

VILLAGER #5: You didn't go to the sea to catch fish!

ANANSI: But I don't like to work!

VILLAGER #6: You're disgusting!

> NOTE
> What characters think

Here the dialogue describes the action and makes clear what others think of Anansi and his wish for a free meal.

Focus on Key Lines and Speeches

Every play has key lines and speeches. These parts of the play usually come at important moments and suggest the playwright's message. To find key lines and speeches, look for parts that tell you important things about the plot or characters. Here's an example from the end of the play.

Drama

from *How Anansi Got a Thin Waist*

NARRATOR: Anansi was never fat again. He stayed the same until today, with his fat head and fat body and thin, little waist in between. *(KUMA and KWAKU let go of the rope and Anansi lets it fall to the floor.)*

ANANSI: *(Admiring his waist.)* How thin I am! Now I'll have to eat more to fatten up!

> NOTE
> What Anansi thinks

Anansi's carefree comment shows that he is a silly character who never learns from his mistakes.

After Reading

After finishing the play, look back at what you learned about the play's language from the stage directions and dialogue. Reread parts of the play to learn anything you may have missed. By paying attention to the stage directions and dialogue when reading a play, you will understand the plot, characters, and theme better.

As you reread, try to read at least some of the play out loud. That's a great way to feel the emotions and mood and zero in on the language. After all, a play is meant to be seen *and heard* by an audience.

Once more with feeling!

Director

Summing Up

- Stage directions "show" you what's happening on stage and give instructions on how to perform the play.

- Dialogue can tell you a lot about characters, plot, and theme of a play.

- A play's key lines and speeches give insight into what the playwright is trying to say.

Focus on Theme

Have you ever read something and then asked yourself,
"What's the point?" The point you're
looking for is probably the **theme**.
The theme is the main idea,
or the author's
statement
about life.

Plays usually have
themes, just as
folktales, short
stories, and novels
do. Sometimes
there's more than
one theme. But
to find the theme
of a play, you need
a plan.

Drama

Goals

Here you'll learn how to:

✔ **find the subject or big ideas of a play**
✔ **look at what characters do and say related to those big ideas**
✔ **determine the author's statement about life**

Before Reading

When you pick up a play to read, start looking for its theme. You do that by figuring out the general subjects or big idea of the play.

1. Find the Subject or Big Idea

The subject is what the play is about, or its big idea. This might be a topic, such as love, friendship, family, or loyalty. It might be a specific idea like "believe in yourself."

Read this passage from the beginning of the play *How Anansi Got a Thin Waist*. What big ideas do you see?

> **from *How Anansi Got a Thin Waist* by Pamela Gerke**
>
> NARRATOR: Long ago in West Africa, Anansi the Spider did not look like he does today. Of course, he had eight legs and lived in a web, but back then, he was big all over and his waistline was very fat. Today he still has a big head and a big body but with a thin waist and this is how it came to pass . . .

NOTE Main character and what he looks like

NOTE What story will explain

This passage tells you the setting, introduces you to the character, and tells you what you'll be hearing more about. But read on to get a better sense of the play's big idea.

from *How Anansi Got a Thin Waist*

ANANSI: *(Eagerly.)* Can I come to the feast?

VILLAGER #3: No! You haven't done any work
to prepare for it!

VILLAGER #4: You didn't plant yams or potatoes
or rice!

VILLAGER #5: You didn't go to the sea to catch
fish!

ANANSI: But I don't like to work!

VILLAGER #6: You're disgusting!

NARRATOR: It was true, Anansi played or slept all
day and never worked. And since it's the custom
to never refuse to feed anyone who comes to your
house, Anansi ate very well by simply visiting all
his friends. In fact, he ate more than they did,
which explains why his waist was so fat.

> **NOTE**
> Big idea=
> laziness

Anansi's conversation with the villagers and the narrator's
comments point to the topic of laziness. Keep it in mind
as you continue to read.

During Reading

Pay attention to what the characters say and do that relates
to any general topic you've found. That's the second step
in finding the theme.

2. Notice What Characters Say and Do

Characters' words often give you clues about theme. Look for
conversations and actions that relate to the big ideas you've
noticed. For instance, in this one short passage six different
people—four villagers, the narrator, and Anansi himself—
mention how the spider avoids doing work. Here's what one
reader wrote about Anansi's laziness.

Drama

375

QUOTES	MY THOUGHTS
"But I don't like to work!"	I can't believe he would say this. Is he stupid? Maybe he's proud of how he can get so much food without working.
"It was true, Anansi played or slept all day and never worked."	Anansi is definitely lazy. There seems no doubt about that because everyone said it.

Details about Characters

Paying attention to details about characters can give you a lot of clues about the theme of a play. Look for repeated words or ideas.

So far, you know that Anansi is lazy and loves to eat. He thinks that others should do all the work for him while he does nothing. Authors often use "good" characters to tell their message, and they use "bad" characters as examples of what *not* to do. What kind of character is Anansi?

Details about Plot

The plot is what happens in a play—its events or actions. As you read, ask yourself why the playwright makes the story turn out a certain way. Think about that as you read another passage from the end of the play. It shows what happens when Anansi tries to get food at two different feasts in two faraway villages. He ties a rope around his waist and gives an end to each of his sons. Anansi tells each boy to take the rope to one of the feasts and pull on it when the food is ready.

from *How Anansi Got a Thin Waist*

NARRATOR: Can you guess what happened? The people in the east village and the people in the west village had their dinners at *exactly the same time!*

(KUMA & KWAKU simultaneously give a pull on the rope. ANANSI cries out in alarm and struggles to go one direction or another, but can't.)

KUMA & KWAKU: *(Simultaneously.)* Why hasn't father come to the feast yet? I'd better pull harder!

(They pull on the rope again while ANANSI jerks around, crying in alarm while being pulled this way and that.)

KUMA & KWAKU: *(Simultaneously.)* He still isn't here! I'd better pull even harder!

(They continue to pull on the rope while ANANSI jerks around, crying out in alarm while surreptitiously pulling the pillows out of his shirt when his back is toward the audience.)

NARRATOR: Anansi was never fat again. He stayed the same until today, with his fat head and fat body and thin, little waist in between.

(KUMA & KWAKU let go of rope and ANANSI lets it fall to the floor.)

ANANSI: *(Admiring his waist.)* How thin I am! Now I'll have to eat more to fatten up! *(ANANSI exits, skipping merrily)*

(LIGHTS DOWN.)

NOTE
What happens

NOTE
What happens in the end

Drama

Anansi's plan to attend both feasts backfired. His laziness is the reason he got so thin. Here's how one reader summarized the key events in the plot.

BEGINNING	MIDDLE	END
Anansi wants to eat food at both the east and west villages.	He ties a rope around his waist and sends one son to each village to tell him when the food is ready.	Anansi's sons both pull on the rope at the same time. His waist gets squeezed more and more. With a thin waist, Anansi now plans to eat all he wants.

A Story Organizer like this one helps you make a simple summary of the plot. It will help you remember what happened and connect the events of the plot to your ideas about theme.

After Reading

After finishing the play, take time to think about what you've learned. Consider the big ideas you've found and how details of the characters and the plot relate to them. Now's the time to begin thinking of possible themes.

3. State an Important Lesson

Ask yourself what lesson about life a reader could learn from the play. What message did the playwright want to get across? Remember that there's a difference between a play's topic and its theme. Laziness is one of the main topics. A theme is the point *about* those topics that the play makes. A reading tool called a Theme Diagram walks through the steps needed to find the theme. Here's one reader's Theme Diagram for *How Anansi Got a Thin Waist*.

THEME DIAGRAM

Step 1. What subject or big idea is the play about?

(laziness)

Step 2. What do the characters do and say that relates to this "big idea"?

Anansi admits he doesn't like to work.	Villagers don't like that Anansi gets free food.	Anansi tries to get free food at two villages.	Anansi's greed causes him to get a thin waist.

Step 3. What do these things tell you that is important to learn about life?

For a good life, you should help with the work and not try to live off others.

Drama

You might have noticed other details or come up with a very different theme statement. Don't worry. Just be sure that you can find several specific details to support your theme.

Summing Up

- The theme is an important statement about life.
- To find the theme, first find the subject or big idea. Second, look at what characters say and do that relates to the subject. Finally, state what these things tell you is important to learn about life.

Elements of Drama

In some ways, plays are like folktales, short stories, and novels. Plays usually are fictional, and they include such elements as characters, setting, plot, and theme. But, unlike folktales, short stories, and novels, plays are written to be performed on a stage.

The written form of a drama is called a *script*, and the play's author is called a *playwright*.

Here are some of the basic elements of drama.

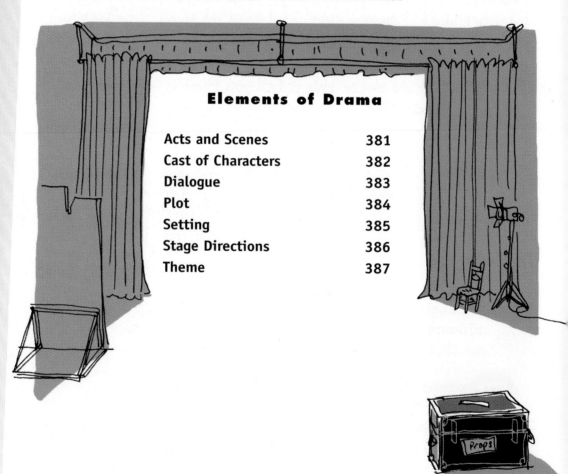

Elements of Drama

Acts and Scenes

Plays often are divided into main sections called acts, and acts are usually divided into smaller sections called scenes.

EXAMPLE

from *Toad of Toad Hall* by A.A. Milne

Act III — Major section

Scene 2 — Smaller section

THE DUNGEON

SCENE. *A Dungeon. On a heap of straw in the corner* TOAD *sleeps uneasily. The door is unlocked and* PHOEBE, *the gaoler's [jailer's] daughter comes in with breakfast on a tray.* TOAD *sits up and takes the straw from his hair.*

PHOEBE: Good morning, Toad.

TOAD *(gloomily)*: Good morning, woman.

DESCRIPTION

A play can have any number of **acts and scenes.** Usually a play is divided into one to five acts. Each act is then divided into two or more smaller scenes. A scene usually changes whenever there is a change in time or place, or both. In *Toad of Toad Hall,* for example, scene 2 takes place in a jail. The previous scene takes place in the courthouse. Each scene takes place on a different day.

DEFINITION

A play's main parts are called acts. An act can be made up of two or more smaller parts called scenes.

Drama

Cast of Characters

At the beginning of most plays, you'll find a cast of characters. This is a list of the persons, animals, or creatures that are in the play.

EXAMPLE

from *Pecos Bill* by John Tichenor

Characters:
Narrator
Ma
Pa
Pecos Bill
Chuckwagon Chuck
Sourdough Sal
Hardtack Hank
Flap Jack
Sluefoot Sue
(Coyotes and Cattle)

DESCRIPTION

Before you read a play, skim through the **cast of characters**. Try to learn a little about who the characters are. Sometimes a short description appears after the character names, telling something about them. The cast of characters is a handy list for the person directing the play, as well as for anyone who reads it. You can often learn something about the play just by skimming through the cast of characters.

DEFINITION

A **cast of characters** is a list of all the play's characters.

Dialogue

Plays are mostly made up of dialogue—that is, the talking or conversation between characters.

EXAMPLE

from *Toad of Toad Hall* by A.A. Milne

MOLE: Oh, Ratty, I don't know how to tell you, and I'm afraid you'll never want me for a companion again, but I can't, I simply can't go all that way now.

RAT: Tired?

MOLE: Aching all over. Oh, Ratty, do forgive me, I feel as if I must just sit here for ever and ever and ever, I'm not a bit frightened now you're with me. And—and I think I want to go to sleep.

Speech tags tell who's talking.

DESCRIPTION

In the **dialogue** in plays, the *speech tag*—the name of the character who is speaking—is printed in capital letters to tell you who is talking. Speech tags help you keep track of who says what. Note, too, that plays do not use quotation marks for dialogue. Dialogue among different characters tells the story, reveals the characters, develops the plot, and explains the play's message.

Drama

DEFINITION

Dialogue is the talking, or conversation, between characters in a play.

Plot

The plot is what happens or the series of events that occurs in a play. Here is a diagram of the usual way that the plot of a play develops.

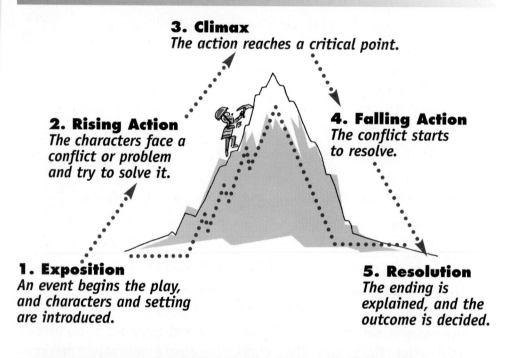

3. Climax
The action reaches a critical point.

2. Rising Action
The characters face a conflict or problem and try to solve it.

4. Falling Action
The conflict starts to resolve.

1. Exposition
An event begins the play, and characters and setting are introduced.

5. Resolution
The ending is explained, and the outcome is decided.

The **plot** of most plays develops the same way that the plot of many stories or novels develops. The play starts with a description of characters in a situation (exposition) that turns into a problem or conflict. The problem gets worse (rising action) and reaches a point of high tension (climax). Then, the problem or conflict begins to resolve (falling action), and the action comes to an end (resolution).

The **plot** is the action or series of events that makes up the play.

Setting

What is the setting—the place and the time—of the scene shown below?

EXAMPLE

from *Star Sisters* by Joseph Bruchac

> Scene I: A Forest at Night
> *Red Star Sister and White Star Sister lie on blankets
> outdoors in the forest.*
> NARRATOR: One night, two sisters went outside
>   to sleep under the stars.
> RED STAR SISTER: Look up into the sky.
> WHITE STAR SISTER: It is beautiful up there.

Time and place

DESCRIPTION

In plays, the **setting** for an act or scene is usually given in the stage directions. Most plays have one general setting— an overall time and place for the whole play. But each scene might take place in its own special place and special time.

The play's setting often influences the mood and reveals what the characters are like. In many plays, setting changes help show how the time has changed—say, from morning to night or from one day to the next.

Drama

DEFINITION

A play's **setting** is the place and time in which it takes place. Stage directions usually name and often describe the setting at the beginnings of acts and scenes.

Stage Directions

Stage directions tell how a play should be performed.

EXAMPLE

from *Toad of Toad Hall* by A.A. Milne

BADGER *(opening the door)*: Well, well, well, what is it, what is it? *(A collection of field mice, half a dozen of them in red mufflers, stand nervously shuffling at the entrance.)*

> What the scene looks like

FIRST FIELD MOUSE *(huskily)*: Oh, please, Mr. Badger, did you want any carols?

BADGER: Any what? Speak up!

FIRST FIELD MOUSE *(swallowing)*: Carols.

BADGER: Let's have a look at them.

SECOND FIELD MOUSE *(striking up)*: "Good King Wenceslas looked out —"

> What the characters do and how they sound

BADGER: Oh, I thought you said carrots. Run along, all of you. Time you were in bed.

DESCRIPTION

Stage directions appear at the beginning of a play and throughout the play script. Stage directions include:

- lists of characters, props, and costumes
- descriptions of settings, lighting, music, and sound
- details on how actors should move, speak, behave, and react to other characters

DEFINITION

Stage directions are the playwright's written instructions about how the play is to be performed and acted.

Theme

A theme is a playwright's message or statement about life. In the Ojibway play *Star Sisters*, the Star Sisters who wanted to marry Red Star and White Star have gotten homesick in Sky Land. What in these lines suggest the play's theme?

EXAMPLE

from *Star Sisters* by Joseph Bruchac

LITTLE STAR: Grandmother, they are sad. They miss their families and their friends.

STAR GRANDMOTHER: Look down through this hole. What do you see?

RED STAR SISTER (*looking*): I see my family's wigwam.

WHITE STAR SISTER (*looking*): I can hear my people singing.

STAR GRANDMOTHER: You are ready to go home.

RED STAR (*standing up*): If you are ready to go home, we will help you.

WHITE STAR (*also standing*): We will miss you.

RED STAR: But you should be with your family.

Key message or statement about life

Drama

DESCRIPTION

Red Star's statement that "you should be with your family" is an important message, or **theme**, of *Star Sisters*. A theme may be stated directly, or it may be something you have to figure out. To find the theme, start with a play's general subject or "big idea." Next, see what the characters say and do that relates to that topic. Then, sum all that up in a statement about life.

DEFINITION

A play's **theme** is the author's statement about life.

Reading on the
Internet

Internet

389

Reading a Website

With the World Wide Web, you have a huge library at your fingertips. The Web offers millions of pages from sources around the world. Sometimes you'll find sites that amaze you—like hundreds of news stories on one event, with videos, sounds, maps, animations, and more.

But the Web also can be very confusing. You might find 20 or even 300 websites when you search for a topic. Which sites do you choose? And, even if you find a good site, you will have the problem of staying on track and not wandering around, clicking on the first link you see. It's easy to click on links. It takes a good reader to find specific information.

Using the reading process and the right strategies can help.

Goals

Here you'll learn how to:

✔ apply the reading process to a **website** and use a plan to evaluate websites

✔ use the strategy of **reading critically** to examine a website

✔ understand **how websites are organized**

Before Reading

When you're using the Web to search for information, use the reading process. It will help you to stay on track.

A Set a Purpose

Start by setting a reading purpose. Ask yourself, "What do I want to find out?" Maybe your teacher has given you a specific subject to research. For example, let's say that you want to learn about the Space Shuttle. In that case, here are some possible reading purposes.

Setting a Purpose

■ **What is the Space Shuttle, and what is it used for?**
■ **What does it look like?**

Write these questions in your notebook or on note cards like the ones below. They will help you stick to your reading purpose when you go to the computer and start surfing the Web for information.

1.

What is the Space Shuttle, and what is it used for?

2.

What does it look like?

Internet

391

B Preview

When you reach a site that you might want to use, start with a quick preview to see whether it has information about your reading purpose. You can use the Preview Checklist below to get a feel for what the NASA KIDS website has to offer. Here are some things to look for:

Preview Checklist

✔ the site name and introductory information

✔ the main menu choices

✔ the site's graphics and overall "look"

✔ the source, or who created and pays for the website

✔ the first few pages of the site

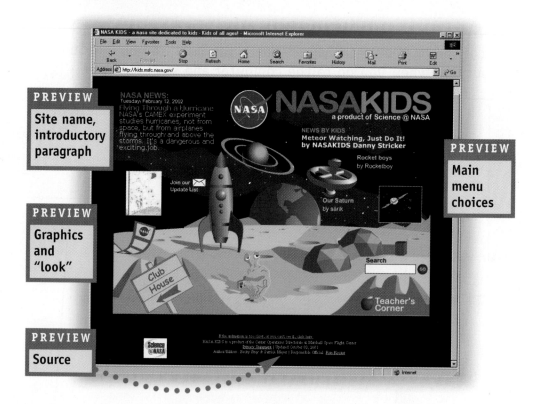

PREVIEW
Site name, introductory paragraph

PREVIEW
Graphics and "look"

PREVIEW
Source

PREVIEW
Main menu choices

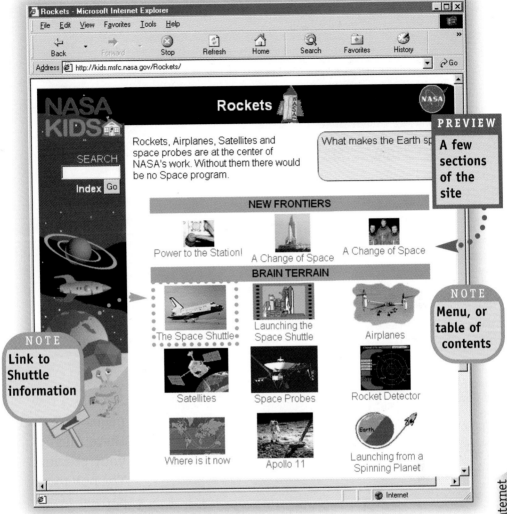

As you preview a website, look back at your reading purpose. Decide whether the website will have the information you'll need to answer your questions. On this site, you'd probably want to click on the link to the Space Shuttle.

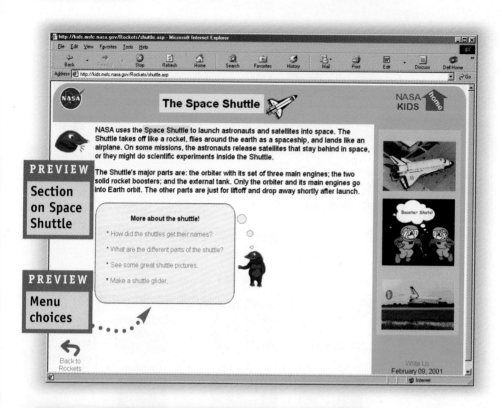

PREVIEW

Section on Space Shuttle

PREVIEW

Menu choices

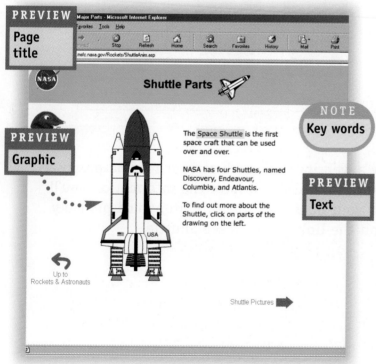

PREVIEW

Page title

PREVIEW

Graphic

NOTE

Key words

PREVIEW

Text

Sample a few pages here and there during your preview. Try not to get carried away clicking on different links. Right now, you mostly want to know whether this website has the kind of information you need.

Plan

In your preview, you probably learned a lot.

- This site is created by NASA, the U.S. government space agency.
- It has a whole section on satellites and airplanes and on the Space Shuttle.
- The Space Shuttle pages have a lot of information and can probably tell you a lot of what you need to know.

When surfing the Web for information, remember two things:

1. Stay on track. *Set a time limit for your research, and focus on your reading purpose questions. That's why it's a good idea to keep your questions with you when you are working at the computer.*

2. Check to see who created the website. *Anybody can create a website, so you need to know whether you can trust the information you find. Some sites give you a lot of opinions, not facts.*

You'll need a good reading strategy to make sure that you're getting reliable information from a website rather than opinions from someone who isn't an expert.

Internet

Reading Strategy: Reading Critically

Reading critically is a very good strategy to use with a website. When you read critically, you ask questions that can help you figure out whether a site contains accurate and reliable information. Use a Website Profiler to help you evaluate a website.

NAME (URL):	
SPONSOR:	DATE:
POINT OF VIEW:	EXPERTISE:
REACTION:	

A Website Profiler like the one above summarizes some of the basic information you need to know about a website. You might even want to put your Website Profiler in your notebook or on another note card with your reading purpose questions.

A Website Profiler raises the questions that will help you decide whether the information on the website is reliable and accurate.

EVALUATING A WEBSITE

Question a website's facts if:

the site's source is not named or described.

the source isn't well known.

the site's goal is to sell a product or to argue for a certain cause or political party.

the information is out-of-date.

the text has obvious errors, grammatical or spelling mistakes, or typos.

During Reading

Now you're ready to begin reading the website for information.

D Read with a Purpose

As you read a website, keep your reading purpose questions handy. Use your Website Profiler to help you decide that a website has the information you're looking for and is reliable.

Website Profiler

Your Website Profiler gives you a way to record basic information about a website. This information helps you determine the accuracy of a source. The Website Profiler also is a useful reference for future web searches.

WEBSITE PROFILER

NAME (URL): NASA KIDS (http://kids.msfc.nasa.gov/)	
SPONSOR: NASA, U.S. Government	DATE: Updated every day
POINT OF VIEW: gives information about space and what NASA does	EXPERTISE: probably the best source for space information
REACTION: It has choices like Projects and Games, Club House, Rockets and Airplanes, Our Earth, Astronauts Living in Space, Creation Station, Teacher's Corner, and a whole section on the Space Shuttle.	

Internet

5W's and H Organizer

A 5 W's and H Organizer gives you an easy way to sort out and keep track of lots of information about almost any topic. It summarizes some of the key facts about the Space Shuttle.

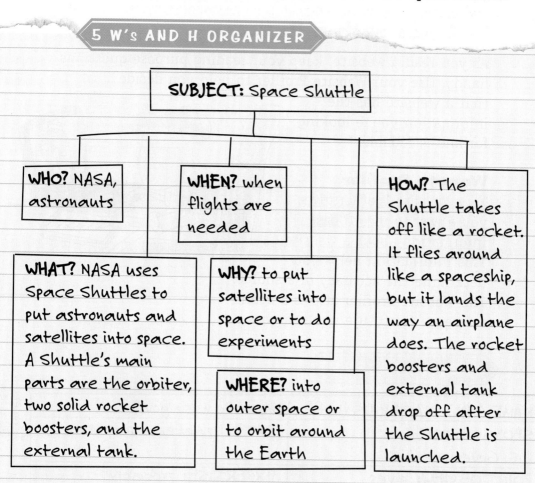

5 W's AND H ORGANIZER

SUBJECT: Space Shuttle

WHO? NASA, astronauts

WHEN? when flights are needed

HOW? The Shuttle takes off like a rocket. It flies around like a spaceship, but it lands the way an airplane does. The rocket boosters and external tank drop off after the Shuttle is launched.

WHAT? NASA uses Space Shuttles to put astronauts and satellites into space. A Shuttle's main parts are the orbiter, two solid rocket boosters, and the external tank.

WHY? to put satellites into space or to do experiments

WHERE? into outer space or to orbit around the Earth

Notice that there aren't any quotes around the sentences and phrases. That's because it's important to put what you learn in your own words. Avoid copying what a website says word for word.

How Websites Are Organized

Think for a minute about the way you read a book and the way you explore a website. A website is a series of "pages." Some sites have only a few pages, and others have thousands. You move around a website by clicking on links. These links take you immediately from page to page.

Websites are organized differently than books. A book puts information in a fixed order. Most people read many books straight through, page by page, from beginning to end.

A website's home page presents many different topics that you can choose in any order. Any page could have links to other topics and pages on the website. You can jump around from topic to topic, following your interests. You do not have to follow a certain order or sequence. But be careful! Clicking on links is easy, but choosing the best links for your purpose takes skill.

BOOK ORGANIZATION vs. WEBSITE ORGANIZATION

E Connect

It's important to read a website actively. React to what you read. Connect what you read with your own life and experiences. Think about what it means to you.

Ask yourself questions like these to create a connection between yourself and what you read:

How can I use what I've learned?

How does this matter to my life or anyone I know?

Am I surprised by what I've learned?

What feelings or opinions do I have about this?

You might find it helpful to write your reactions in a journal or notebook.

JOURNAL ENTRY

About the NASA KIDS website:

1. I never knew that NASA has four shuttles. I wonder if more are being built.
2. I saw a space shuttle launch on TV last year.
3. On my next visit to the site, I'll join NASA KIDS. I'd love to be an astronaut!

By recording your thoughts about your reading, you will remember more and understand which parts are most important.

After Reading

After gathering information from a website, stop to make sure you've got everything you need.

F Pause and Reflect

Think about your reading purpose questions. Did you find enough information to answer them completely? Look over any notes you took and ask yourself several questions about what you've read.

Looking Back

- **Can I explain what the Space Shuttle is and what it is used for?**
- **Do I know what it looks like?**
- **Is there other information I need to find?**

Sometimes the answers you find aren't complete, or the information is confusing. Sometimes you come up with new questions as you read. Perhaps you forgot to jot down the web address or want to check when the site was last updated. When this happens, go back to the website again for another look.

Internet

G Reread

Rereading is a natural and important part of the reading process. When rereading for information, try a new strategy.

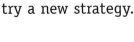

Skimming is a helpful strategy with websites. When you skim for information, you glance over the text for specific words or phrases. Instead of reading every word, you try to find headings, labels, and key words that can lead you to the information you want.

For example, perhaps you have a new question about the Space Shuttle. What happens to the solid rocket boosters and external tank that drop away from the Shuttle during launch? Go back to reread the site pages. How would you skim for that information?

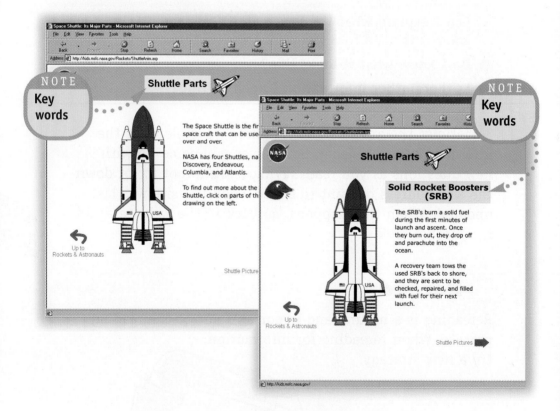

The key to using the rereading strategy of skimming is to focus on finding information about your key words. If you want to find information about "solid rocket boosters," then look for those words on the site.

H Remember

To help you remember what you've learned from reading a website, try the activity below.

Email a Friend

Write an email to a friend describing or recommending the site. Tell your friend what the site has to offer—information, graphics, features, and anything else that he or she might find interesting. You might also want to keep a list of websites your friends recommend to you.

Summing Up

When you read a website for information, remember to use the reading process and the strategy of **reading critically.** Be careful to evaluate the site's reliability and pay attention to **how a website is organized.** Try using tools like these:

■ Website Profiler

■ 5 W's and H Organizer

When you reread, **skimming** can help you to find what you want quickly.

Internet

Elements of the Internet

The Internet links computers around the world. The World Wide Web is a set of connected sites and files that can be reached with a type of software called a browser.

The Internet can bring you endless amounts of information, including graphics, sound, movies, live camera shots, and more. On the Web, you can shop, search for information, send messages, and almost effortlessly click your way around the world in seconds—all from your own computer!

This section describes some basic elements of the Internet.

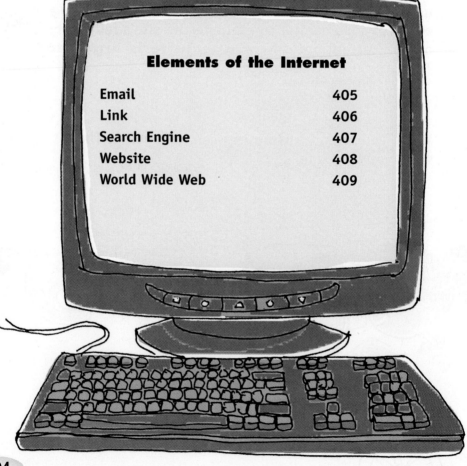

Elements of the Internet

Email

An email is a kind of letter or message. Through the Internet, people can send email messages almost instantly to any place in the world. Email gives people a fast, cheap, and easy way to connect with each other.

EXAMPLE

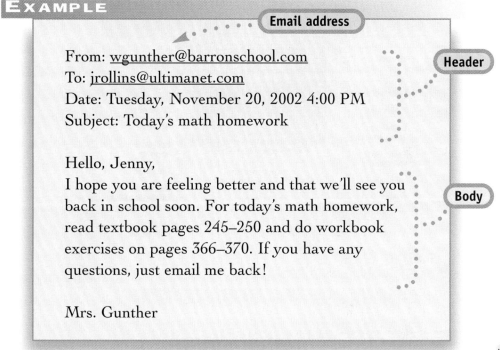

Email address

From: wgunther@barronschool.com
To: jrollins@ultimanet.com
Date: Tuesday, November 20, 2002 4:00 PM
Subject: Today's math homework

Header

Hello, Jenny,
I hope you are feeling better and that we'll see you back in school soon. For today's math homework, read textbook pages 245–250 and do workbook exercises on pages 366–370. If you have any questions, just email me back!

Body

Mrs. Gunther

DESCRIPTION

An **email** usually has two main parts, the header and the body. The term *email* is short for "electronic mail"— a message sent electronically over the Internet.

The header includes the sender's address, the receiver's address, the date and time the message was sent, and the subject. The body contains the actual message.

DEFINITION

An email is an electronic message sent over the Internet.

Internet

Link

A link is a word, phrase, or graphic that you click on to jump from one place to another on the World Wide Web.

EXAMPLE

DESCRIPTION

On a website, a **link** connects you with another page or another website. Text links often are underlined, as in the example above. Graphics and text often are links, too. To find out whether something is a link, use the mouse to pass the arrow of your cursor over it. If the item is a link, the arrow will change to a hand with a pointed finger. That means that you can click on that item to go to another page or website.

Most websites have lots of links. To avoid wasting time, skim through all of the links before choosing one to follow.

DEFINITION

A link is a word, phrase, or graphic that you click on to reach another page or website.

Search Engine

From the billions of website pages, search engines give you a way to find what you need. Many different search engines are available, so try using more than one.

EXAMPLE

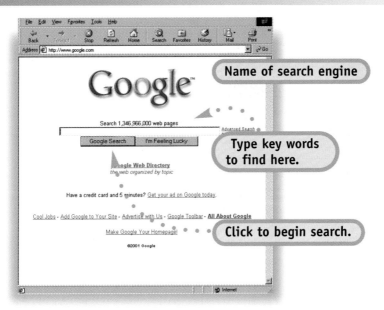

DESCRIPTION

Search engines keep huge databases (organized collections) of information about websites. Computer programs called "robots" or "spiders" build some of these databases by following site links all over the Web and indexing sites.

When you visit a search engine, find the input area marked "Search." Next, type in a word or phrase (such as "mountain climbing") and click "search." The search engine will display a long list of "matches," or "hits." These are websites that mention your search terms.

DEFINITION

A **search engine** is a tool that helps you find information on the World Wide Web.

Internet

Website

A website is a page or group of pages on the World Wide Web. Websites usually include text, graphics, and other features.

EXAMPLE

DESCRIPTION

A **website** might have one page or thousands of them. Websites make it easy for you to jump around from one place to another. On the first page (the "home page"), you usually find a table of contents (sometimes called a "navigation bar") that names the main parts of the site.

DEFINITION

A **website** is a single page or a group of linked pages on the World Wide Web.

World Wide Web

The World Wide Web is a "web" of computers that reaches all over the world. Using the Web, you can almost instantly send and receive messages and connect with any one of millions of websites around the globe.

EXAMPLE

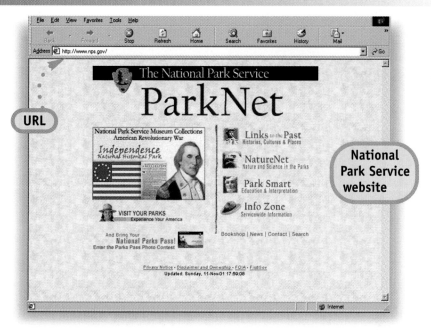

URL

National Park Service website

DESCRIPTION

The **World Wide Web** is made up of millions of documents on large and small computers that "talk" to each other. The Web offers a huge collection of websites and an enormous universe of information.

Through the World Wide Web, you can find almost anything you can think of. Each website has its own unique address, called a *URL*, which stands for "uniform resource locator."

DEFINITION

The **World Wide Web** is an ever-changing system of computers that share information. The files on the Web can be viewed with a kind of software called a *browser*.

Internet

Reading
Graphics

Reading Tables and Graphs

Elements of Graphics

T F S

Reading Tables and Graphs

Tables and graphs pack a lot of information into a form that is small and visual.

A **table** organizes information into columns and rows. A **graph** is a kind of chart that shows the relationship between numbers or amounts.

You'll find tables and graphs wherever you find facts—in magazines and newspapers, almanacs, biographies, textbooks, and more.

As a reader, you often "look at" tables and graphs, but it takes practice to "read" them and find out what they mean.

Goals

Here you'll learn how to:

✔ identify the **major parts of tables and graphs**

✔ use the reading strategy of **paraphrasing**

✔ understand the **way that tables and graphs are organized**

Before Reading

Before you read a table or graph, decide on your reading purpose. Then, preview the graphic and choose a strategy for reading it.

A Set a Purpose

Your basic purpose in reading a table or graph is to answer these two questions:

Setting a Purpose

■ **What main idea is the table or graph trying to show?**

■ **What conclusions can I draw from the table or graph?**

B Preview

Use the Preview Checklist below to look over the table and graph on the next two pages. When you preview, look at:

Preview Checklist

✔ the title
✔ the labels and column headings
✔ any numbers, amounts, or measurements
✔ any symbols, keys, or legends

Graphics

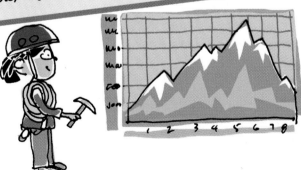

413

1. Bar Graph

A bar graph compares numbers and amounts, usually to show a trend or make comparisons. What is this one about?

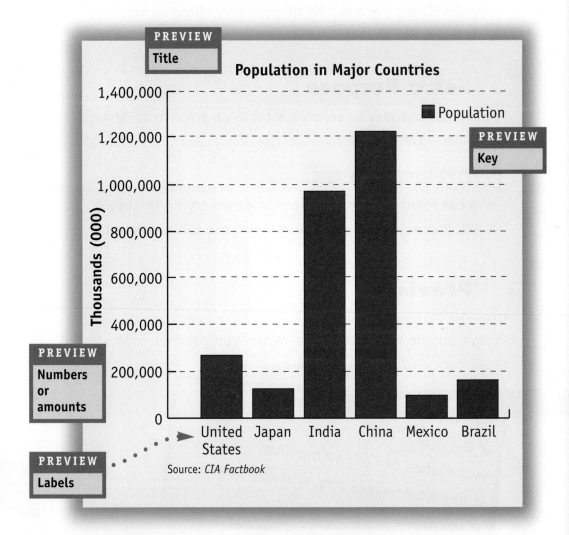

Bar graphs use either vertical or horizontal bars to show or compare amounts of something. The graph above shows the population of six countries.

2. Table

Tables present information in columns and rows. Maybe you've seen tables that list bus or train schedules. Or maybe you have used a table to solve a word problem in math. The table below lists information about the items in a sporting goods store. The table shows how many of each item have been sold, which ones are available, which are on order, and which are lost or damaged.

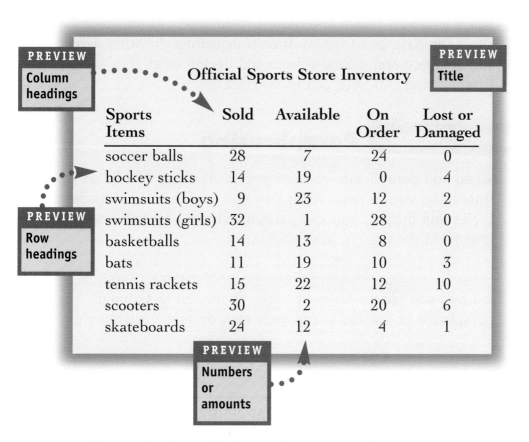

PREVIEW
Column headings

PREVIEW
Title

PREVIEW
Row headings

PREVIEW
Numbers or amounts

Official Sports Store Inventory

Sports Items	Sold	Available	On Order	Lost or Damaged
soccer balls	28	7	24	0
hockey sticks	14	19	0	4
swimsuits (boys)	9	23	12	2
swimsuits (girls)	32	1	28	0
basketballs	14	13	8	0
bats	11	19	10	3
tennis rackets	15	22	12	10
scooters	30	2	20	6
skateboards	24	12	4	1

Tables pack a lot of information in a small space. When you read a table, be sure first to read the title. Then read the row headings and column headings. Often you will be looking for one bit of information, and to find it you'll need to be familiar with the headings.

Graphics

C Plan

Even a quick look at the two example graphics probably showed you a lot:

■ The graph compares the populations in several countries.

■ The table gives information about items in a sports store.

■ What a graph or table is saying may not always be clear right away.

When you read tables and graphs, your job is to pull together all of the data and then to draw conclusions. In other words, you compare and combine facts and decide what they mean. Paraphrasing can help you to do this.

Reading Strategy: Paraphrasing

When you paraphrase, you use your own words to explain something you've read. After you pull together the data from tables and graphs, you use **paraphrasing** to explain the most important details—*in your own words*.

Use a Paraphrase Chart to make sense of a table or graph. It gives you spaces for your notes about the facts, your paraphrase of the facts, and your own opinions or thoughts.

PARAPHRASE CHART

NOTES	MY PARAPHRASE
MY THOUGHTS	

During Reading

Once you have a general idea of what tables and graphs are about, go back and study the details.

D Read with a Purpose

To make sense of tables and graphs, take some notes. You will find it helpful to record even one or two things you learn from each table or graph you read.

Reading a Bar Graph

Try to write one or two notes in a Paraphrase Chart. Look again at the bar graph on page 414. Be sure to read all the important parts of the graph—the title, the numbers on the left, and the names of the countries along the bottom.

What conclusions can you draw from this information?

PARAPHRASE CHART

BAR GRAPH: Population

NOTES	MY PARAPHRASE
Subject: how many people live in different countries around the world 1. Population is shown in the thousands. 2. China has the largest population by far.	• India and China have a lot more people than other countries. • The United States is big, but not even close to China or India. China's population is more than 1,200,000 thousand.
MY THOUGHTS I'm surprised that the countries with the most people are India and China.	

Graphics

Reading a Table

Go back to page 415 read the table on sporting goods one more time. Begin by carefully reading the title and headings. You might even want to put your finger on them as you read. Often readers "look" at charts and tables and forget to "read" them.

Let's say that part of a math problem asked you about the numbers of scooters and skateboards that were sold and are on order. Find the headings for these two items. Think about jotting down the key facts. Try using another reading tool called Summary Notes. This tool can help you to record two or three bits of key information. Here are the notes one reader made about scooters and skateboards.

SUMMARY NOTES

SUBJECT:
Sports Store Inventory

1. SOLD: 30 scooters
            24 skateboards

2. ON ORDER: 20 scooters
             4 skateboards

The test of your reading ability comes in "reading" a table and answering questions about it. For instance, can you answer these questions?

▪ Which item has sold the most?

▪ What are the two items that have been lost or damaged the most?

▪ How many more skateboards are available than scooters?

How Tables and Graphs Are Organized

To read and use the information in tables and graphs, you need to understand how they are organized.

1. In Grids

You can think of bar graphs as being in the shape of an "L." On one side, one kind of thing is measured, and on the bottom something else. The horizontal line across the bottom of the "L" is called the "x axis," and the vertical part of the "L" is called the "y axis."

ORGANIZATION OF A BAR GRAPH

y axis

x axis

To read a bar graph, you read "up and over" or "over and up," depending on what you are looking for. For example, to find out how many people are in China, you follow these steps:

1. Go across the bottom to China.

2. Then, go up to the top of the bar for China.

3. Read across to the left, and you see it goes just over 1,200,000. Because the numbers are in thousands, you add three more zeroes (000), making the total 1,200,000,000.

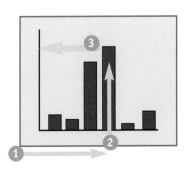

Graphics

419

2. In Columns and Rows

Tables use columns and rows to organize information. The column headings tell you what kind of data is being shown.

To read a table, first figure out its subject by reading the title. Then, read the column and row headings on the top and on the left. Touch the title and headings as you read them. Be sure you know what they mean.

For example, suppose you wanted to know which item the store had the fewest of. How would you find the answer?

1. First, read across the column headings. The one you want is the heading called "Available."

2. Then, read down the column to find the lowest number.

3. Next, look over to see which item is shown. You should find that the answer is girls' swimsuits.

READING A TABLE

Official Sports Store Inventory

Sports Items	Sold	Available	On Order	Lost or Damaged
soccer balls	28	7	24	0
hockey sticks	14	19	0	4
swimsuits (boys)	9	23	12	2
swimsuits (girls)	32	1	28	0
basketballs	14	13	8	0
bats	11	19	10	3
tennis rackets	15	22	12	10
scooters	30	2	20	6
skateboards	24	12	4	1

 **Connect**

When you read a table or graph, think about what this data means to you. How do you feel about what you're reading? How can you connect it with your own life and experience?

As an active reader, you can jot down your thoughts on sticky notes to connect what you're reading to your own life. Write down any thoughts or ideas that are important to you.

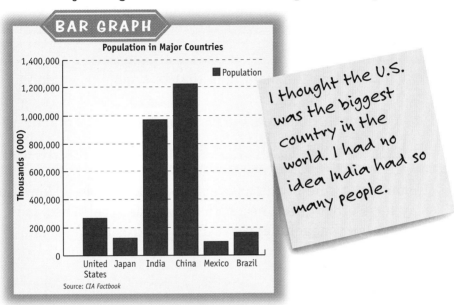

BAR GRAPH

Population in Major Countries

Source: *CIA Factbook*

I thought the U.S. was the biggest country in the world. I had no idea India had so many people.

By making a connection to what you read, you will find yourself remembering it better and understanding it more.

TABLE

Official Sports Store Inventory

Sports Items	Sold	Available	On Order	Lost or Damaged
soccer balls	28	7	24	0
hockey sticks	14	19	0	4
swimsuits (boys)	9	23	12	2
swimsuits (girls)	32	1	28	0
basketballs	14	13	8	0
bats	11	19	10	3
tennis rackets	15	22	12	10
scooters	30	2	20	6
skateboards	24	12	4	1

My tennis racket is broken, too. Maybe they just break easily.

Graphics

After Reading

Tables and graphs often look simple, but reading them takes some work. After you've read them, make sure you understand what you've read.

F Pause and Reflect

Can you answer your original reading questions?

If you're not sure of the answers, go back to reread. You also may have other questions, such as whether the tables and graphs show enough data and if the sources are reliable.

G Reread

Some tables and graphs are easier to understand than others. When you decide it's a good idea to reread, try the strategy of close reading.

Rereading Strategy: Close Reading

Doing a **close reading** of a graphic means paying attention to every detail. You don't skip over anything. A quick glance at the population bar graph might tell you that China has the most people. But what if you needed to know something more specific—such as what's the population of China and Mexico combined? Look closely at the graph again and make a few notes.

SUMMARY NOTES

Population of China is about 1,200,000,000.

Population of Mexico is about 100,000,000.

Population of China and Mexico combined = 1,300,000,000.

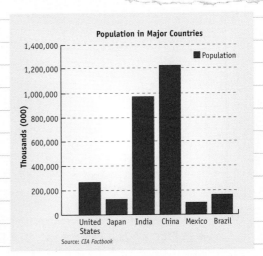

Population in Major Countries

■ Population

Thousands (000)

1,400,000
1,200,000
1,000,000
800,000
600,000
400,000
200,000
0

United States Japan India China Mexico Brazil

Source: *CIA Factbook*

H Remember

To help remember what you've learned about how tables and graphs are organized, apply it to your own life, as in the activity below.

Graph Your Life . . .

Make a graph that shows the main events of your life so far. First, pick out four or five key things that have happened to you over your lifetime. Rank the events from 0 to 5, with 0 being the low point and 5 being the high point. List the events across the bottom of your graph, starting with the event that happened first. Mark off the vertical part of your graph from 0 to 5. Put a dot where the first event ranked. Then, do the same for the other events. Use the graph on the next page as an example.

Graphics

423

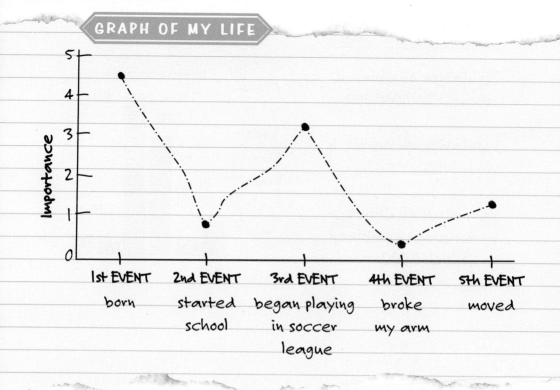

Importance

5 — 4 — 3 — 2 — 1 — 0

| 1st EVENT | 2nd EVENT | 3rd EVENT | 4th EVENT | 5th EVENT |
| born | started school | began playing in soccer league | broke my arm | moved |

Summing Up

When you read tables and graphs, use the reading process and the strategy of **paraphrasing.** Remember to think about what you're learning from tables and graphs. Record what you find with one of these reading tools:

■ Paraphrase Chart

■ Summary Notes

Pay attention to **how tables and graphs are organized.** Remember, too, that **close reading** is a good strategy for rereading because it helps you find specific information.

Elements of Graphics

The term *graphics* includes graphs, cartoons, maps, photos, timelines, and more. These graphics often pack a lot of valuable information into small spaces. But they require careful reading, just as words do.

Here you'll learn about many different types of graphics that you'll find in your reading.

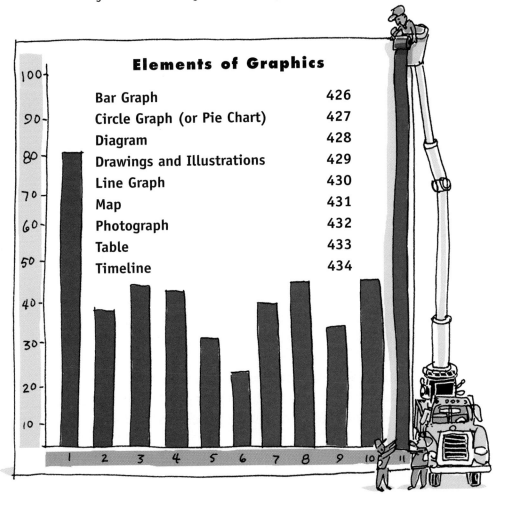

Elements of Graphics

Graphics

Bar Graph

Bar graphs show quantities or compare amounts. You'll find bar graphs in nonfiction, in textbooks, and on websites.

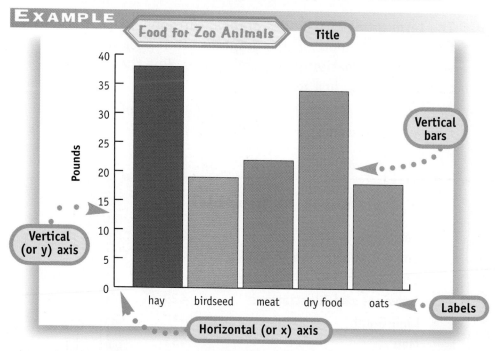

Food for Zoo Animals — Title

Vertical bars

Vertical (or y) axis

Labels

Horizontal (or x) axis

DESCRIPTION

The **bar graph** above compares the amount of food animals at the zoo eat in a week. It's easy to recognize bar graphs because they use solid bars to represent numbers or amounts. The title of a bar graph usually gives you the subject or main idea. A bar graph has a *vertical* (or *y*) *axis* and a *horizontal* (or *x*) *axis*. Each side of the graph shows or measures something different. To figure out what's being shown, read the title and the labels. In this graph, the vertical axis shows pounds, and the horizontal axis shows kinds of food.

DEFINITION

A **bar graph** uses vertical or horizontal bars to show or compare quantities or amounts.

Circle Graph (or Pie Chart)

Circle graphs (also called pie charts) show how a whole thing is divided. They are often used to show comparisons.

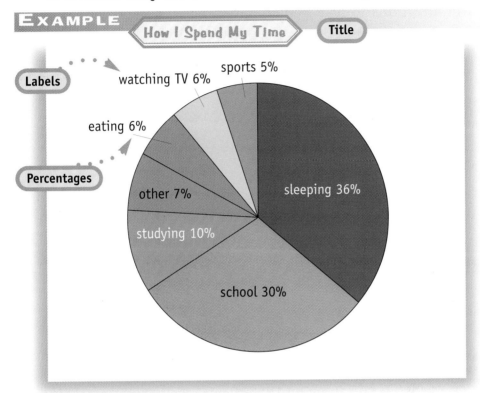

How I Spend My Time — **Title**

Labels

sports 5%
watching TV 6%
eating 6%

Percentages

other 7%
studying 10%
sleeping 36%
school 30%

The **circle graph,** or **pie chart,** above gives you information about how one student spends his or her time. The complete circle stands for the whole thing. Here that means 24 hours. Parts of the circle stand for bits of the whole. As in the example, the parts often have different colors to help you tell the different pieces apart.

A **circle graph,** or **pie chart,** is based on a circle. It shows fractions, percentages, and the sizes of various parts in relation to the whole.

Graphics

Diagram

A diagram is a drawing that can show parts of the earth, machines, the human body, and more. Diagrams are also used in directions to help people put things together.

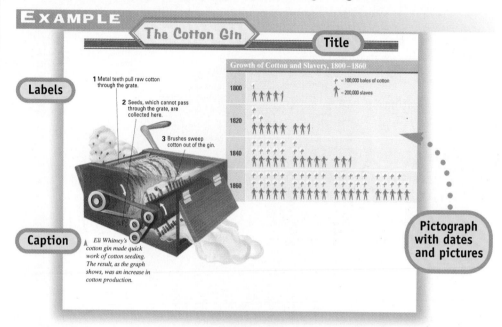

The Cotton Gin

Title

Labels

Growth of Cotton and Slavery, 1800–1860

1 Metal teeth pull raw cotton through the grate.

2 Seeds, which cannot pass through the grate, are collected here.

3 Brushes sweep cotton out of the gin.

= 100,000 bales of cotton
= 200,000 slaves

1800
1820
1840
1860

Pictograph with dates and pictures

Caption Eli Whitney's cotton gin made quick work of cotton seeding. The result, as the graph shows, was an increase in cotton production.

DESCRIPTION

A **diagram** is a drawing that shows or explains something. This diagram of a cotton gin appears with a *pictograph*, which is a kind of bar graph. The caption ties the two graphics together. To understand a diagram, read all of the text— the titles, labels, captions, and numbered parts. Then try to sketch or re-create a diagram from memory to be sure you understand it.

DEFINITION

A **diagram** is a drawing with labels that shows the parts of something or how something works.

Drawings and Illustrations

Drawings and illustrations add variety and interest to readings. When you see drawings and illustrations in textbooks or works of nonfiction, ask yourself what idea or point they are making.

DESCRIPTION

Drawings and illustrations generally make points or add something to what you have been reading. In the example, the illustrations go with a part of a chapter entitled "Different Armies, Different Ideals." The illustration shows differences in how soldiers in the British and American armies were dressed.

EXAMPLE

The Uniforms of Two Soldiers

Title

Goatskin pack

Homemade shirt

Brush for musket

Box for ammunition

Bayonet

Trousers

Breeches

Labels

Musket

Stockings

British Soldier

Continental Soldier

Graphics

DEFINITION

Drawings and illustrations are pictures made with lines and colors to represent or explain something.

Line Graph

Line graphs show changes over time. For example, line graphs are excellent tools for showing yearly changes, predicting trends, and showing rates of change.

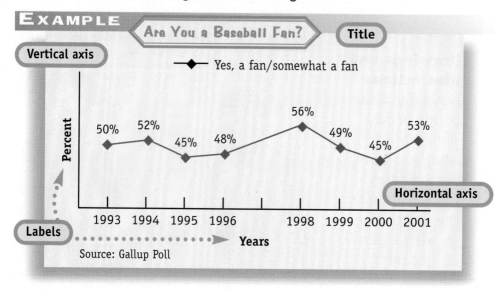

EXAMPLE

Are You a Baseball Fan? — Title

Vertical axis

Yes, a fan/somewhat a fan

Percent

50% 52% 45% 48% 56% 49% 45% 53%

Horizontal axis

1993 1994 1995 1996 1998 1999 2000 2001

Labels

Years

Source: Gallup Poll

DESCRIPTION

A **line graph** is like a bar graph, except that it is better at showing trends, or changes over time. In this example, the horizontal (or x) axis shows years. The vertical (or y) axis shows percent of people who answered "yes" to the survey question. Line graphs usually help you see at a glance how something has changed over time.

DEFINITION

A **line graph** is a graph that plots changes over time.

430

Map

Maps show all or part of the earth's surface or the heavens. They give information in lines, shapes, colors, and symbols.

DESCRIPTION

Maps usually show the basic shape of the land or the heavens. *Physical maps* show mountains, rivers, and other geographic features. *Political maps* show states, countries, and locations of cities. Maps can also show other kinds of information, such as highways, population, and so on.

EXAMPLE

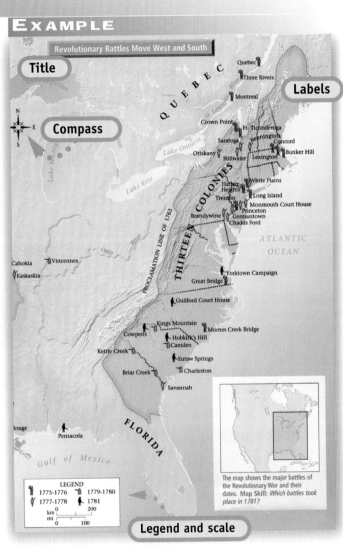

Revolutionary Battles Move West and South

Title

Compass

Labels

Legend and scale

The map shows the major battles of the Revolutionary War and their dates. Map Skill: *Which battles took place in 1781?*

Graphics

DEFINITION

A **map** is a drawing that shows the basic shape of the land and other geographic, political, or historical features.

Photograph

Photographs are snapshots of real life that add realism.

EXAMPLE

Photo of Harriet Tubman

Reaching the first house just after dawn, Tubman presented her slip of paper. The woman of the house responded by giving her a broom and telling her to sweep the walk. Tubman was shocked. Was this a betrayal? Was she now this woman's slave? But she soon realized the move was for camouflage. A black woman with a broom would hardly be noticed, certainly not suspected as a runaway.

Text

Tubman *(far left)* is shown here with some of the former enslaved African Americans she led to freedom.

Caption

Photo

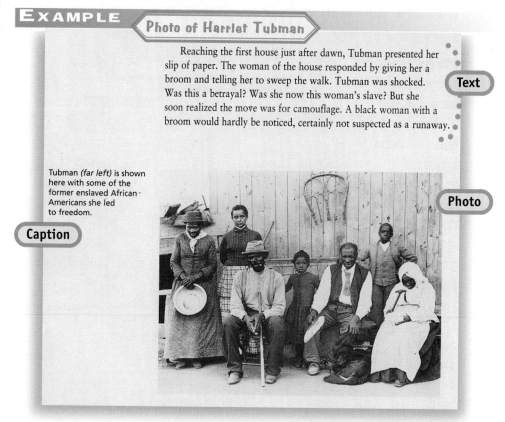

DESCRIPTION

Photographs add human interest and reinforce the main ideas of the text. For example, the photo above shows you African Americans who were once enslaved, along with the great antislavery activist Harriet Tubman. Be sure to read the *caption* next to a photograph. It can tell you what is shown in the photo and why it is important to what you're reading.

DEFINITION

A **photograph** is an image of a real scene captured by a camera and printed.

Table

Tables can organize large amounts of information in a small space. Tables present all kinds of data, from numbers and amounts to calendars and menus.

EXAMPLE

Title

Column headings

Pony League Statistics

League Leaders	Wins	Losses	Points Scored	Points Allowed	TDs	Turnovers
Chargers	5	2	68	23	8	5
Tigers	4	3	71	59	9	9
Eagles	3	3	60	58	8	5
Streaks	3	3	58	56	7	8
Buffaloes	2	4	48	66	6	9
Rangers	2	4	46	72	6	8

Row headings

DESCRIPTION

The information in a **table** is usually organized in columns and rows. To read a table:

1. First, read the title.

2. Then, read the row and column headings.

3. To find specific information (such as the points allowed by the Buffaloes), read down and then across to the correct row and column information, or read across and then down.

4. Compare the information in the rows and columns, looking for similarities, differences, and patterns.

5. Think about whether any information has been left out.

DEFINITION

A **table** is a list of numbers or other facts, usually arranged in both columns and rows.

Graphics

Timeline

Timelines show dates on a line, with key events connected in chronological order.

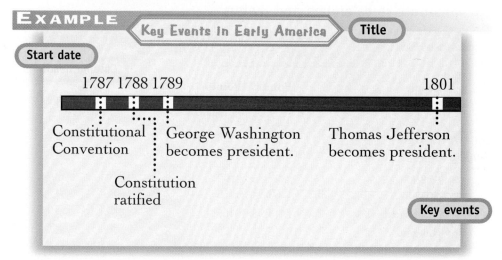

EXAMPLE

Key Events In Early America — Title

Start date

1787 1788 1789   1801

Constitutional Convention

George Washington becomes president.

Thomas Jefferson becomes president.

Constitution ratified

Key events

DESCRIPTION

A **timeline** usually starts with a horizontal line that shows time. Entries added to the timeline show key events and the order in which they occurred. To read a timeline:

1. Read the title. That usually helps you know the overall subject.

2. Be sure also to read any labels.

3. Then, read the key events along the line.

4. To find a specific date or event, read across. Look first for the date or event you were asked about.

Timeline, continued

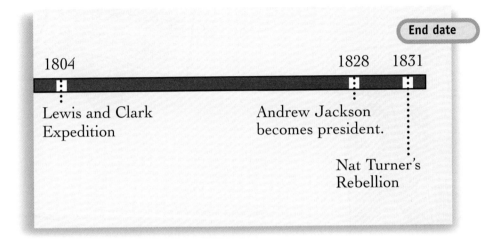

Timelines such as the one above give you a clear picture of the order in which events occurred. Make a Timeline of your own to keep track of key dates in a biography, events in a history book, or scenes in a novel or play.

DEFINITION

A **timeline** shows events in chronological, or time, order. It usually shows key events and includes specific dates.

Graphics

435

Reading
for Tests

Tests

Reading a Test and Test Questions

Everybody likes to bring home good test scores. The good news is that it isn't as hard as it looks. A few good tips may be all that you need to improve your test grades.

In this lesson, you will read a sample test and look at the kinds of questions in it. Knowing the kinds of questions in a test will help you know what you're looking for as you read.

Goals

Here you'll learn how to:

✔ prepare for **different kinds of tests and test questions**

✔ use the reading strategy of **skimming** to find answers

✔ understand **ways that tests are organized**

Before Reading

You become a good athlete by training hard, and the same goes for test-taking. Get yourself ready for each test.

- Study each subject as you go along. Make study guides and notes to help you study.

- Learn all you can about the test ahead of time.

- Start studying early, not at the last minute.

- Go to sleep early the night before the test.

A Set a Purpose

On any test, you want to answer the questions correctly, so focus on one reading purpose.

Setting a Purpose

- **What is each test question asking, and what information do I need?**

B Preview

At test time, you get your test and are told to begin, but what should you do first? Relax. First, take a few deep breaths, and start previewing the test. Look for:

Preview Checklist

✔ the main sections of the test

✔ the kinds of readings and questions

✔ how much time you have

✔ any directions about how to mark answers or whether it's better to guess or leave an answer blank

Tests

Time: 60 minutes

Directions: Read "The Runaway Apprentice."
Then answer each of the questions that follow.

The Runaway Apprentice

It was October, 1723, early on a cold Sunday
morning. A boat pulled up to the Market Street
wharf in Philadelphia. The weary crew and
passengers had rowed for most of the night.

One of the passengers was a young man of 17.
He was a printer's apprentice from Boston. His
master in Boston was his older brother James.
James had taught him the trade of printing. But the
two brothers did not get along. So the young man
had broken his contract and run away.

Years later, he described his arrival in Philadelphia:

> "I was in my working-dress, my best clothes [were]
> to come round by sea. I was dirty from my journey;
> my pockets were stuffed out with shirts and stockings;
> I knew no soul, nor where to look for lodging. I was
> fatigued with traveling, rowing, and want of rest,
> I was very hungry; and my whole stock of cash
> consisted of a Dutch dollar, and about a shilling
> in copper."

The young man walked up Market Street.
A boy directed him to a baker. He asked the
baker for three pennies' worth of bread.

"I was surprised at the quantity, but took it, and having no room in my pockets, walked off with a roll under each arm, and eating the other. Thus I went up Market Street as far as Fourth Street, passing by the door of Mr. Read, my future wife's father; when she, standing at the door, saw me, and thought I made, as I certainly did, a most awkward, ridiculous appearance."

By 1733, ten years after he landed in Philadelphia, the young man owned the best print shop in the city. He had been married for three years to Deborah Read. He published a newspaper, the *Pennsylvania Gazette.* He also wrote and printed a yearly book, *Poor Richard's Almanac.*

Within 25 years after he arrived in Philadelphia, he had made enough money to retire from business. By 1753, he was already on his way to becoming world famous as a scientist and inventor.

He became one of early America's leaders. He represented the American colonies in Great Britain, pleading the cause of freedom. Later, he was the first U.S. ambassador to France. Thanks to him, France supported the American Revolution. He helped to write both the Declaration of Independence and the United States Constitution.

Yes, that awkward, ridiculous young man was Benjamin Franklin.

Tests

Multiple-choice Questions

PREVIEW
Directions

Directions: Read each question and decide which choice is the correct answer. Circle the letter of the correct answer. If you do not know an answer, make the best guess you can.

PREVIEW
Multiple-choice questions

1. Who is the hero of "The Runaway Apprentice"?
   A. Benjamin Franklin
   B. Mr. Read
   C. James Franklin
   D. Poor Richard

NOTE
Fact or recall question

2. Based on the reading, about how long do you think it took Franklin to reach Philadelphia?
   A. a few hours
   B. half an hour
   C. some days or even weeks
   D. ten years

NOTE
Inference question

3. What does the word *apprentice* mean?
   A. someone with no job skills
   B. a runaway
   C. a person who is under contract to learn a trade
   D. a person who works for a family member

NOTE
Vocabulary question

4. In what year did Franklin marry Deborah Read?
   A. 1723
   B. 1730
   C. 1733
   D. 1753

NOTE
Drawing a conclusion

Reading and Writing Test, continued

5. Which of these events happened first?
   A. Franklin helped write the Declaration of Independence.
   B. Franklin left Boston.
   C. Franklin became a scientist and inventor.
   D. Franklin arrived in Philadelphia.

NOTE
Fact or recall question

6. Which is the best summary of this selection?
   A. Franklin should have stayed in Boston.
   B. Franklin looked awkward and ridiculous to his future bride.
   C. Franklin arrived in Philadelphia with nothing, but he later became famous and successful.
   D. Franklin wrote a lot of different important works.

NOTE
Inference question

Essay Question
Directions: Read the question below. Write your answer to the question in one or two paragraphs. Use details from "The Runaway Apprentice" to support your answer. Then check your work.

PREVIEW
Directions

   How would you summarize the changes in Ben Franklin's life between 1723 and 1733?

PREVIEW
Essay question

Tests

C Plan

During your preview, you probably learned a lot:

■ This test has three parts: a reading passage, six multiple-choice questions, and an essay question.

■ The test time is 60 minutes.

■ On the multiple-choice questions, it's better to guess than not to answer.

Now you need a plan for taking the test. First, divide up your time. Think about everything you have to do and decide about how long each part should take. Your plan might be something like this:

PLANNING CHART

WHAT TO DO	TIME I'LL SPEND
Read the selection.	10 minutes
Do multiple-choice questions.	20 minutes
Answer essay question.	20 minutes
Check answers.	10 minutes
TOTAL	60 minutes

The test questions are based on the reading, so start by carefully reading the passage. With reading tests, one reading rarely is enough. That's the secret of doing well on reading tests. Even after reading the whole passage once, you'll need to go back again and again, looking for specific answers. That's where the strategy of skimming comes in.

Reading Strategy: Skimming

When you are **skimming,** you go back and glance through a reading, searching for key words or phrases. You "read lightly" through the text, watching only for key words. Sometimes it helps to run your finger down the page as you skim.

During Reading

Now you're all set to begin taking the test.

D Read with a Purpose

As you start each new part of a test, remember to read the directions very carefully. Watch for key information.

1. Read the Passage

Start by reading "The Runaway Apprentice" slowly and carefully. Here are some tips for reading:

TIPS FOR READING TESTS

Focus on what you're reading. Try not to rush.

Watch for key words in the questions, such as names and events.

Key words

In each paragraph, look for the main subject.

If you can mark the test itself, circle a key word or sentence in each paragraph.

2. Answer the Multiple-choice Questions

Now it's time to read and answer the multiple-choice questions. Take your time. Good test-takers read every word in a question and then think about what the question is asking them to find. The most common mistake made by test-takers is to rush through the reading of the passage or the questions themselves. If you're allowed to mark on the test, highlight or circle key words in each question. Be sure you know what information you are being asked to find.

Most tests have two main types of questions—fact or recall questions and inference questions. Some tests also have vocabulary questions and ask you to draw conclusions.

Tests

445

FACT OR RECALL QUESTIONS

With fact or recall questions, you'll find the answer *stated right there* in the reading. That's great. All you have to do is look back at the reading to find the answer.

The first question is an example of a fact or recall question. Read the question carefully, marking the key words. What is this question asking you to recall?

NOTE
Key words

1. Who is the hero of "The Runaway Apprentice"?
   A. Benjamin Franklin
   B. Mr. Read
   C. James Franklin
   D. Poor Richard

The key words are *hero* and *"The Runaway Apprentice."* You know that *hero* means "main character" and that *"The Runaway Apprentice"* is the title of the test reading. When you read the answer choices, you see that they all are names of people, so the information you want is the name of the main character.

You may remember immediately that the right answer is Benjamin Franklin. If you're not sure, go back to the reading and skim. Look for names of people. Names are easy to spot because they begin with capital letters. When you find a name, skim the sentence. Decide whether it is someone important enough to be the main character. This reading refers to "he" until the very end of the passage, where you find the name Benjamin Franklin. That's the correct answer.

INFERENCE QUESTIONS

Inference questions take a little more thought. To answer these kinds of questions, you take information from the reading and put it with what you already know to draw a conclusion of your own.

| information from the reading | + | what you already know | = | a conclusion or inference |

First, read the question carefully. What are the key words? What is the question asking you to find?

---

from Reading and Writing Test

2. Based on the reading, about how long do you think it took Franklin to reach Philadelphia?

   A. a few hours
   B. half an hour
   C. some days or even weeks
   D. ten years

NOTE
Key words

The key words and phrases are *about how long* and *to reach Philadelphia*. To find the right answer, look back at the reading. Skim until you find the paragraphs about Franklin's trip. They are the first and the third paragraphs of the reading. What clues did you find?

Tests

447

1st Paragraph

It was October, 1723, early on a cold Sunday morning. A boat pulled up to the Market Street wharf in Philadelphia. The weary crew and passengers had rowed for most of the night.

NOTE
Clues

3rd Paragraph

Years later, he described his arrival in Philadelphia:

"I was in my working-dress, my best clothes [were] to come round by sea. I was dirty from my journey; my pockets were stuffed out with shirts and stockings; I knew no soul, nor where to look for lodging. I was fatigued with traveling, rowing, and want of rest, I was very hungry; and my whole stock of cash consisted of a Dutch dollar, and about a shilling in copper."

Here are some of the clues:

- Passengers and crew had traveled by sea, rowing all night.
- Franklin was dirty and worn out from traveling, rowing, and lack of sleep.
- He also was very hungry and out of money.

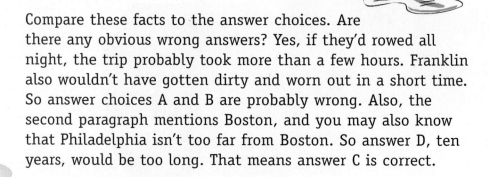

Compare these facts to the answer choices. Are there any obvious wrong answers? Yes, if they'd rowed all night, the trip probably took more than a few hours. Franklin also wouldn't have gotten dirty and worn out in a short time. So answer choices A and B are probably wrong. Also, the second paragraph mentions Boston, and you may also know that Philadelphia isn't too far from Boston. So answer D, ten years, would be too long. That means answer C is correct.

3. Answer the Essay Question

The last part of the test is an essay question. You've allowed 20 minutes for this, so you can take your time and work your way through it. Start by reading the directions carefully. Break down what the essay question asks you to write.

What are the key words and phrases?

from Reading and Writing Test

Directions: Read the question below. Write your answer to the question in **one or two paragraphs.** Use details from "The Runaway Apprentice" to **support your answer.** Then **check your work.**

NOTE
Key words

How would you **summarize the changes** in Ben Franklin's life **between 1723 and 1733?**

NOTE
Key words in question

The key instructions here are to:

1. write one or two paragraphs

2. support your answer with details

3. check your work for correctness

Before you begin writing, make some notes on what you want to say. Go back to the reading. Skim until you see the dates 1723 and 1733, and read for important changes in Franklin's later life. Your notes about his life might look like the notes on the next page.

<u>1723</u>

1. arrived in Philadelphia
2. alone and poor
3. had no job or home

<u>1733</u>

1. owned a print shop
2. married
3. published a newspaper and wrote a book

Then, organize your notes into one or two paragraphs. Your finished essay might look something like this:

SAMPLE ESSAY

Changes in Franklin's Life

Benjamin Franklin's life changed a lot in the ten years between 1723 and 1733. In 1723, he was a poor printer's apprentice who had run away to Philadelphia. He was alone and poor and had no home.

But he was lucky. He already knew how to be a printer, so he started a print shop. By 1733, the shop was very successful. Franklin also printed a newspaper and a yearly book called <u>Poor Richard's Almanac.</u> He was also married to Deborah Read. Life in 1733 was very different for Ben Franklin than it was in 1723.

Note how the essay above does the three things called for in the directions.

■ The essay is two paragraphs long.

■ It is supported by details from the passage.

■ It is mistake-free.

How Tests Are Organized

Test questions usually move from easier questions to harder questions. As you work through a test, be sure to answer the questions you know the answer to first.

Questions about a reading often go in the same order as the reading. That means that if you're not sure how to answer question #1, you should start by looking in the first paragraphs. And if you're stumped by a question toward the end of the test, reread the end of the passage. Of course, there are no guarantees. All tests are different, but many questions do follow the order of the reading. Knowing this can make it easier for you to find the answers to test questions.

ORGANIZATION OF TEST QUESTIONS

1. *Information about question 1 is usually found in first paragraphs.*

2. *Information about question 2 is found in middle paragraphs.*

3. *Information about question 3 is found in middle paragraphs.*

4. *Information about question 4 is found in last paragraphs.*

E Connect

When you read a test selection, be an active reader. Think about how this selection connects with your life. How does what you're reading affect you personally or fit with what you may already know?

Try to make a personal connection with every reading. You will understand the reading better, and it will become more important to you. This can help improve your test scores, especially on essay questions that ask for a personal response.

Here are the notes one reader made on part of "The Runaway Apprentice."

"I was in my working-dress, my best clothes [were] to come round by sea. I was dirty from my journey; my pockets were stuffed out with shirts and stockings; I knew no soul, nor where to look for lodging. I was fatigued with traveling, rowing, and want of rest, I was very hungry; and my whole stock of cash consisted of a Dutch dollar, and about a shilling in copper."

This must have been a hard trip!

It must be scary being in a new place and not having much money.

After Reading

After you have worked through all of the questions, you should have a little time left over. Use this time to review the questions and to check your answers.

F Pause and Reflect

After the test, pause to think about how it went. Are there parts of the test you're unsure of? As you pause and reflect, review your reading purpose to see whether you've met it.

Looking Back

- **Do I know what each test question is asking and what information I need?**
- **Do my answers make sense?**
- **What do I need to spend more time on?**

G Reread

Make the most of the time you have to go back over the test. Reread the questions you didn't answer or whose answers you are not sure about. Check your answers again, but try not to outsmart yourself and change answers that might be correct. Look for careless mistakes or questions you may not have understood correctly on your first reading.

Tests

Rereading Strategy: Visualizing and Thinking Aloud

With the questions that are hard for you, try **visualizing and thinking aloud.** This means trying to picture information in your mind and talking yourself through the answer.

Try the strategy with this question. What are the key words?

from Reading and Writing Test

6. Which is the best summary of this selection?
   A. Franklin should have stayed in Boston.
   B. Franklin looked awkward and ridiculous to his future bride.
   C. Franklin arrived in Philadelphia with nothing, but he later became famous and successful.
   D. Franklin wrote a lot of different important works.

NOTE
Key words

First, read the question carefully. Note the words *best summary.* You know that *summary* means including all of the main points. Next, read the answers carefully. Visualize the reading and think through the answers. For instance, go back to the reading to make a simple Timeline of Franklin's life.

TIMELINE

1723	1730	1733	1748	1753	1775-76
arrives by boat in Philadelphia	gets married	has good print shop and publishes and writes	is rich enough to retire	is a famous scientist and inventor	is a leader in the American Revolution

Visualizing can help you make sense of and sort out the information you've just read. Timelines, diagrams, and sketches can help you talk your way through a question.

THINK ALOUD

The Timeline goes from 1723 when Franklin left Boston to after 1753. The right answer has to be the one that covers the whole period. B and D both must be wrong. They don't tell the whole story. The reading talked about much more than his bride and his writing. Answer A doesn't make sense either. C must be the right answer because it hits on all of the main points I remember.

Putting ideas into words for yourself helps you think through a question. When you think aloud, you go step by step, explaining the problem to yourself. That can often make the answer clearer.

Tests

H Remember

Are you one of those students who doesn't stop thinking about a test once it's over? Try the activities below to help you learn what you can from the test experience.

1. Talk about It with a Friend

After the test is over, talk to a friend about it. Compare your answers. What kinds of questions gave you the most trouble? Talking with a friend might help you understand some of the questions you found hard.

2. Write Down Questions

When you get your test back, read it over carefully. If you got a question wrong, go through it again and make sure you understand why you missed it. Look again for the right answers.

Take the attitude that each test helps you to prepare for the next one. Learn a little from each test, and you'll be better prepared for the next one.

Summing Up

When you read a test, use the reading process. Preview the test carefully and apply the reading strategy of **skimming** to find the right answers. Remember to think about the kinds of questions and **how the test is organized.**

When you recheck your answers, try the rereading strategy of **visualizing and thinking aloud** to answer the more difficult questions.

Focus on Writing for Tests

Lots of tests ask you to write something. You usually find the writing question at the end of the test. Sometimes you're asked to write a story. Other times you are asked to read something and then write about it. Or you might even be asked to write a persuasive essay.

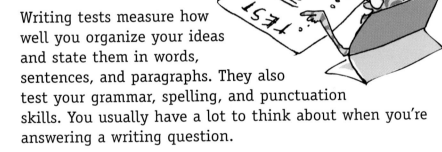

Writing tests measure how well you organize your ideas and state them in words, sentences, and paragraphs. They also test your grammar, spelling, and punctuation skills. You usually have a lot to think about when you're answering a writing question.

But writing questions are not always as hard as they look, if you're prepared.

Goals

Here you'll learn how to:

✔ **read directions and questions on a writing test**
✔ **write a story and an essay on a test**
✔ **use organizers to help you plan your writing**

Tests

Before Reading

Start planning for success on the writing part of a test before you even pick up a pen or pencil. Follow these three tips as you get ready to write.

1. Before the test day, find out as much as you can about what kind of writing you'll be asked to do.

2. When you get the test, look it over quickly. Read through any writing questions. Get an idea of what you'll be writing about later.

3. Plan your test time. Save at least 15 minutes for writing, plus 5 minutes for checking your work.

During Reading

Once you've finally reached the writing question, how do you begin? Try following these four steps:

STEPS IN WRITING FOR TESTS

1. Read the directions carefully—twice.

2. Plan what you'll write, using a graphic organizer.

3. Write out your answer.

4. Check your writing for mistakes.

Now you've got a plan, and you're ready to get started.

Reading the Directions

With test directions, your first step is to read them carefully. Make sure that you know exactly what the assignment is.

SAMPLE WRITING TEST

Directions: Write a story about the best birthday you ever had. You may write about real events or a story that you make up. Write at least two paragraphs. Be sure to proofread your work.

What exactly is the question asking? Read the question a second time, looking for key words.

SAMPLE WRITING TEST

NOTE
Key words

Directions: Write ① a story about the ② best birthday you ever had. You may write about ③ real events or a story that you make up. Write at least ④ two paragraphs. Be sure to ⑤ proofread your work.

Here's what you can learn from these key words:

① **a story** The assignment is to write a story.

② **best birthday you ever had** This is the subject.

③ **real events or a story that you make up** The story can be real or made up.

④ **two paragraphs** Write about two main ideas—about ten sentences.

⑤ **proofread** Check for spelling, punctuation, and other errors after writing.

Tests

Writing a Story

Your next step is planning what you will write. Start by deciding whether you'll tell a real story or make one up.

Make some planning notes in a Story Organizer. It can help you map out your story's events and give your story a clear beginning, middle, and end.

Here is how one reader used a Story Organizer to plan a story.

STORY ORGANIZER

TITLE: The Best Birthday I Ever Had

BEGINNING	MIDDLE	END
• move to St. Louis • two years ago on June 22	• trouble in school • sad and lonely • surprise— video and phone call	• Old friends made it the best birthday.

You may not have time to plan in detail. But having a few notes like these will help you feel confident when you start to write.

Writing an Essay on a Reading

Many tests ask you to write an essay. Sometimes you are asked to write your opinion about something or to explain how to do something step by step. Other times you're asked to write about a selection you've just read.

Here are directions for an essay question. Read them carefully. What are the key words? What main things should you remember?

SAMPLE WRITING TEST

Directions: Read the selection called "How to Wash a Dog." Then explain the process in your own words.

NOTE
Key words

The key words are *Read the selection, explain the process,* and *your own words.* In other words, after you read about how to wash a dog, you need to explain it in your own words.

For this question:

◼ Start by reading the selection carefully.

◼ Circle or number the main steps of the process.

◼ Use Process Notes to help you keep track of the steps of the process.

Tests

461

TITLE: How to Wash a Dog

STEP 1: Find a good place.

STEP 2: Get the dog wet all over.

STEP 3: Rub in the soap or shampoo.

STEP 4: Rinse the dog off.

STEP 5: Dry the dog with towels.

Once you understand what you've read, it's time to write your essay. Remember that you need to keep the steps in order and explain the process in your own words. To help the reader understand the process, use signal words such as *First, Second,* and *Third* to introduce the steps.

SAMPLE ESSAY

How to Wash a Dog

Washing a dog is easy and fun. First, find a good place. If your dog is big, wash him outside or in the bathtub. If he's small, wash him in the sink. Second, get your dog wet all over with warm water. Use a pitcher or a spray. Talk to him a lot while you do this. Third, rub in the soap or shampoo. Save his face for last. Fourth, rinse off the soap. Be careful to get all of it. Fifth, dry him off with towels and let him go. You're probably all wet, too, but you're done!

Writing a Persuasive Essay

Sometimes a test asks you to write your own views about a topic or issue. Take the question below, for example. What are the key words and question in these directions?

SAMPLE WRITING TEST

Directions: Write your views about the question below. Use five to ten sentences and support your opinion.

NOTE
Key words

Is TV bad for kids?

NOTE
Question

The directions tell you to do four things.

1. Give your views.

2. Write on the subject given in the question.

3. Write five to ten sentences.

4. Support your opinions with reasons.

What is your opinion on this topic? Use a Main Idea Organizer to plan your argument. Start with an opening statement. Then, list three reasons, and add a concluding sentence.

MAIN IDEA ORGANIZER

OPINION: TV can be good for kids.		
DETAIL 1: can help kids relax	DETAIL 2: can teach them new things	DETAIL 3: Parents can control what kids watch.
CONCLUDING SENTENCE: If kids do homework and parents control what they watch, TV can be good for kids.		

Tests

After Reading

After you finish writing, take the time to reread your answer. Check to see that you did what the directions asked.

Use these tips to make sure that you've answered the question well and that your writing is clear and free of mistakes.

TIPS FOR CHECKING YOUR WRITING

1. *Reread the directions word by word. Make sure that you followed the instructions.*

2. *Reread your answer carefully. Does it answer the question? Does it make sense? Are your ideas clear? Are all your sentences complete?*

3. *Check your writing for mistakes in spelling, punctuation, and indenting.*

Summing Up

- Plan your time and allow at least 15 minutes for a writing question.

- Read the directions carefully and read them at least twice.

- Choose organizers—such as a Story Organizer, Process Notes, or a Main Idea Organizer—to help you plan your writing.

- Write your answers with care, using complete sentences. Then, check your work.

Focus on Math Tests

When you open your math book, you see numbers, charts, and diagrams. You don't see many words, except for the word problems. But good reading skills can make a big difference in math. Reading skills are especially important on math tests.

Math tests check your understanding of math ideas. They also test how well you can solve math problems. Your reading skills can help you to be better at both things.

Goals

Here you'll learn how to:

✔ **prepare for a math test**

✔ **use a four-step plan to read math tests and answer test questions**

✔ **use visualizing and thinking aloud to help solve problems on math tests**

Tests

Before Reading

Would you like to do better on math tests? It's not as hard as you might think. Follow these steps to get ready.

How to Prepare for a Math Test

- Find out as much as you can about the test ahead of time.
- Read or review textbook sections that will be tested.
- Review the key math terms and processes you have learned.
- Look back over previous math quizzes and homework.
- Study textbook drawings, charts, and diagrams. Math questions often test how well you read graphics.

When test time comes and the teacher passes out the test, quickly preview it. Look for information such as how much time you have and what kinds of questions the test includes. Before you start the test, plan your time. Make sure you allow enough time for the tougher questions and for double-checking your answers.

Now preview the math test on the next two pages.

PREVIEW

Time limit

Math Test

Time: 20 minutes

Directions: Read and work each problem. Circle the letter of the correct answer. Use a blank sheet of paper to work the problems.

PREVIEW

Directions

1. Which numeral expresses 4 hundreds, 9 tens, and 3 ones?
   A. 439
   B. 493
   C. 49.3
   D. 4,903

PREVIEW

5 multiple-choice questions

2. Carla bought a new computer for $899. She also spent $200 for a printer and $250 for a monitor. All prices included tax. How much did Carla spend altogether?
   A. $1,554
   B. $560
   C. $8,990
   D. $1,349

3. The school cafeteria served 270 hot meals on Monday. Exactly one-third of the meals were barbecued chicken. How many people were served the chicken?
   A. 90
   B. 70
   C. 75
   D. 750

Tests

4. Which answer expresses the same idea as these two diagrams?

    A. 3/8 > 1/2

    B. 2/4 > 5/8

    C. 5/8 < 2/8

    D. 5/8 > 2/4

5. The sides of a pyramid are shaped like triangles. If the base of a pyramid has four sides, how many flat surfaces, or faces, does the pyramid have?

    A. 5

    B. 12

    C. 3

    D. 4

During Reading

You learned some important things in your preview. You have 20 minutes to do five multiple-choice problems. One of the questions has graphics. Answer the questions that you're sure of first. If you get stuck on a question, don't panic. Eliminate any answers that are obviously wrong. If you still aren't sure how to solve a problem, just go on to the next one. You can always come back to the ones you skip.

Use this four-step plan to solve problems on a math test.

HOW TO SOLVE MATH PROBLEMS

1. Read the directions and the questions.

2. Decide how to solve the problem.

3. Do the math.

4. Check your answer.

1. Read the Directions and the Questions

The first step is to read the directions and the questions well. Start with the test directions. These are very important. If you don't follow these directions exactly, you can lose points on the test.

Read the directions on the sample test again. What key words and phrases stand out?

Tests

NOTE
Key words

Directions: Read and work each problem. Circle the letter of the correct answer. Use a blank sheet of paper to work the problems.

You probably saw that you should mark a correct answer by circling the letter. You also noticed that you should use a blank piece of paper to work the math problems.

Now try reading a test question. This time look for key numbers you need and for key words that tell you how to solve the problem. Look at this question.

from **Math Test**

NOTE
Key numbers

NOTE
Key words

2. Carla bought a new computer for $899. She also spent $200 for a printer and $250 for a monitor. All prices included tax. How much did Carla spend altogether?

    A. $1,554
    B. $560
    C. $8,990
    D. $1,349

You found the key numbers right away: $899, $200, and $250. That's what you know. But what do you need to find out? The question asks you to find how much Carla spent.

2. Decide How to Solve the Problem

When you read the question, you probably saw key words and phrases that gave you clues about how to solve the problem. These key words are in the last sentence: *"How much did Carla spend altogether?"*

Think about what these key words tell you. Try the reading strategy of thinking aloud to figure out the problem. You have to keep quiet during a test, but you can still think aloud to yourself.

THINK ALOUD

"How much" means a total. "Spend" means that the answer is about money, the money that Carla spent. "Altogether" tells me to put all of the numbers together, or add them up. This is an addition problem.

3. Do the Math

Reread the problem again and look over the choices. Can you see any answers that are clearly wrong?

from Math Test

2. Carla bought a new computer for $899. She also spent $200 for a printer and $250 for a monitor. All prices included tax. How much did Carla spend altogether?

NOTE
Obvious wrong answers

A. $1,554
B. $560
C. $8,990
D. $1,349

Tests

First, I eliminate wrong answers. Answer B is lower than the cost of the computer itself, so it has to be wrong. I can eliminate Answer C, too. It's way too high. That leaves me just two choices: A and D.

Now go on to do the math. You can often save some time if you do a quick estimate of the right answer.

THINK ALOUD

Next, I'll try to estimate the answer. $899 is almost $900, so the problem is about $900 + $200 + $250. That's about $1,350. Now I'll do the math, but it looks like it's Answer D.

The right answer is D.

$$\begin{array}{r} 899 \\ 200 \\ +\,250 \\ \hline 1,349 \end{array}$$

4. Check Your Answer

Finish the problem by checking your answer. Reread the question, double-checking your work and your way of solving the problem. Then, double-check your math and make sure you marked the correct answer.

With some problems, the reading strategy of visualizing can also be a big help. When you visualize something, you try to see what it looks like by sketching it on paper.

Take question 5, for example. Start by reading the question carefully. Find the key words and decide how to solve the problem.

from Math Test

5. The sides of a pyramid are shaped like triangles. If the base of a pyramid has four sides, how many flat surfaces, or faces, does the pyramid have?

    A. 5
    B. 12
    C. 3
    D. 4

NOTE
Key words

You see that the key words of the problem are *sides of a pyramid, shaped like a triangle,* and *base . . . has four sides.* The problem asks *how many flat surfaces* the pyramid has. You may need to make some sketches to understand the problem and find the right answer.

VISUALIZING AND THINKING ALOUD

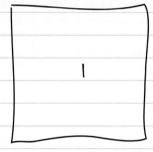
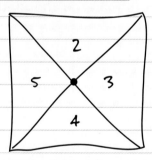

view of base   view from the top

OK. The problem says the base—the bottom of the pyramid—has four sides. I'll draw that like a square. That would be Face 1. From the top, it would have a point where all the triangle sides come together. The problem says I should find how many "faces" the pyramid has. There are 4 sides plus the base. That's a total of 5, so A is the right answer.

Tests

After Reading

If you have time, recheck your work. Make sure you have answered all the questions you can. Go back to check your work, using the list below.

- Reread each question. Did you do what the question asked? Is your answer reasonable?

- Recheck your numbers. When you worked the math, did you copy all of the numbers correctly?

- Is your answer readable?

Summing Up

- **Get ready for math tests by preparing in advance. Be sure to review textbook pages, key terms, math processes, and previous tests.**

- **Follow a four-step plan for a math test: read the directions and the questions, decide how to solve the problem, do the math, and check your answers.**

- **Use visualizing and thinking aloud to help you answer math test questions. Double-check your work afterward.**

Focus on Science Tests

You heard that you've got a science test on Monday. What should you expect? Most science tests usually have two types of questions: questions that ask for science facts and questions that ask you to think like a scientist.

To do well on science tests, sharpen your reading skills. Reading skills can help you follow directions and find key words in test questions and answers. They can also help you to read charts, tables, and maps.

Goals

Here you'll learn how to:

✔ prepare for science tests

✔ use the reading process to read science tests and test questions

✔ read graphics such as charts and maps to answer test questions

Tests

Before Reading

Give yourself time to prepare for a science test. If you can, start preparing a week ahead of time. First, ask your teacher about what the test covers, the kinds of questions it has, and how long it will be. Then dig in and study.

Remember that most science tests look for two things:

1. science facts, such as names (parts of a plant), definitions (what is energy?), and processes (stages of plant growth)

2. scientific thinking when you read a graph, chart, or diagram or explain the results of an experiment

How to Prepare for a Science Test

Skim your textbook chapters, quizzes, and tests.

Practice summarizing key ideas and facts after you study each chapter.

Learn key science facts—names, definitions, and processes—covered in the textbook.

Practice reading charts, tables, and maps to develop your ability to get information from them.

When the actual test begins, start with a preview. Look for the amount of time you have. Note the number and types of questions. Then, plan your test-taking time. You'll want to allow extra time for tougher questions and for double-checking at least some of your answers.

Now preview the science test on the next few pages.

Science Test

PREVIEW

Test time

Time: 20 minutes

Directions: Read each multiple-choice question. Circle the letter of the correct answer.

PREVIEW

Directions

1. What is the lowest level in a food web?
   A. plants
   B. herbivores
   C. carnivores
   D. water

PREVIEW

5 multiple-choice questions

2. Which sentence explains how the moon controls the tides?
   A. Moonlight causes less evaporation than sunlight.
   B. The moon's gravity exerts a pull on the ocean.
   C. The earth's gravity pulls against the moon's gravity.
   D. The earth and moon rotate in opposite directions.

3. While hiking in the mountains, you pick up a rock. You see that it has tiny shells in it. What is the correct conclusion to draw from this observation?
   A. Ancient peoples buried shells in the mountains.
   B. Floods rose so high that they covered the mountains.
   C. Shell collectors once hiked in these mountains.
   D. The rock was formed under the ocean.

Tests

4. What is the correct conclusion to draw
from the data on the chart and map below?

A. Temperatures in the Tropics do not vary
from season to season.

B. Cities on the ocean are colder than cities
located inland.

C. January and July temperatures are reversed
in the Southern and Northern Hemispheres.

D. Temperatures vary a great deal between
North America and Asia.

Average High Temperatures °F		
City	January	July
Athens, Greece	56	89
Buenos Aires, Argentina	86	60
Cape Town, South Africa	79	63
Montreal, Canada	22	79
Sydney, Australia	80	62

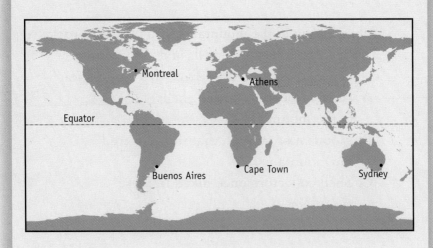

5. Which sentence best describes a successful experiment?
   A. The results are better than what you had hoped for.
   B. If other scientists do the experiment in exactly the same way, they get the same results.
   C. The experiment follows the scientific method, including the details to do at every step.
   D. The possible causes are carefully controlled.

During Reading

After you've previewed the questions, make a plan about how to use your time. In your preview, you found out that you have 20 minutes to do 5 multiple-choice questions. One question has a chart and a map in it. You decide to spend 5 minutes on the easiest questions, saving 10 minutes for the chart and map question. Use the last 5 minutes for checking your answers.

Now that you have a general idea about what's on the test, it's time to begin your more careful reading.

Tests

Read the Question

Take the time to read each question closely. Reread it if necessary. Look for key words that help you find the right answer. What are the key words in question 1?

NOTE
Key words

1. What is the lowest level in a food web?
   A. plants
   B. herbivores
   C. carnivores
   D. water

You probably see that *lowest level* and *food web* are the key words. So the question is asking about a key term, *food web*. Do you remember what the levels of a food web are?

Find the Answer

With the key words in mind, look at the answer choices.
If you're not sure of the answer, try to make a good guess.
Do you see any answers that are obviously wrong?

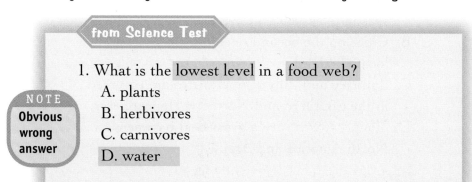

from Science Test

1. What is the lowest level in a food web?
   A. plants
   B. herbivores
   C. carnivores
   D. water

NOTE
Obvious
wrong
answer

You might remember that the food web is about who eats
what. You rule out D, water, because water isn't food. That
leaves A, B, and C. Try to recall what each of them eats. You
remember that herbivores eat plants and carnivores eat
herbivores and other carnivores. So plants, answer A, must
be the lowest level in a food web.

Draw Conclusions from Charts, Tables, and Maps

Science tests often ask you to draw conclusions from the
data shown in charts, tables, and maps. Here are some tips
for answering those questions:

1. Read the title and other key parts of the graphic to find
   out what information is shown.

2. Read the test question carefully and figure out what
   information you need to find in the graphic.

3. Go back to the chart, table, or map and find the
   information you need.

Go back to the test and try question 4 again. Study the
question, its chart, and the map.

Tests

4. What is the correct conclusion to draw from the data on the chart and map below?

A. Temperatures in the Tropics do not vary from season to season.

B. Cities on the ocean are colder than cities located inland.

C. January and July temperatures are reversed in the Southern and Northern Hemispheres.

D. Temperatures vary a great deal between North America and Asia.

NOTE
Key words

You see that the key words in the question are *correct conclusion* and *data on the chart and map.* You realize that your conclusion needs to come as a result of summarizing all of the data.

Now check the answers. Are any of them obviously wrong? You might rule out B and D, because there isn't enough data to draw those conclusions. Next, you test answer C by using the reading strategy of visualizing and thinking aloud. Making a sketch can help you make sense of the information and see that answer C is correct.

VISUALIZING

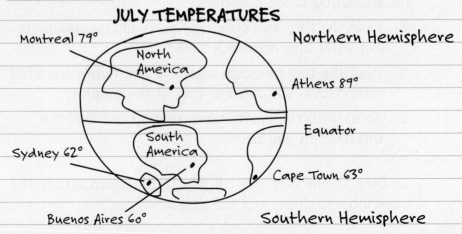

JULY TEMPERATURES

Montreal 79°   North America   Northern Hemisphere

Athens 89°

Equator

Sydney 62°   South America

Cape Town 63°

Buenos Aires 60°   Southern Hemisphere

THINK ALOUD

Answer C talks about Southern and Northern Hemispheres. The Equator is the dividing line. Montreal and Athens are in the Northern Hemisphere. The other three cities are in the Southern Hemisphere. I'll write in their July temperatures and compare them. OK. From them, it looks like answer C is correct.

After Reading

After taking the test, go back and double-check your work. Follow these tips for checking a science test:

- Reread the test directions to make sure that you marked answers correctly.
- Scan the test for skipped questions or answers that are hard to read.
- Reread every question against your answer. Did you do what the question asked? Is your answer reasonable?
- Spend any extra time rethinking the hard questions.

Summing Up

- **Prepare for science tests by rereading text and quizzes, summarizing key ideas, studying key terms, and practicing how to read graphics.**
- **During the test, read questions carefully, looking for key words. Rule out all wrong answers first.**
- **After the test, carefully check your answers.**

Tests

Focus on Social Studies Tests

Social studies tests demand a lot from you. They check your knowledge of facts, big ideas, names, dates, and places. They ask you to show your skill at reading maps, graphs, timelines, and tables. And they ask you to summarize, draw conclusions, give your opinion, and use critical reading skills.

That may seem like a lot to do, but knowing how to study and how to use reading strategies can make your job a lot easier.

Goals

Here you'll learn how to:

✔ **prepare for social studies tests**
✔ **read and answer questions on social studies tests**
✔ **interpret graphs and maps to answer test questions**

Before Reading

When you hear about an upcoming social studies test, try to get some information about it. Find out what the test will cover, what types of questions it will have, and how long it will take. Then, get started on your studying. Use the guide below as a checklist of what to do.

How to Prepare for a Social Studies Test

- Look over your textbook and past quizzes.
- Study terms, concepts, names, dates, people, and places.
- Make a list of ten things you would put on a test and learn something about each one.
- Review how to read graphs, tables, maps, timelines, and other graphics, because they are almost sure to be on the test.

Once the test begins, do a quick preview. Look for what type of questions the test includes and how much time you have. Then, plan your test time.

Answer the easier questions first. Set aside extra time for the harder questions. Last, save a few minutes at the end to double-check your answers.

Now that you have a plan, preview a sample social studies test.

Tests

Social Studies Test

Time: 30 minutes

Part I. Multiple Choice

Directions: Read each sentence. Circle the letter of the correct answer.

1. Most early English and German settlers came to America _____.
   A. to fight in the Revolutionary War
   B. for religious freedom
   C. because they had relatives here
   D. because Native Americans offered them land

2. William Penn was _____.
   A. the founder of New York City
   B. a cousin of King George III
   C. a wealthy Quaker leader
   D. the governor of Massachusetts

3. The most important result of the American Revolution was _____.
   A. independence from Great Britain
   B. freeing the slaves
   C. removing all European colonies from the Americas
   D. more wealth for the former 13 colonies

4. When the war ended, North America was divided among _____.
   A. Great Britain, Canada, and Russia
   B. Spain, Canada, and the United States
   C. the United States, Spain, and Native American peoples
   D. all of the above

Social Studies Test, continued

Part II. Reading a Map

Directions: The questions below are based on information found in the map. Read the questions. Circle the letter of the correct answer.

PREVIEW
Directions

PREVIEW
Map

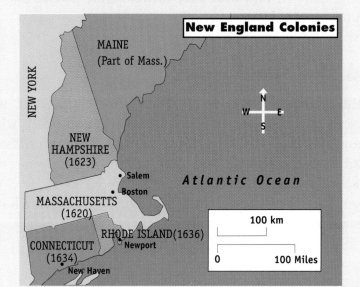

1. Which New England colony is farthest south?
    A. Massachusetts
    B. New Hampshire
    C. Maine
    D. Connecticut

2. Which of these conclusions is correct, based on this map?
    A. Rhode Island, the smallest colony, was settled before Massachusetts was.
    B. Newport is closer to Boston than New Haven is.
    C. The largest colony shown is Connecticut.
    D. Connecticut and New Hampshire were settled in the 1630s.

Tests

During Reading

In your preview, you saw that the test has four multiple-choice questions and two questions based on a map. Plan how to use the 30 minutes you have. Because the test has two parts, divide the time in half and save a little time at the end to check your answers.

Read the Questions

First, start slowly. Take a deep breath and relax. Then, read the first question carefully. Under pressure you often will hurry and not read the question carefully. Take your time and read each question twice.

When you read a test question, look for key words. What are the key words in the question?

> **from Social Studies Test**
>
> 1. Most early English and German settlers came to America _____.
>   A. to fight in the Revolutionary War
>   B. for religious freedom
>   C. because they had relatives here
>   D. because Native Americans offered them land
>
> **NOTE**
> **Key words**

Here, the key words are *early* and *settlers came to America.* They tell you that you're looking for the reason that settlers came to America.

Read the Answers

Read through all the multiple-choice answers before you mark your choice. Then, if you know the correct answer, mark it. If you don't know the answer, try to rule out any answers that are obviously wrong. You might know, for instance, that A must be wrong because the early settlers came to America a long time before the Revolutionary War. If you can rule out some answers, even if you guess, you have a better chance of being right.

Read Maps

Social studies tests almost always include questions based on maps. Before the test, review how to read them. Here are some tips to remember.

TIPS

1. *First, read the title. It should give you a clear idea of the subject.*

2. *Look at the map, key, or legend to find out what the colors or symbols mean. Notice the compass directions.*

3. *Read the other labels on the map. Focus on what kind of information is shown.*

4. *Put into your own words what you learn from the map. Too often you will "look at" a map but never "read" it. Sum up what the map shows in one or two sentences.*

Now, let's work through the two map questions you previewed earlier.

1. Which New England colony is farthest south?
   A. Massachusetts
   B. New Hampshire
   C. Maine
   D. Connecticut

Here the key word in the question is *south*. You need to look carefully at the *compass* to be sure you know which way south is. Once you are sure of that, then put your finger on the farthest south point of the map. What colony are you touching? If you said Connecticut, you're right. That's the correct answer, D.

Now try the second map question. It is a little harder to answer.

2. Which of these conclusions is correct, based on this map?
   A. Rhode Island, the smallest colony, was settled before Massachusetts was.
   B. Newport is closer to Boston than New Haven is.
   C. The largest colony shown is Connecticut.
   D. Connecticut and New Hampshire were settled in the 1630s.

Finding the correct conclusion means paying attention to all the parts of the map. Some of the choices focus on years and others on location. Look carefully at the labels, the dates, and the scale. Here's how one reader worked through the possible answers.

Answer A can't be right because the Massachusetts date (1620) is earlier than the Rhode Island date (1636). Answer B seems right, but I should check the others. I can tell that Answer C isn't correct. I can rule out D too, because the New Hampshire date is not in the 1630s. Answer B is definitely correct.

After Reading

After you've answered the questions, take the last five minutes to double-check the test.

- Scan the test for any missed questions or careless mistakes.

- Reread the questions you found the hardest to answer. Did you understand each question? Do your answers still make sense to you?

Summing Up

- **Prepare for social studies tests by reviewing the text and past quizzes, studying key terms and facts, and reviewing how to read graphics.**

- **During the test, be sure to read the questions carefully and look for key words. Be sure also to read the graphics as well as the questions about them.**

- **Save a few minutes to double-check your answers.**

Tests

Improving
Vocabulary

Learning New Words

Building Vocabulary Skills

Understanding New Terms

Mastering Vocabulary Tests

Improving Vocabulary

When you were about a year old, you could probably say and understand only a small number of words. When you reached age five or six, you were just beginning to read.

Think about how far you've come and how much you've built your vocabulary since then. You've added a few words to your vocabulary every day, week by week.

Words help you all the time, everywhere you go. Whether you are thinking, speaking, reading, or writing, you can't do very much without words.

Here you'll learn a number of different ways to improve your vocabulary.

Learning New Words

The more words you know, the more you can do with language. You're like a magician with more tricks, a baseball pitcher with more pitches, a dancer with more steps. You can read a wider range of books, write better papers, speak well, and even impress a few people along the way.

Learning new words involves three things: collecting new words, using your new words, and exercising your word skills.

Collect New Words

What do you like to collect—coins? baseball cards? magnets? Whatever you collect, you want to find as many different items as you can. With each new item, you learn something new, and you become more of an "expert."

The same is true for collecting words. The more you collect, the more you learn. One of the best ways to improve your vocabulary is to start a Vocabulary Journal. Keep your Vocabulary Journal in one part of your school notebook.

Four-step Plan for Collecting Words

Here's an easy plan to follow to help you become more of a word expert and build your vocabulary.

1. WRITE IT DOWN

When you read or hear a new word, write it down in your notebook. Record where you found it, the page number, and any other important information.

> **VOCABULARY JOURNAL**
>
> English class—10/12
> "The White Deer" told by
> the Lenape
>
> treaty, p. 23
>
> pleaded, p. 24
>
> National Geographic
> TV special—12/8
>
> excavate

Vocabulary

2. USE CONTEXT CLUES OR LOOK IT UP

Figure out the meaning of each word. You can use context clues, or you can look it up in a dictionary. Read the definition of the word, and see how the word works in a sentence.

Now read this dictionary entry for the word *excavate*. Do the sample sentences make the word's meaning clear?

from *The American Heritage Children's Dictionary*

excavate *verb* **1.** To dig or dig out: *The workers excavated a hole for the swimming pool.* **2.** To uncover by digging and expose to view: *They excavated the ruins of an ancient Roman city.*

ex•ca•vate (ĕks′ kə vāt′) *verb* **excavated, excavating**

3. WRITE THE DEFINITION

Write the definition next to the word in your notebook. Choose the definition that best fits the way the word was used in the book or by the person who was speaking. For example, the definition you may want for *excavate* is "to uncover by digging and expose to view."

4. SAY IT ALOUD

To help you remember the word, read it and the definition aloud. If you need help, look at the way the word is divided into syllables and use the dictionary to help you pronounce it.

excavate

Use Your New Words

To master any skill takes practice. Even the most talented gymnasts can't perform perfectly on the balance beam on the first try. The best baseball players don't hit home runs in every game. But the more they practice, the better they get.

The same holds true for building your vocabulary. The more you use new words when you speak, read, and write, the faster they will become a part of your vocabulary. Experts say you need to hear or read a word about eight or more times before you *really* know it.

The best way to build your vocabulary is to read a lot and pay attention to words. Then, practice using them.

How to Learn New Words

The excavation was cavernous and subterranean.

1. Set aside 8 to 10 minutes a day every week.

2. Choose several new vocabulary words to practice.

3. Read each word. Try to remember what it means. Make up a sentence that uses the word.

4. Check to see whether you got it right. If you did, go on to another word.

5. If you can't remember the word and what it means, try rereading its definition aloud.

6. Put a check mark next to all the words you know.

7. Circle or highlight the words you need to study again.

Once you've learned some new words, try using them whenever you can. Make a point of using the new words in your conversation or your writing. Before you know it, you'll be adding more words to your everyday vocabulary.

Vocabulary

Exercise Your Word Skills

Here are some ideas for exercising your word skills.

1. Look for a Word of the Day

Try to find one new word every day. Just write it down in your Vocabulary Journal. Then, when you have time, write down what it means. Try this even for a month or two, and you'll add a number of new words to your vocabulary.

2. Search for Synonyms and Antonyms

With a friend, look at your word lists and choose two or three words that you both want to know more about. Look up their meanings. Then search books or newspapers for words that mean the same (*synonyms*) and words that mean the opposite (*antonyms*). For example, you might find these synonyms for the word *astonished: amazed, marveled, astounded,* and *surprised.* Add them to your Vocabulary Journal.

3. Hunt for Homophones

Homophones are pairs of words, such as *sea* and *see,* that sound alike but are spelled differently and have different meanings. Start a special collection of homophones. Be sure to match the right spellings and definitions. If it helps you remember, write sentences for each of them.

4. Keep a List of Interesting Words

Lots of words are fun and interesting, such as *level*. It's spelled the same way backward and forward.

Some words come from the names of people or places. These words are called *eponyms*. The *graham cracker,* for example, is named for Dr. Sylvester Graham. Can you make a guess about the eponym *hamburger?* These meat patties were first cooked in Hamburg, Germany.

Do you know any other eponyms? Use the word history in a dictionary to find out where these names came from: *candy, Ferris wheel, sandwich, teddy bear.*

Look for interesting words from other languages (such as *cuisine*) or words from the ancient world (such as *myths*). What other interesting words can you find?

5. Play Word Games

Try your word skills by playing word games and doing crossword puzzles or word searches. You'll find these in magazines and newspapers and in books of word games. Try having fun with words, and you'll find your vocabulary increasing.

6. Stump Your Friends

Every now and then, give those new words in your Vocabulary Journal some exercise. Pair off with a friend. Take turns quizzing each other on what the new words mean. If your partner can define the word, he or she gets 1 point. Keep a running score. The first person to get 5 points wins. You can also challenge each other to make up words using prefixes, suffixes, and roots.

Vocabulary

Building Vocabulary Skills

How do people improve their vocabulary? How do vocabularies grow? You learn words naturally—by listening, by reading, and by talking. But you can also learn words by learning about context clues, word parts, and word tools, such as a dictionary.

Look at Context Clues

A word's *context* is the words, phrases, and sentences that surround it. If you look closely at the context of an unknown word, you often get clues about that word's meaning.

Understanding Context Clues

Read the sentence below. What context clues help you understand the word *anxiously?*

> **from *The Midnight Fox* by Betsy Byars**
>
> She moved anxiously toward the bushes and there was a tension to her steps, as if she were ready to spring or make some other quick, forceful movement.

What words help you understand how "she" moves? Note the words *tension, ready to spring,* and *make some other quick, forceful movement*. These context clues tell you that, in this sentence, *anxiously* means "tensely, quickly, and forcefully."

Kinds of Context Clues

When you're reading and see a word you don't know, check the surrounding words to see if you can figure out its meaning. Here are some ways to understand a word from its context.

1. LOOK FOR SYNONYMS

Watch for words that repeat the same meaning.

> **from _Boys Against Girls_ by Phyllis Reynolds Naylor**
>
> Just because she was supposed to be super smart— "precocious," the grown-ups called it—didn't mean he had to like her.

You probably see that the words _super smart_ and _precocious_ both mean the same thing. In this sentence, _super smart_ and _precocious_ are synonyms.

2. STUDY THE SURROUNDING SENTENCES

Look closely at the sentence containing the word, as well as the sentences that come before and after it. Be patient when you come upon a word you don't know. Read on.

> **from _The Sultan's Perfect Tree_ by Jane Yolen**
>
> There was once a sultan who loved perfection. In his palace he would allow only the most perfect things. Each fruit that he ate had to be without blemish. Each cup that he drank from had to be without flaw.

By reading the whole passage, you learn that the word _blemish_ means "a flaw." Something that is perfect would not have a blemish.

Vocabulary

3. CHECK FOR ANTONYMS

Sometimes authors use words with opposite meanings, called antonyms, to make a point. In the paragraph below, the word *but* points to antonym clues.

from "Nomi and the Magic Fish" by Judy Sierra

When Nomi was a little girl, her mother died, and her father married another woman. This woman had a daughter called Nomsa. Nomi was a beautiful, tall child, but Nomsa was very short and ugly.

In this example, the author uses two pairs of antonyms to show that Nomi and Nomsa looked very different from each other.

4. LOOK FOR A DEFINITION

When you come across an unfamiliar word, you'll often find it defined nearby. Sometimes you'll see words and phrases—such as *or*, *that is*, and *in other words*—with a definition right after it in parentheses.

from "Census Surprise!" from *Junior Scholastic*

The U.S. Census Bureau conducts a **census** (people count) every 10 years. Since 1960, the population growth rate had been slowing down. But no longer.

Notice that the word being defined—*census*—is printed in boldface type, and its meaning is given right after it in parentheses.

5. LOOK FOR AN EXAMPLE

Sometimes an author gives you an example that explains what a word means. Examples often follow words or phrases, such as *for example, such as, like,* and *especially.*

> **from *Boys Against Girls***
>
> Actually, nobody knew if there was an abaguchie in Buckman at all, and if there was, just what kind of creature it was. For several years various people in Upshur County claimed to have seen a large animal, something like a cat, lurking around in the shadows, running along the edge of the woods, or even crawling about under somebody's window.

The word *abaguchie* is unfamiliar. But you soon learn that it's a "creature," "a large animal, something like a cat."

6. CHECK FOR REPETITION OF AN UNKNOWN WORD

Sometimes a difficult word is mentioned more than once. You may not understand what the word means the first time you see it but can figure out its meaning when it's repeated.

> **from *Creeps from the Deep* by Leighton Taylor**
>
> The deeper you go in the sea, the more pressure is on you. In the deepest part of the ocean, almost 35,000 feet down, water has a pressure of 16,000 pounds on every square inch. A school bus weighs about 16,000 pounds. Now that's seriously heavy pressure!

Seeing how *pressure* is used in several sentences helps you understand that it means "the feeling of being pressed or weighed down."

Vocabulary

Learn about Word Parts

You often can figure out what a new word means by learning about the three basic word parts:

- **Word Roots** main parts of words
- **Prefixes** word beginnings
- **Suffixes** word endings

Word Roots

A *root* is the main part of a word. If you know the root, you can often figure out what a word means. For example, the word root *fin* means "end." So, when you see the word *final*, you know that it means "the end or last of something." Here are some other examples.

WORD ROOTS

Word Root	Meaning	Examples
aud	"hear" (Latin)	*aud*io, *aud*itorium
dic	"say, tell" (Latin)	*dic*tate, pre*dic*t, *dic*tionary
fac, fact	"do, make" (Latin)	*fac*tory, manu*fact*ure
photo	"light" (Greek)	*photo*graphy, *photo*synthesis
pop	"people" (Latin)	*pop*ular, *pop*ulation
scrib, scrip	"write" (Latin)	pre*scrib*e, *scrip*t
therm	"heat" (Greek)	*therm*ometer, *therm*al
voc	"call" (Latin)	*voc*abulary, *voc*al

To learn more about word roots, see pages 563–565.

Prefixes

Prefixes are word parts that come before a root word. A prefix can change the meaning of a word. For example, the prefix *anti-* means "against." When you add *anti-* at the beginning of a word like *freeze*, you form the word *antifreeze*. You change the meaning to "a liquid that works *against* freezing."

Here is a table of some common prefixes.

PREFIXES

Prefix	Meaning	Examples
co-	"together"	co*operate*, *correspondent*
counter-	"against"	counter*attack*, counter*clockwise*
ex-	"out of, away from"	ex*haust* ex*tract*
non-	"not, against"	non*sense*, non*fiction*
tri-	"three"	tri*angle*, tri*pod*

To learn more about prefixes, see pages 560–561.

Suffixes

A *suffix* is a word part that comes at the end of a word. The suffix *-ist* means "a person who." What does the word *motorist* mean? It means "a person who does motoring, or driving."

Sometimes a suffix helps tip you off about what part of speech a word is. For example, many words that end with the suffix *-ist* are nouns. They name a person, place, or thing. Examples are art*ist* and chem*ist*. Remember that adding prefixes and suffixes often changes the spelling of the root word. To learn more about suffixes, see pages 561–562.

Vocabulary

Use Word Parts

When you use word parts to figure out the meaning of a word, it's like taking your bike apart to see how it works. Here are some tips that can help you to do it.

- If the word has a prefix, try to say the word, and then take the prefix off.
- If the word has a suffix, try to say the word, and then take the suffix off.
- Look at the root word that is left. Does it look like another word you know? Try saying it.
- Use the strategy of thinking aloud and explain the meaning of each part of the word that you know. Here's an example of what you might say about the word *inflexible*:

THINK ALOUD

The prefix in- means not. The root flex means bend. And -ible is a suffix. That probably means it's an adjective. I guess the word inflexible means that someone or something does not bend.

Remember that words do not always have a prefix or a suffix. Some examples are *sleep, meter, believe,* and *cloud.*

Practice Using Word Parts

To learn some common prefixes, suffixes, and roots, read through the Word Parts section in the Reader's Almanac on pages 560–565. Add the word parts that you think are most useful in your Vocabulary Journal. Another good idea is to test yourself on the meaning of word parts. Write a word part on one side of an index card, and write its meaning and a few examples on the other side. Then, quiz yourself on a few cards each week.

Breaking Apart Words

Practice using what you know about word parts to understand unfamiliar words.

> Word: *telegram*
> Root: *tele* "far off, distance"
> Root: *gram* "letter"

You might figure out that if *gram* means "letter," and *tele* means "distant or distance," then a *telegram* might be "a letter sent over a distance."

What can you learn from breaking apart the word *biology?*

> Word: *biology*
> Root: *bio* "life"
> Suffix: *-logy* "study, science"

You might say that if *bio* means "life" and *-logy* means "study or science," then *biology* means "the study of life."

Here's another example.

> Word: *intersection*
> Root: *sect* "cut"
> Prefix: *inter-* "between"
> Suffix: *-tion* "state of" (suggests that the word is a noun)

You can use the root, prefix, and suffix to figure out that *intersection* means a place where two or more things cross.

Vocabulary

507

Use a Dictionary

As a word collector, you'll want to have all the tools you need to understand new words. Every smart reader has or can find a good dictionary. Why should you use a dictionary?

The top three reasons to use a dictionary are to find:
- the spelling and pronunciation of a word
- the meaning of a word
- how to divide a word into syllables

Here are some of the features you'll find in a dictionary.

FEATURES OF A DICTIONARY

Feature	Description	Use It to
1 Guide words	tell first and last word on that page	find the word you want
2 Entry words	are the words being defined, listed alphabetically	check a word's spelling and capitalization
3 Definitions	list all possible meanings for the word	find the right meaning for your word, as shown by the context
4 Sample sentence	is a sentence that uses the word	see how to use the word
5 Pronunciation	shows how you should pronounce, or say, the word	learn how to say a word
6 Part of speech	tells whether a word is a noun, verb, adverb, and so on	use a word properly in a sentence
7 Other forms	lists related forms of the word	find spellings of related words
8 Syllable divisions	are shown with a space or heavy black dots (•) to separate syllables and to show how to divide a word into syllables	check how to divide a word into syllables or at the end of a line of writing

A Sample Dictionary Page

Note the key parts of this page from a dictionary.

from *The American Heritage Children's Dictionary*

(1) **erupt ➤ establish** (3)

(2) **erupt** *verb* To burst out violently: *Lava and ash erupted from the volcano.*
e·rupt (ĭ rŭpt′) ◊ *verb* **erupted, erupting**

eruption *noun* A sudden bursting forth of something, such as water in a geyser or lava from a volcano.
e·rup·tion (ĭ rŭp′shən) ◊ *noun, plural* **eruptions**

escalator *noun* A moving staircase that carries people between floors of a building.
es·ca·la·tor (ĕs′kə lā′tər) ◊ *noun, plural* **escalators**

(4) **escape** *verb* **1.** To get free: *The prisoners escaped by climbing the wall.* **2.** To succeed in avoiding: *I fell off the ladder but managed to escape injury.* ◊ *noun* **1.** The act of getting free or avoiding something bad. **2.** A way of getting one's mind off worries or cares.
(5) **es·cape** (ĭ skāp′) ◊ *verb* **escaped, escaping** ◊ *noun, plural* **escapes**

escort *noun* **1.** One or more persons going along with another to give protection or show respect: *The visiting foreign leader was given a police escort.* **2.** One or more ships or planes traveling with another to give protection. **3.** A man who goes with a woman to a party or other social event. ◊ *verb* To go with as an escort: *Police escorted the senator during the parade.*
es·cort ◊ *noun* (ĕs′kôrt′), *plural* **escorts** ◊ *verb* (ĭ skôrt′) **escorted, escorting**

Eskimo *noun* **1.** A member of a people of the Arctic regions of North America and Asia. **2.** The language of the Eskimo. ◊ *adjective* Of or relating to the Eskimo or their language.
Es·ki·mo (ĕs′kə mō′) ◊ *noun, plural* **Eskimo** or **Eskimos** ◊ *adjective* (6)

esophagus *noun* The tube that connects the throat with the stomach.
e·soph·a·gus (ĭ sŏf′ə gəs) ◊ *noun*

especially *adverb* **1.** In a special way; specifically: *These coats are designed especially for tall people.* **2.** More than usually; very.
es·pe·cial·ly (ĭ spĕsh′ə lē) ◊ *adverb*

espionage *noun* The use of spies by a government to get secret information about another country.
es·pi·o·nage (ĕs′pē ə näzh′) ◊ *noun*

essay *noun* A short piece of writing that gives the author's opinions on a certain subject; composition.
es·say (ĕs′ā′) ◊ *noun, plural* **essays** (7)

essence *noun* The basic quality of a thing that makes it what it is: *The essence of democracy is faith in the people.*
es·sence (ĕs′əns) ◊ *noun, plural* **essences**

essential *adjective* **1.** Very important; vital: *It is essential that you pay attention.* **2.** Being an absolutely necessary part of something; basic: *Eating regularly is essential to good health.* ◊ *noun* A basic thing that cannot be done without: *Bring a small bag with your toothbrush and other essentials.*
(8) **es·sen·tial** (ĭ sĕn′shəl) ◊ *adjective* ◊ *noun, plural* **essentials**

–est The suffix *–est* forms the superlative of adjectives and adverbs and means "most." The *happiest* person in a group is the person who is the most happy. The *hoarsest* person with a cold is the person who is most hoarse. The *thinnest* person in a room is the person who is the most thin. The runner who runs *fastest* is the runner who runs faster than anyone else.

establish *verb* **1.** To begin or set up; found; create: *My grandparents established the lumber company in 1920.* **2.** To show to be true: *I established my identity by showing my passport.*

Understanding New Terms

When you start reading about a new subject, you'll find many words you do not know. Each subject tends to have its own set of terms, or language, that you need to learn.

Many of the new, or specialized, terms are highlighted in the textbook so they stand out. They might be in *italic type,* in **boldface type,** or in colored type. For example, in an American history book, you might find some of these terms in a chapter about the development of the Southwest: *dam, reservoir, aqueduct.*

Use Concept Maps to organize information about specialized terms. Add them to your Vocabulary Journal. Here's one reader's Concept Map of the new words in a chapter about the Southwest.

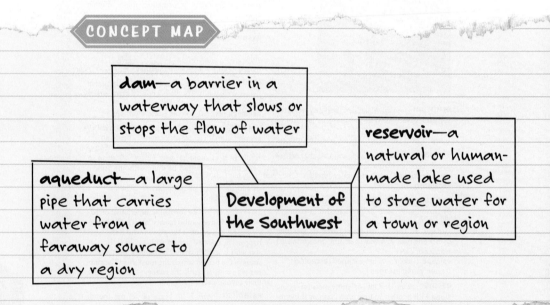

CONCEPT MAP

dam—a barrier in a waterway that slows or stops the flow of water

reservoir—a natural or human-made lake used to store water for a town or region

aqueduct—a large pipe that carries water from a faraway source to a dry region

Development of the Southwest

Use Concept Maps like the one above to help you study and remember new words.

Mastering Vocabulary Tests

By now, you've probably taken one or more vocabulary tests. Here are some tips that might help you to improve your scores for common types of vocabulary questions.

Remember, the test will seem simpler if you rule out obvious wrong answers.

1. Definition Questions

Start by looking for prefixes, suffixes, and roots. For example, try this question.

SAMPLE QUESTION

To <u>mechanize</u> means:
  a. to memorize
  b. worker who repairs machines
  c. a robot
  d. to equip with machines

Here is a good example of why you should study word parts. If you know your prefixes, suffixes, and roots, you can figure this question out. For example, you might know the root *mech* means "machine." The suffix *-ize* signals a verb. That rules out answer b, because worker is a noun. So the answer probably is d. to equip with machines.

Vocabulary

2. Synonym Questions

Standardized tests often ask you to choose a synonym (a word with the same or similar meaning). For example, try this question.

Which of these is a synonym of <u>subterranean</u>?
a. under water   b. near the sea
c. less healthy   d. under the earth

If you've studied word parts, you might know that the root word *terr* means "land" or "earth." You might also know the prefix *sub-* means "under." This information can help you to rule out all answer choices except d. under the earth.

3. Antonym Questions

Use the same process to help choose a word that is an antonym, or opposite. Try this question.

Which is an antonym of <u>avoid</u>?
a. stay away   b. hole in space
c. seek out   d. fight

Suppose that you don't know what *avoid* means. If you recognize it as a verb, you know that its antonym will be a verb, too. So you can at least rule out choice b. hole in space, because *hole* is a noun.

If you know that *avoid* means "stay away," it's much easier to find its antonym. You'll quickly figure out that the opposite of "stay away" is c. seek out.

4. Words in a Paragraph

On many vocabulary tests, you're asked to read a paragraph and then to define a word found in it. Try the example below.

> from *Bridge to Terabithia* by Katherine Paterson
>
> "Sure," Jess agreed quickly, relieved that there was no need to plunge deeper into the woods. He would take her there, of course, for he wasn't such a coward that he would mind a little exploring now and then farther in amongst the ever darkening columns of the tall pines.
>
> In this passage, what does the word <u>relieved</u> mean?
> a. scared   b. angry
> c. thankful   d. sad

To answer this question, go back and find the word *relieved.* If you don't know its meaning, read the sentences around it. In this example, the first sentence says there's "no need to plunge deeper into the woods." Later you see the words "he wasn't such a coward." From these, you can infer that, if Jess doesn't have to go into the woods, he would have been "thankful," so that c. thankful is correct.

Vocabulary

5. Analogy Questions

Many standardized tests have analogy questions. An analogy shows a relationship between two things.

How to Read Analogy Questions

Here is one common type of analogy question.

Finger is to *ring* as *ear* is to _____
a. bracelet   b. earring   c. necklace   d. pin

First, figure out how *finger* and *ring* are connected. Look for a relationship between the words. A *finger* is the place where you wear a *ring*. Now finish the analogy. If a finger is the place for a ring, what is it that you wear on your ear? The answer is b. earring.

Now try another analogy question on your own. Notice that it is written a little differently than the one above.

cry : pain :: laugh : _____
a. joke   b. hurt   c. sad   d. unhappy

The first colon (:) means "is to." The double colon (::) means "as." Read this question like this: "Cry **is to** pain **as** laugh **is to** _____." Pain can cause you to cry. What can cause you to laugh? The answer is a. joke.

Other Types of Analogy Questions

You will find many different kinds of analogy questions. Here are some common ones used on standardized tests.

1. SYNONYMS

A *synonym* is a word that has the same or similar meaning as another word. Examples are *toss, throw,* and *pitch.* Here is an example of an analogy question that uses synonyms.

> **SAMPLE QUESTION**
>
> pull : tug :: push : _____
> a. shove   b. talk   c. lift   d. find

You would read this analogy as: "Pull **is to** tug **as** push **is to** _____." Think about *pull* and *tug*. They mean the same thing. So you're looking for a word that means the same as *push*. The answer is a. shove.

2. ANTONYMS

Antonyms are words that mean the opposite of other words. *Hate* is an antonym of *love. Ceiling* is an antonym of *floor.* Here is an example of an analogy question that uses antonyms.

> **SAMPLE QUESTION**
>
> fast : slow :: neat : _____
> a. tidy   b. sloppy   c. clean   d. nasty

You'd read this analogy as: "Fast **is to** slow **as** neat **is to** _____." You first figure out the relationship between *fast* and *slow*. They're opposites, or antonyms. So what is an antonym for *neat?* The answer is b. sloppy.

Vocabulary

3. RHYMING WORDS

How are the first two words below alike? They don't have much in common, so what do you do? Think about what they might have in common. You'll find that the words *deep* and *weep* rhyme, or sound alike.

Once you've figured out how the words are related, the analogy is easy to solve. The answer is c. hook because it rhymes with *book*.

4. HOMOPHONES

Homophones are words that sound alike but have different meanings. Examples are *steak, stake* and *foul, fowl*. Here is an example of a homophone analogy question.

Look for the relationship between the first two words. You see that they're homophones. *Real* and *reel* sound the same but are spelled differently, so you look for a homophone for *stare*. Be careful here. It's a bit tricky. The answer b. stair is correct.

5. PARTS OF THINGS

Here's another type of analogy test question.

> **SAMPLE QUESTION**
>
> kitchen : living room :: _____
> a. shoe : head   b. sister : brother
> c. flower : water   d. dog : baseball

A *kitchen* and *living room* are both parts of a home. So the correct answer is b. A *sister* and *brother* are both parts of a family.

6. AN ITEM AND WHO USES IT

What is the relationship between *pen* and *writer?*

> **SAMPLE QUESTION**
>
> pen : writer :: book : _____
> a. reader   b. kitchen   c. scissors   d. page

A *reader* uses a book just as a *writer* uses a pen. The correct answer is a. reader.

7. AN ITEM AND WHAT IT DOES

See if you can figure out this analogy.

> **SAMPLE QUESTION**
>
> hose : waters :: _____
> a. flower : rains   b. airplane : flies
> c. oven : table   d. light : dark

How would you complete the analogy? What's the relationship? A *hose waters*. The relationship is a pair of words that name an item and what it does. The answer is b. airplane : flies.

Vocabulary

8. A GROUP AND AN EXAMPLE OF THAT GROUP

How would you describe the relationship of the first pair of words in the question below?

> ### SAMPLE QUESTION
>
> fruit : plum :: building : _____
>
> a. car   b. apple
>
> c. shed   d. garden

The first word, *fruit,* names a particular kind of food. The second word, *plum,* is one kind of that particular group (fruit). So, if your first word is *building*, what is an example of that kind of thing? The correct answer is c. shed.

9. AN ACTION AND WHERE IT TAKES PLACE

How would you identify the relationship here?

> ### SAMPLE QUESTION
>
> sleep : bed :: swim : _____
>
> a. bank   b. pool
>
> c. airplane   d. bathtub

You see that *sleep* is an action that takes place in a *bed.* Where does a person *swim*? The answer is b. pool.

10. SEQUENCE OR ORDER

The first two words below have another type of relationship. How would you describe it?

SAMPLE QUESTION

breakfast : lunch :: spring : _____
a. night   b. summer
c. vacation   d. kitchen

You see that *breakfast* and *lunch* are names of meals. You also realize that *breakfast* happens before *lunch* does. So *breakfast* is followed by *lunch*. That means that the right answer for *spring* will be a season that comes after it. That leads you to the answer b. summer.

Summing Up

Become a collector of words. Start by beginning a Vocabulary Journal and watch your vocabulary grow. Practice using context clues and word parts to figure out the meanings of unfamiliar words. Use your dictionary to review and practice the words in your Vocabulary Journal. Learn what you can about analogies so you can master standardized vocabulary tests. If you do all that, you'll soon turn into a word expert.

Vocabulary

Reader's
Almanac

- Strategy Handbook
- Reading Tools
- Word Parts: Prefixes, Suffixes, and Roots

Strategy Handbook

This part of your *Reader's Handbook* explains strategies that can help you improve your reading.

A strategy is a plan for approaching reading. Different types of readings call for different strategies. Before reading a selection, you set your purpose and preview the reading. Then, you choose an appropriate reading strategy.

Here is a list of the key strategies used in this handbook.

Almanac

Close Reading

When you read something slowly and carefully, word by word and line by line, you are "close reading." In close reading, your goal is to examine one part of a reading in great detail to make sure you understand its full meaning.

Using the Strategy

Close reading works best with short readings, such as poems, speeches, or key passages in longer works. Whenever you aren't sure about the meaning of an important passage, close reading can help.

Here's how to use this strategy:

1. Select a Passage
As you read through a selection, choose a few passages that call for more careful study. Mark these passages with a highlighter or sticky notes. Or, you can copy them as direct quotes into a Double-entry Journal.

2. Read the Passage
Examine the passage you selected word by word. Ask yourself questions and record your thoughts in the Double-entry Journal. You might ask questions like these:

- Why did the writer use this word?
- Why does the writer mention this point?
- What is the importance of this statement?
- What is special or unusual about these words?
- What does this passage mean?

3. Make Inferences

As you think about the passage, make inferences about what you think it means. Put what you've read with what you already know and ask a question or draw a conclusion.

For example, read the Double-entry Journal below. It uses close reading with some sentences from the novel *Skylark* by Patricia MacLachlan.

DOUBLE-ENTRY JOURNAL

QUOTES	MY THOUGHTS
"Sarah had written one word in the prairie dirt. Sarah."	I wonder why she wrote her own name? Is it important that she wrote her name in the dirt?
"But the prairie is home, the sky so big it takes your breath away, the land like a giant quilt tossed out."	The prairie sounds beautiful and rich. You get a good feeling from this part.

This strategy helps you "create meaning." Through a close and very careful reading, you see what you can learn from each word and sentence.

DEFINITION

Close reading means reading something slowly and carefully, word by word, line by line, and sentence by sentence. With close reading, you assume that every word you read is important and ask yourself why the author wrote it that way.

Almanac

Looking for Cause and Effect

When you read about *why* an event happened or *why* a person did something, you're reading about cause and effect. The "cause" is the event that happened first. The "effect" is the event or events that resulted from that cause.

Using the Strategy

You'll find cause-effect relationships in history and science textbooks, in news stories, and in biographies and auto-biographies. As you read about people, events, and scientific facts, ask yourself *why*. Try to see why a certain cause might lead to certain effects.

Here's how to use this strategy:

1. Read and Make Notes
Read the selection from beginning to end. Watch for cause-effect relationships, noting them with a highlighter or on sticky notes.

2. Use an Organizer
After reading, create a graphic organizer to show the causes and effects. Reflect on the events you read about and how the events are related to each other. Write the causes (or what happens first) in the organizer. Then write what came next, or resulted, from them.

Here are examples of two kinds of Cause-Effect Organizers that you can make.

CAUSE-EFFECT ORGANIZERS

ONE CAUSE, SEVERAL EFFECTS

CAUSE

In 1773, England taxed the tea sold to American colonies.

EFFECTS

Colonists got angry at the King of England.

In the Boston Tea Party, colonists dressed like Indians dumped tea into Boston Harbor.

The colonies moved closer to rebellion.

SEVERAL CAUSES, ONE EFFECT

CAUSES

Spring has arrived with warmer, sunny weather.

Mrs. Potter plants seeds in her garden.

It rains almost every week.

EFFECT

Mrs. Potter's garden is in bloom.

DEFINITION

Looking for **cause and effect** means focusing on the relationship in which one event brings about another. The "cause" is the event or situation that happens first. The "effect" is the event or events that happen as a result of the cause.

Almanac

525

Note-taking

Taking notes helps you understand and remember what you're reading. Good readers take notes before, during, and after reading a selection. As they read, they watch for important parts of the text and write them down. The act of writing something down helps you to remember it.

Using the Strategy

When you take notes while reading, choose the method that seems most appropriate. Here are three types of note-taking.

1. Summary Notes

Use Summary Notes to keep track of the most important details, terms, or events. Chapter-by-chapter notes work well with longer readings, such as novels, plays, and textbooks.

SUMMARY NOTES

Chapter 1: "Factories Bring Change"

DATES AND PLACES	NAMES
• 1789, England • Rhode Island	• Samuel Slater knows how to build cotton-spinning machines (and wants to go to the U.S.)
PROBLEM	OUTCOME
• The English didn't want countries to have or know about their cotton-spinning machines. • Workers were discouraged from sharing the plans for building their machines.	• Slater dresses up as a farmer and sails for the U.S. • He carries in his head the plans for building a cotton-spinning machine.

2. Timeline

Use this type of notes to keep track of the order of events and the dates on which they occurred.

TIMELINE

Lewis and Clark Expedition explores route to the west.	United States claims Texas.	Mexican and American War fought.	Homestead Act passed and settlers go west.
1804–06	1843	1846–48	1862

3. Key Word Notes

Use Key Word Notes to collect information about major topics. In the left column, write key words or ideas. In the right-hand column, write notes related to those key words.

KEY WORD NOTES

KEY WORDS	NOTES FROM "FACTORIES BRING CHANGE"
Rhode Island	location of Slater's first cotton-spinning mill
Samuel Slater	made fast, water-powered machines to help bring down the cost of making yarn
steam engines	allowed factories to be built away from rivers

DEFINITION

Note-taking is a way of recording key information to help you remember facts and details from a reading or from class. Writing down information when you read helps you understand and remember it.

Almanac

Paraphrasing

When you paraphrase, you use your own words to tell about what you have read, seen, or heard. Paraphrasing can help whenever you're having trouble understanding a written passage or a graphic.

Using the Strategy

Use paraphrasing to help you understand any reading or graphics, such as maps, charts, diagrams, and pictures. Paraphrasing works well with poetry, too.

Here's how to use this strategy with a written passage.

1. Preview the Reading
Glance through the reading to get an overview.
As you preview, ask yourself questions like these:

■ What is the main subject of this selection?

■ What clues hint at the meaning or main idea?

■ What facts or details stand out?

2. Read and Take Notes
Then, read the selection carefully. Take notes in the margins, on sticky notes, or in a notebook. You already know the subject of the reading. Now find three or four things that the author has to say about it. You might use a Web to keep track of your notes.

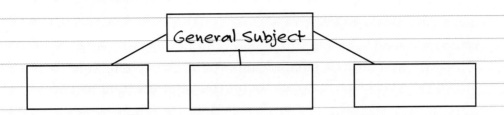

WEB

General Subject

3. State in Your Own Words

Now paraphrase what you've read. The key part of paraphrasing is *using your own words*. Think of paraphrasing as explaining something to a friend or to someone in your family. Talk through what you would say. Most of the words should be your own. Use quotation marks around any key phrases that you use from the source. Here is how one reader paraphrased a line from a poem by Alfred, Lord Tennyson.

PARAPHRASE CHART

LINE	MY PARAPHRASE
"He clasps the crag with crooked hands...!"	He uses his claws to hang on tightly to the rock.
MY THOUGHTS	
I like this description of an eagle on a mountain.	

HOW TO PARAPHRASE A GRAPHIC

When paraphrasing a graphic, follow these steps:

1. Study the graph, table, photo, or cartoon.
2. Read any text, such as the title or headings.
3. Write a one-sentence summary of it, using your own words.

DEFINITION

Paraphrasing is using your own words to describe what you have read, seen, or heard.

Questioning the Author

When you read, you might wonder why an author wrote in a particular way or created these particular characters. Of course, you can't just call the author and ask him or her your questions. But you can look in the reading selection for clues about the author's decisions.

Using the Strategy

The strategy of questioning the author works with all types of readings, both fiction and nonfiction.

1. Ask Yourself Questions

While reading, imagine that the author is sitting in front of you. Write down questions that you'd ask him or her about the reading. You might ask questions like these:

- What is the author trying to teach me or say to me?
- Why did the author include *that* event, *that* detail, or *that* character?
- How does this compare with what the author said earlier?
- What am I supposed to think of this?
- What point is the author trying to make?
- Why did the author say it that way?
- What does that statement mean?
- Why did the author begin this way?
- Why did the author choose this title?
- How am I supposed to feel after I read this?

2. Infer the Answers

The author won't answer your questions, but he or she probably has left clues in the reading that can help you to make inferences about the answers.

As you read, think about your questions and anything you learn from the reading that relates to them. Take the information you learned from the reading and what your common sense tells you. What answer does all this suggest? Some questions might be tough to answer, but answer them the best you can.

3. Evaluate the Author's Purpose

After reading, ask yourself what the author's purpose was and how well it was met. First, decide whether you think that the author intended to explain something, to entertain, to persuade, or to teach. Then, sum up your own personal response to the reading.

EVALUATE THE AUTHOR'S PURPOSE

If the Author's Purpose Was to . . .	Then Ask Yourself:
Explain	Did I learn something from the reading?
Entertain	Did this reading entertain me? Would I tell others to read it?
Persuade	Did this reading change my mind about something?
Teach	Did the reading teach me something new or interesting?

DEFINITION

Questioning the author means asking questions of the author during reading and inferring why he or she made those specific choices as a writer.

Almanac

531

Reading Critically

When you read critically, you first understand and then evaluate the point a writer is making. You grasp the writer's argument and then evaluate the argument itself.

Critical readers know that usually there are two sides to a story and that sometimes readers aren't given the whole story. As they read, critical readers ask themselves questions such as these:

- What is missing here?
- Has the author considered both sides of the question?
- How believable or good is this evidence?
- How well has the writer supported the point of view?

Using the Strategy

Reading critically works especially well with newspaper and magazine articles and any type of persuasive writing. Whenever a writer wants to change your mind about something, that's the time to read critically.

1. Start with Questions

Before you read, make a list of critical reading questions:

- What is the main idea or viewpoint?
- How does the author support the main idea with evidence?
- How authoritative and reliable are the sources?
- Is the evidence convincing?
- What's the other side of the story?

2. Read the Selection

As you read, look for answers to your critical reading questions. Be sure to pick out the author's main idea and note the supporting evidence. Think about whether the evidence is reliable, and make notes about your ideas in your notebook or on sticky notes.

3. Evaluate What You've Read

A Critical Reading Chart can help you look closely at an argument or point of view to decide whether or not you can believe what you've read. Here's a Critical Reading Chart one reader made to evaluate an article that suggested that kids should go to school all year.

CRITICAL READING CHART

QUESTION	MY THOUGHTS
1. Is the main idea or viewpoint clear?	Yes.
2. What evidence is presented?	a. Students waste summer. b. Other countries do it. c. It will help test scores.
3. Are the sources reliable?	Writer gives no sources, specific information, or proof.
4. Is the evidence convincing?	not very
5. Is there another side to the story?	Yes, mine! Kids need a break.

DEFINITION

Reading critically means first finding and then evaluating the author's main idea or viewpoint. Critical reading means testing the evidence to see whether it supports the author's viewpoint and is authoritative and reliable.

Almanac

Skimming

When you skim, you glance through a selection looking for specific words and phrases. Use skimming when you're previewing a selection, when reading a test, or when rereading for specific information.

Using the Strategy

Skimming works well with almost any kind of reading. It is especially helpful when a reading is long and challenging. But skimming is essential for previewing, taking a test, and rereading.

Here's how to use this strategy:

1. How to Skim for General Ideas
When skimming for general ideas, glance over the whole text to get a general sense of the subject. Look for these things:

- titles and headings
- repeated words
- names, dates, and places
- words in boldface type
- first and last paragraphs
- illustrations, photographs, and their captions

2. How to Skim for Specific Information
Often as a reader you're hunting for one tiny bit of information in a sea of details. When you need a single fact or name in an article, skimming will help. Read only for the word or name you need to find. Ignore everything else. Instead, zero in only on the information you need.

3. How to Skim for Tests

When answering test questions, you need to find key words in the test question and then skim for them in the reading selection. Try this example:

SAMPLE QUESTION

1. Who was the leader of the Plymouth Colony?
   A. Benjamin Franklin
   B. Betsy Ross
   C. George Washington
   D. John Smith

NOTE
Key words

What are the most important words in the question? If a question asks about the leader of the Plymouth Colony, go back to the test passage and skim until you find the words *leader* or *Plymouth Colony*. These are the key words. Then skim until you find a name and the word *leader* nearby. You might also skim the test passage looking for the names used in the answers. Skimming for names is easy because they begin with a capital letter.

DEFINITION

Skimming means glancing quickly through a selection, looking for specific words or phrases. When you skim, you quickly read through a selection to get a sense of the topics and important information.

Summarizing

When you summarize, you retell the main events or ideas in a selection using your own words. With this strategy, you leave out all of the smaller details and focus on the main points.

Using the Strategy

Summarizing works well for any type of reading. The key to summarizing is knowing what you want to find and being able to pick out the main points or ideas. Remember, a summary should be much shorter than the reading itself.

Here's how to use this strategy:

1. Summarizing Fiction and Drama

To sum up a folktale, story, novel, or play, first read the selection all the way through. As you read, take notes with a tool such as a Story Organizer or a Fiction Organizer. A good summary will include key information for each part of the organizer.

STORY ORGANIZER

TITLE:		
BEGINNING	MIDDLE	END

FICTION ORGANIZER

CHARACTERS

SETTING

AUTHOR AND TITLE

PLOT

THEME

2. Summarizing Nonfiction

To summarize nonfiction readings such as a news story, essay, or biography, first read the selection. Remember that a nonfiction selection usually has three parts: introduction, body, and conclusion.

A Nonfiction Organizer can help focus you on the important information for your summary.

NONFICTION ORGANIZER

SUBJECT
INTRODUCTION
BODY
CONCLUSION

DEFINITION

Summarizing means telling the main events or ideas in a selection in your own words.

Synthesizing

When you synthesize, you look at a number of parts of a text and pull them together. Your goal is to learn how they affect the reading as a whole. Think of synthesizing as completing a jigsaw puzzle. You piece together different parts of a reading into a single, unified picture.

Using the Strategy

You can use synthesizing with almost any kind of text, fiction or nonfiction. Synthesizing can be especially helpful with long works. It helps you to keep track of details from the beginning to the end of a reading in a number of areas, such as characters, plot, setting, and style.

Here's how to use this strategy:

1. Using Synthesizing with Fiction

When evaluating a folktale, story, novel, or play, you look at different parts of a story. You need to look at plot, characters, setting, and so forth. Synthesizing can help you to pull these elements together and show their connections. For example, you can also use synthesizing to look closely at how a character is described throughout a novel.

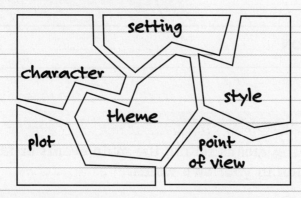

SYNTHESIZING FICTION

setting

character

style

theme

plot

point of view

2. Using Synthesizing with Nonfiction

When reading nonfiction, you connect details into a picture that makes sense. For example with a news story, you're interested in finding the subject and facts about the subject— *who, what, when, where, why,* and *how.* Your goal in synthesizing is to pull these details together into a clear overall picture.

SYNTHESIZING NONFICTION

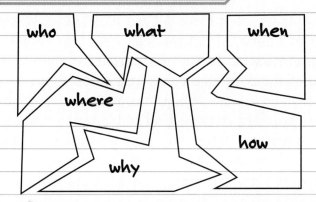

who   what   when

where

how

why

With nonfiction, such as a biography, you can pull together events into a Timeline.

TIMELINE

1723	1730	1753	1776
Ben Franklin leaves Boston at 17.	Franklin marries Deborah Read.	Franklin becomes known as a scientist and inventor.	Franklin helps write Declaration of Independence.

DEFINITION

Synthesizing means thinking about a number of elements in a selection, pulling them together, and deciding how they affect the subject or selection as a whole.

Almanac

Using Graphic Organizers

Graphic organizers are "word pictures." A graphic organizer arranges details in a visual form, which can make them easier to understand and remember.

Using the Strategy

Graphic organizers work for any type of reading. When you read fiction or drama, organizers can help you keep track of all the different events in the plot. Organizers are also useful for showing changes in characters and clues about setting, point of view, and theme. When you read poetry, organizers can help you sort out details, find hidden meanings, and record your reactions. When you read textbooks or nonfiction, organizers can help you sort through and record information, see relationships between facts, and evaluate evidence.

1. Graphic Organizers for Fiction

Use a Character Map to take notes on main characters you read about in fiction or drama. A Character Map helps you to view a character from many points of view.

CHARACTER MAP

WHAT CHARACTER SAYS AND DOES	WHAT OTHERS THINK ABOUT THE CHARACTER
HOW CHARACTER LOOKS AND FEELS	HOW I FEEL ABOUT THE CHARACTER

NAME

2. Graphic Organizers for Nonfiction

Filling in a 5 W's and H Organizer helps you to get key information from a magazine article, news story, or other nonfiction reading. After you answer questions beginning with *who, what, when, where, why,* and *how,* you'll have all of the key facts about the subject.

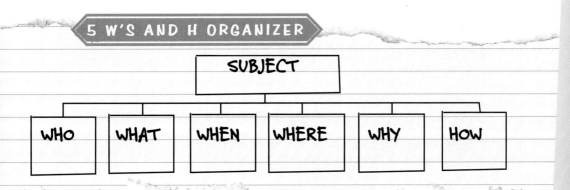

3. Graphic Organizers for Textbooks

A Concept Map works well for the big ideas or terms in your textbooks. You write the term or idea in the center, and then write related examples, definitions, and steps around it.

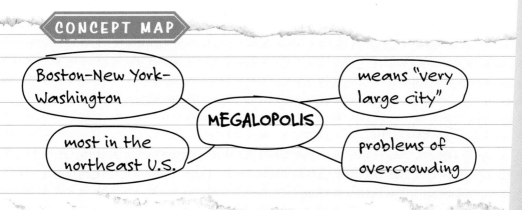

Try different kinds of organizers as you read. Then, stick with the ones that work best for you.

DEFINITION

Graphic organizers are word pictures. They are diagrams that can help you understand what you read.

Almanac

541

Visualizing and Thinking Aloud

Sometimes you need to "see" something in your mind or say it out loud in order to understand it. This is visualizing and thinking out loud. This strategy works with both fiction and nonfiction—from figuring out math problems to imagining what a setting looks like.

For example, the strategy works well with word problems.

SAMPLE WORD PROBLEM

In the first week of April, Juan's class used the computer lab for 30 minutes on Monday and 30 minutes on Wednesday. In the second week, they used it 40 minutes on each of those days. In the third week, they didn't use the computer lab at all. In the fourth week, they used the lab for 30 minutes each on Monday, Wednesday, and Friday. How many minutes did Juan's class use the computer lab in April?

NOTE
Key facts

Visualizing
Try to make mental pictures as you read the problem. Focus on the mental pictures you see as you read. Then draw an image of what you see.

Thinking Aloud
When you think aloud, you talk to yourself about what you're reading. This helps you clarify your thinking and go step by step. Thinking aloud and visualizing go together. When you do one, it helps if you also do the other.

Using the Strategy

You can use visualizing and thinking aloud with any kind of text. It can help you to picture settings and characters in fiction, to diagram facts, and to block out solutions to math problems.

Follow these steps:

1. Read and Sketch

Read the word problem again carefully. Then, use your notebook to draw a quick sketch.

VISUALIZING

	M	T	W	Th	F	TOTALS
week 1	30		30			60 min.
week 2	40		40			80 min.
week 3						
week 4	30		30		30	90 min.

$60 + 80 + 90 =$
230 minutes

2. Listen to Your Thoughts

As you draw what you visualize, talk to yourself about what you're doing. Explaining it to yourself helps you make better sense of it.

3. Review and Reflect

Then, after reading, your sketches will remind you about important details and help you check that you did your work carefully.

DEFINITION

Visualizing and thinking aloud involves making a mental picture of the words on the page and talking through ideas about what you're reading.

Almanac

543

Reading Tools

When you want to do a good job, the right tools can make a big difference. Think of this part of the handbook as your toolkit. As you read, you can use these tools to organize, clarify, and interpret what you're reading.

Get to know these reading tools so you can always choose the best tool for the job at hand.

Reading Tools

ARGUMENT CHART

Use an Argument Chart to evaluate an author's argument in a speech, magazine article, or editorial.

Viewpoint	Support	Opposing Viewpoint
Put the writer's viewpoint here.	*Write three to four ways the writer supports the position here.*	*Note whether the writer considers other viewpoints here.*

See an example on page 172.

CAUSE-EFFECT ORGANIZER

A Cause-Effect Organizer helps you to determine causes and their related effects. The causes can be listed first, followed by effects. Or the effects can be listed first, followed by causes.

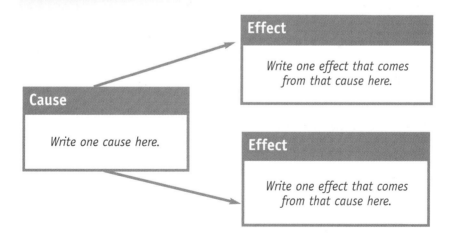

See an example on page 183.

CHARACTER DEVELOPMENT CHART

A Character Development Chart tracks ways that characters change during a story, play, or novel. It's an easy way to see the character's changes that can suggest the work's theme.

Beginning	Middle	End
Write what the main character is like at the beginning.	*Write what the character is like in the middle of the story.*	*Note how the character is at the end of the story here.*

Possible Themes:	
	Write one or two ideas about the theme here.

See an example on page 248.

CHARACTER MAP

A Character Map gives you a detailed picture of a single character from a story, play, or novel. With this tool, you look at the character from several points of view.

Create an organizer with four boxes.

What character says and does	What others think about character
Write one to two key things the character says here.	*Write what other characters think about him or her here.*

Name

How character looks and feels	How I feel about character
Write how the character looks and feels here.	*Write how you as a reader feel about the character here.*

See an example on page 245.

CLASS AND TEXT NOTES

Class and Text Notes pull together what your teacher says in class (class notes) with what you've read in the textbook (text notes). Use this tool whenever you want to organize information from these two sources.

Class Notes	Text Notes
Note key ideas from class here.	*Write notes you took from reading the textbook here.*

See an example on page 80.

CONCEPT MAP

A Concept Map is a great tool for organizing important ideas with lots of elements—especially big topics or ideas (for example, *life cycle, food chain,* or *Constitution*).

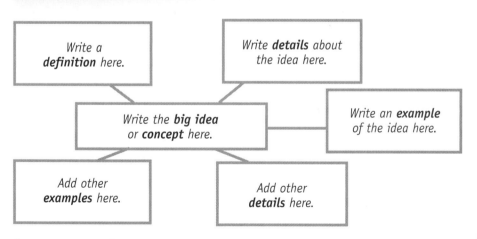

See an example on page 510.

CRITICAL READING CHART

A Critical Reading Chart helps you analyze the facts, opinions, evidence, and viewpoint in a reading.

1. Is the main idea or viewpoint clear?	*Record the main point here.*
2. What evidence is presented?	*Note the evidence here.*
3. Are the sources authoritative and reliable?	*List and comment on sources here.*
4. Is the evidence convincing?	*Evaluate the evidence here.*
5. Is there another side of the story?	*Write another viewpoint here.*

Create an organizer with these five questions.

See an example on page 142.

DOUBLE-ENTRY JOURNAL

A Double-entry Journal is a key tool for understanding and making inferences about part of a reading. Use the first column to record lines from the reading—ideas, quotes, or an important passage. Use the second column to record your own thoughts, ideas, or feelings about each one.

Quotes	My Thoughts
Write a key quote or several lines here.	*Write what you think or feel about the lines of the text here.*

See an example on page 302.

FICTION ORGANIZER

A Fiction Organizer gives you a great tool for keeping track of all of the key information in a story, play, or novel. Fill in the information from the novel or story in the boxes of the organizer below.

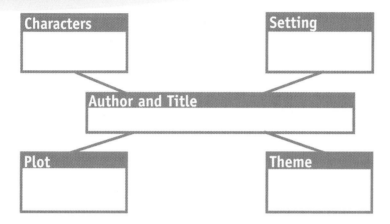

See an example on page 241.

5 W'S AND H ORGANIZER

Use the 5 W's and H Organizer to gather key information from any reading. Once you've answered questions that begin with *who*, *what*, *when*, *where*, *why*, and *how*, you'll have learned the most important information about a subject.

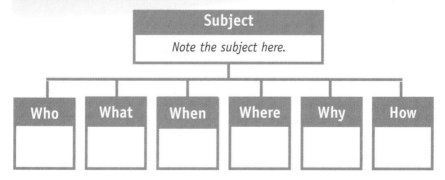

Label each box below the subject with one of the 5 W's and the H.
Write notes that answer each question in the boxes.

See an example on page 149.

INFERENCE CHART

An Inference Chart gives you a good way to look more closely at a difficult passage, character, or description. This chart can help you to "read between the lines," draw conclusions, and make inferences about what you've read.

Text	What I Conclude
Write part of the text, a detail, or an event here.	*Write what conclusions you draw about the meaning of it here.*

See an example on page 137.

KEY WORD OR TOPIC NOTES

Key Word or Topic Notes help you list the main ideas from your reading and make notes as you go. Use this tool to take notes on nonfiction, such as textbooks, essays, and news stories.

Divide your notebook into two columns. Make the right side wider than the left side.

Key Words or Topics	Notes
Note the key words or main topics here. These are the main things to study.	*Take notes about each key word or topic here.*

See an example on page 99.

K-W-L CHART

With nonfiction, use a K-W-L Chart. It can help you record what you already know about a subject and what you want to know. After reading, use it to write down what you've learned.

Divide the paper in your notebook into three columns.

What I Know	What I Want to Know	What I Learned
Jot down what you already know about the topic here.	*Write two to four questions you have about the topic here.*	*Write important information and answers to your questions after you read here.*

See an example on page 68.

MAIN IDEA ORGANIZER

With a Main Idea Organizer, you record important ideas and their supporting details. This tool works best with nonfiction, such as textbooks, biographies, magazine and newspaper articles, and persuasive writing.

Title	*Write the title here.*	
Main Idea	*Write what you think is the biggest, most important idea here.*	
Detail	**Detail**	**Detail**
Write the first detail here.	*Write another detail here.*	*Write another detail here.*
Conclusion	*Finally, write the conclusion the author makes here.*	

See an example on page 151.

NONFICTION ORGANIZER

A Nonfiction Organizer helps you sort out what you learn from reading essays, articles, and editorials. This organizer divides works into three parts: introduction, body, and conclusion.

Title	Write the title here.
Subject	Write the general subject here.
Introduction	Describe the ideas in the first one or two paragraphs here.
Body	Write three or four details, points, or topics from the middle paragraphs here.
Conclusion	Note what happens or what the author says in the last paragraph or two here.

See an example on page 170.

PARAPHRASE CHART

A Paraphrase Chart helps you to think through what a reading means. Use this tool with readings that are hard to understand. Record a few lines from the reading. Then, put what those words mean into your own words. Last, write what you think and feel about the passage.

Lines	My Paraphrase
Write two or three lines or facts from a text here.	Tell in your own words what these lines mean here.

My Thoughts
Note your own ideas or reaction.

See an example on page 308.

PLOT DIAGRAM

A Plot Diagram helps you to see the main plot stages of a folktale, story, novel, or play. It highlights the five main parts of a fictional plot—exposition, rising action, climax, falling action, and resolution.

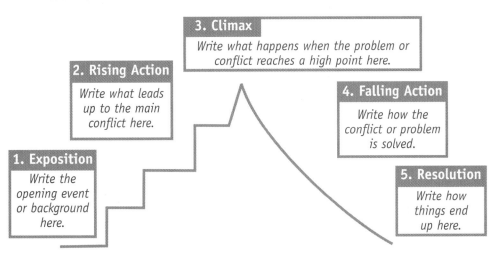

3. Climax
Write what happens when the problem or conflict reaches a high point here.

2. Rising Action
Write what leads up to the main conflict here.

4. Falling Action
Write how the conflict or problem is solved.

1. Exposition
Write the opening event or background here.

5. Resolution
Write how things end up here.

See an example on page 220.

PROCESS NOTES

Process Notes work well whenever you want to keep track of a series of steps, stages, or events. This tool can be valuable when you're reading science or history. It helps you keep track of how things develop or work.

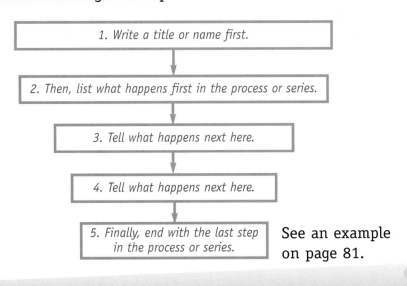

1. Write a title or name first.

2. Then, list what happens first in the process or series.

3. Tell what happens next here.

4. Tell what happens next here.

5. Finally, end with the last step in the process or series.

See an example on page 81.

Almanac

553

SETTING CHART

A Setting Chart is a tool to help you keep track of when and where something happened in a major scene or setting.

Title	Write the title here.
Clues about Time	**Clues about Place**
Write details about the time here—dates, seasons, years, general time periods, and so on.	Write details about where the story is happening here—places, names, cities, states, countries, and so on.

See an example on page 234.

STORYBOARD

A Storyboard is a series of drawings that gives you a way of retelling the events of a folktale, story, novel, or play. It works best for longer works that have a lot of events. The Storyboard helps you remember both what happened and the order in which it happened.

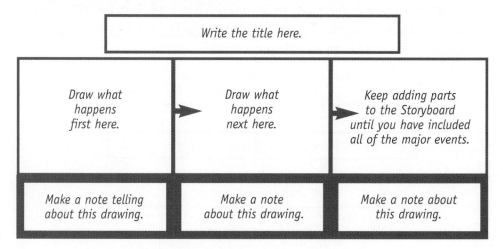

See an example on page 265.

STORY ORGANIZER

With the Story Organizer, you break down the events of a plot into beginning, middle, and end. By looking at a story in these three stages, you get a better sense of the plot and what changes.

Write the title here.		

Beginning	Middle	End
Write what happens first here.	*Write what happens in the middle of the story here.*	*Write what happens at the end of the story here.*

See an example on page 219.

STORY STRING

A Story String links together events so that you can keep track of what's going on. Use it with a folktale, story, play, or novel. It is especially useful when the plot has a lot of twists and turns.

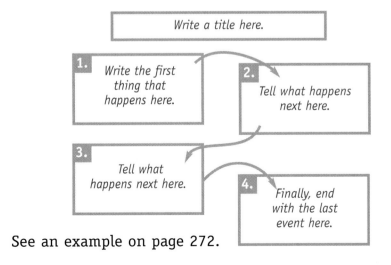

Write a title here.

1. *Write the first thing that happens here.*

2. *Tell what happens next here.*

3. *Tell what happens next here.*

4. *Finally, end with the last event here.*

See an example on page 272.

Almanac

SUMMARY NOTES

Summary Notes help you to focus on the most important parts of a reading. You can write a summary for a single page, a poem, a graphic, a scene in a play, or a textbook chapter.

Title	Write the subject here.
Main Point	Write what you think is the main point or idea here.
1.	
2.	List three to four smaller, related points that support the main idea here.
3.	

See an example on page 86.

THEME DIAGRAM

A Theme Diagram can be a big help when you're trying to figure out the theme of a folktale, story, novel, or play. Start by recording the work's major topics. Then, look for what characters and plot tell you about the topics. Finally, analyze the details and draw conclusions about the theme.

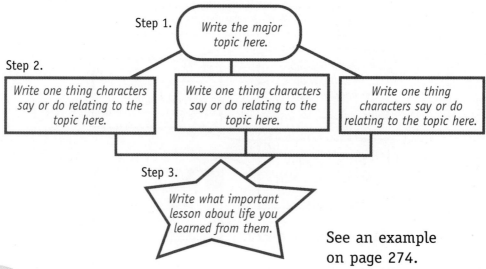

Step 1. *Write the major topic here.*

Step 2.
Write one thing characters say or do relating to the topic here.
Write one thing characters say or do relating to the topic here.
Write one thing characters say or do relating to the topic here.

Step 3.
Write what important lesson about life you learned from them.

See an example on page 274.

THINKING TREE

A Thinking Tree is a great way to organize information as you read. It connects ideas and details into different branches, helping you to see the relationships among them.

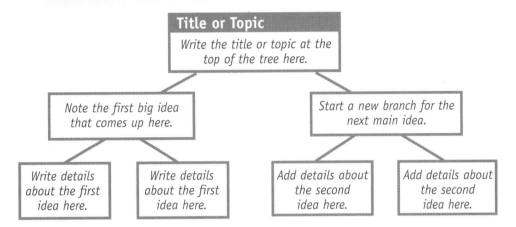

See an example on page 140.

TIMELINE

Use a Timeline to keep track of a series of events. Because it lists events in time order, a Timeline gives you a clear idea of what happened and when it happened. It is especially useful when the reading is jumping back and forth in time.

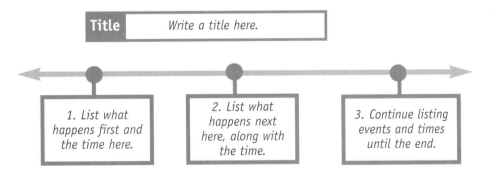

See an example on page 64.

Almanac

TWO PER LINE

A Two Per Line organizer can help you to understand poetry or fiction. First, choose a key paragraph or passage and write it in the first column. Mark the two most important words in each line. In the second column, write your ideas about what the two words mean.

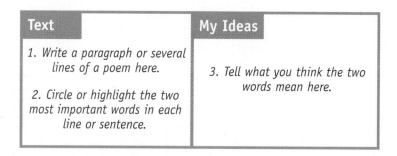

Text	My Ideas
1. Write a paragraph or several lines of a poem here. 2. Circle or highlight the two most important words in each line or sentence.	3. Tell what you think the two words mean here.

See an example on page 303.

VENN DIAGRAM

A Venn Diagram helps you to compare two things. Use it as a way to understand what is similar and different about two characters, ideas, or works.

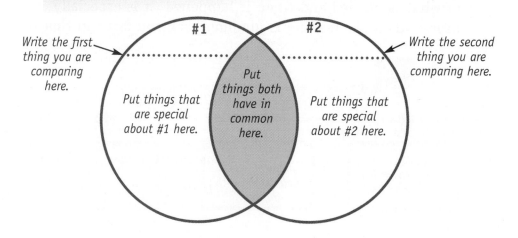

See an example on page 266.

WEB

A Web is an excellent, all-purpose note-taking tool. It's useful for any type of reading. Webs help you to organize information and to brainstorm ideas.

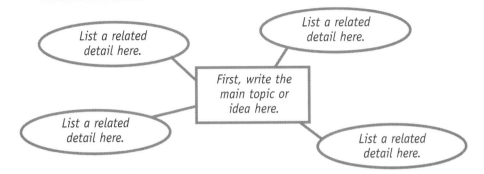

See an example on page 65.

WEBSITE PROFILER

A Website Profiler helps you figure out how much you should trust a particular website. It pulls together information on the site, its sponsor, the date it was last updated, its point of view, its level of expertise, and your reaction to it.

Name (URL)	
Write the name and URL here.	
Sponsor	**Date**
Tell who created or pays for the site here.	Note when the site was last updated here.
Point of View	**Expertise**
Write the site's point of view here.	Tell where the information on the site comes from here.
Reaction	
List your thoughts about and reaction to the site here.	

See an example on page 397.

Word Parts:

Prefixes, Suffixes, and Roots

Prefixes

Prefixes are word parts that create a new meaning when added to the beginning of a root or base word.

Prefixes	Meanings	Examples
a-	not, without	apart, avoid
ab-	away from	absent, abnormal
ad-	to, toward, against	addition, admire
anti-	against, opposite	antiwar, antidote
arch-	original, chief	archbishop, archangel
auto-	self	automobile, automatic
be-	to cause, become	beneath, befriend
bi-	two	bilevel, bicycle
co-	together	coworker, cooperate
con-	with, together	construct, confide
counter-	against	counteract, counterspy
de-	down, away from	descend, detract
dis-	the reverse of	disagree, disable
en-	to cause, provide	enlighten, enable
ex-	out of, away from	expel, external
extra-	outside, beyond	extracurricular, extraordinary
fore-	previously, in front of	forefathers, forefront
il-	not	illegal, illegitimate
im-	not	immovable, immobile
in-	not	incapable, incorrect
inter-	between	interstate, interview
ir-	not	irregular, irresponsible
mal-	bad	malnutrition, maladjusted
micro-	small	microwave, microscope
mid-	middle	midterm, midtown

Prefixes	Meanings	Examples
mis-	wrongly, badly	mistake, mistrust
non-	not, against	nonsense, nonfiction
post-	after, later	postscript, postwar
pre-	earlier, before	prejudge, preview
pro-	in favor of	proclaim, project
re-	back, again	reappear, return
sub-	under, less than	subhead, subzero
trans-	across, through	transport, transact
tri-	three	triangle, tricycle
un-	not, reverse of	unaware, unsafe
under-	below, beneath	underground, underwear
uni-	single, one	unicycle, uniform

Suffixes

Suffixes are combinations of letters (such as -*ance*) or single letters (such as -*y*) that are added to the end of a base word. Here are some examples of common suffixes and the parts of speech that they form.

Suffixes that form nouns	Examples
-age	garbage, luggage
-al	funeral, portal
-ance	reluctance, allowance
-ant	claimant, attendant
-ee	devotee, employee
-ence	independence, audience
-ent	dependent, student
-er, -or, -ar	peddler, monitor, cellar
-ess	actress, address
-ette, -et	kitchenette, booklet
-hood	neighborhood, statehood
-ian, -ion	musician, information
-ism	Buddhism, communism
-ist	journalist, novelist
-logy	psychology, biology
-ment	judgment, amusement
-ness	kindness, happiness
-ure	future, creature

Almanac

Suffixes that form adjectives	Examples
-able	dependable, readable
-al	personal, optional
-er	messier, better
-est	cutest, smartest
-ful	disdainful, hopeful
-ible	edible, incredible
-ic	bionic, tonic
-ical	historical, tropical
-ish	bluish, skittish
-ive	divisive, pensive
-less	childless, mindless
-ous	joyous, religious
-some	loathsome, worrisome
-y	tasty, worthy

Suffixes that form adverbs	Examples
-erly	easterly, westerly
-fully	beautifully, dutifully
-ly	angrily, slowly
-ward	backward, forward
-ways	sideways, always
-wise	likewise, clockwise

Suffixes that create verb forms	Examples
-ate	congratulate, concentrate
-ed	joked, ripped
-en	brighten, eaten
-fy, -ify	personify, solidify
-ing	frightening, stunning
-ize, -yze	familiarize, analyze
-n	known, grown

Greek and Latin Roots

Knowing the meanings of common Greek and Latin roots can help you figure out the meaning of dozens of related words.

Roots	Origins	Meanings	Examples
act	Latin	do	action, transact
aero	Greek	air	aerobics, aerate
alt	Latin	high	altitude, alto
amo	Latin	love	amorous, enamored
anim	Latin	life, spirit	animate, animal
ann, enn	Latin	year	annual, biennial
aqua	Latin	water	aquatic, aquarium
astro, astr	Greek	star	asteroid, astronaut
aud	Latin	hear	audio, auditorium
bio	Greek	life	biology, biosphere
cam	Latin	field	campus, campaign
cand	Latin	glow, white	candle, candidate
cardi	Greek	heart	cardiac, cardiogram
cede, ceed	Latin	go, yield	precede, succeed
ceive, cept	Latin	take, receive	receive, accept
centr	Latin	center	central, eccentric
cert	Latin	sure	certain, certify
chron	Greek	time	chronic, chronicle
claim, clam	Latin	shout	exclaim, clamor
clar	Latin	clear	clarity, declare
commun	Latin	common	communal, commune
cred	Latin	believe	credit, incredible
cur	Latin	care	cure, manicure
cycl	Greek	circle, ring	bicycle, cyclone
dem	Greek	people	democrat, epidemic
dic	Latin	say, tell	dictionary, predict
div	Latin	separate	divide, division
domin	Latin	rule	dominate, dominion
duc	Latin	lead	conduct, educate
fac, fact	Latin	do, make	factory, manufacture
firm	Latin	strong	affirm, confirm
form	Latin	shape	transform, uniform
gen	Greek	birth, race	generate, generous

Roots	Origins	Meanings	Examples
geo	Greek	earth	geography, geology
grad	Latin	step, stage	grade, gradual
gram	Greek	letter	grammar, telegram
graph	Greek	write	autograph, graphic
grat	Latin	pleasing	gratify, ungrateful
hosp, host	Latin	host	hospital, hostess
hydr	Greek	water	hydrant, hydroelectric
imag	Latin	likeness	image, imagery
jud, jur, jus	Latin	law	judge, jury, justice
liber	Latin	free	liberate, liberty
loc	Latin	place	locate, location
luna	Latin	moon	lunar, lunatic
man	Latin	hand	manual, manipulate
mater, matr	Latin	mother	maternal, matron
mech	Greek	machine	mechanic, mechanize
mem	Latin	mindful of	memory, remember
meter	Greek	measure	diameter, centimeter
migr	Latin	depart	migrate, migrant
miss, mit	Latin	send	missile, submit
mob	Latin	move	automobile, mobility
narr	Latin	tell	narrate, narrative
nat	Latin	born	nation, native
nav	Latin	ship	naval, navigate
not	Latin	mark	denote, note
nun, noun	Latin	declare	enunciate, announce
opt	Latin	best	optimal, optimist
ord	Latin	row	order, ordinal
orig	Latin	be born	origin, originality
path	Greek	feeling	pathetic, sympathy
phon	Latin	sound	telephone, phonics
photo	Greek	light	telephoto, photograph
phys	Greek	nature	physical, physician
poli	Greek	city	metropolis, police
pop	Latin	people	populace, popular
port	Latin	carry	import, porter
psych	Greek	mind	psyche, psychology

Roots	Origins	Meanings	Examples
put	Latin	think	deputy, computer
ques	Latin	ask, seek	quest, question
rad	Latin	ray, spoke	radio, radius
scend	Latin	climb	ascend, transcend
sci	Latin	know	conscience, science
scrib, scrip	Latin	write	prescribe, script
sect	Latin	cut	dissect, intersect
sens	Latin	feel	sensation, senses
sign	Latin	mark	insignia, signal
sim	Latin	like	similar, simile
solv	Latin	loosen	solvent, resolve
son	Latin	sound	sonar, sonnet
spec	Latin	see	inspect, spectator
sta	Latin	stand	stationary, stagnant
struct	Latin	build	construct, instruct
sum	Latin	highest	summary, summit
tele	Greek	far off	telephone, telescope
ten	Latin	hold	tenant, tenure
terr	Latin	land	terrace, terrain
therm	Greek	heat	thermal, thermos
trib	Latin	give	contribute, tribute
var	Latin	different	variety, vary
vid	Latin	see	evidence, video
voc	Latin	call	vocabulary, vocal
void	Latin	empty	avoid, devoid

Acknowledgments

44, 109, 112, 121 From THIS IS MY COUNTRY in HOUGHTON MIFFLIN SOCIAL STUDIES by Armento et al. Copyright © 1997 by Houghton Mifflin Company. Reprinted by permission of Houghton Mifflin Company. All rights reserved.

46, 227-229, 231-233, 235, 237, 239 Used by permission of HarperCollins Publishers.

51, 60-62, 69-70, 428 From AMERICA WILL BE in HOUGHTON MIFFLIN SOCIAL STUDIES by Armento et al. Copyright © 1999 by Houghton Mifflin Company. Reprinted by permission of Houghton Mifflin Company. All rights reserved.

53, 176-179, 181-182 From LINCOLN: A Photobiography by Russell Freedman. Copyright © 1987 by Russell Freedman. Reprinted by permission of Clarion Books/Houghton Mifflin Company. All rights reserved.

54-55, 76-78, 84 Excerpt pp. A26-A28, D14 from SCOTT FORESMAN SCIENCE Grade 4 by Timothy Cooney et al. Copyright © 2000 by Addison-Wesley Educational Publishers Inc. (Reprinted by permission of Pearson Education, Inc.)

90-91, 96 From HOUGHTON MIFFLIN MATHEMATICS by Vogeli et al. Copyright © 2002 by Houghton Mifflin Company. Reprinted by permission of Houghton Mifflin Company. All rights reserved.

117, 120, 123, 125 From EXPLORE OUR LAND in WE THE PEOPLE, by Hartoonian et al. Copyright © 1997 by Houghton Mifflin Company. Reprinted by permission of Houghton Mifflin Company. All rights reserved.

118-119, 122, 124 Text from pages iv, A-1, A-2, A-4, and B-43 in HARCOURT SCIENCE, Grade 5. Copyright © 2000 by Harcourt, Inc., reprinted by permission of the publisher.

130-134, 137, 140 From JUNIOR SCHOLASTIC, April 10, 2000 issue. Copyright © 2000 by Scholastic Inc. Reprinted by permission of Scholastic Inc.

146-147, 152-153 From JUNIOR SCHOLASTIC, March 12, 2001 issue. Copyright © 2001 by Scholastic Inc. Reprinted by permission of Scholastic Inc.

159-161 Reprinted with permission from Stone Soup, the magazine by young writers and artists, © 2001 by Children's Art Foundation.

168 © Gurdeep Sareen. Reprinted by permission of the author.

189, 194 Courtesy of the San Francisco Bay Area Rapid Transit District (BART).

202 From THE NEW YORK TIMES UPFRONT, March 5, 2001. Copyright © 2001 by Scholastic Inc. Reprinted by permission of Scholastic Inc.

214-216, 221, 269-270 Reprinted by permission of Chelsea House Publishers.

243-247, 295, 500 From THE MIDNIGHT FOX by Betsy Byars, copyright © 1968 by Betsy Byars. Used by permission of Viking Penguin, an imprint of Penguin Putnam Books for Young Readers, a division of Penguin Putnam Inc.

255, 257-258, 293 From SALSA STORIES by Lulu Delacre. Copyright © 2000 by Lulu Delacre. Reprinted by permission of Scholastic Inc.

284, 289 Reprinted in part courtesy of BOOKSPAN. © 1982 by Joanna Cole.

300, 304-306 Copyright © 1981 by Evil Eye Music, Inc.

311, 314 Reproduced with permission of Curtis Brown Ltd, London, on behalf of Grace Nichols. Copyright Grace Nichols.

318, 321 Reprinted with the permission of Margaret K. McElderry Books, an imprint of Simon & Schuster Children's Publishing Division from THE RAINBOW HAND by Janet S. Wong. Copyright © 1999 by Janet S. Wong.

324-327 Text Copyright © 1993 by Jack Prelutsky

330 From WAY TO GO! Sports Poems by Lillian Morrison. Copyright © 2001. Published by Wordsong of Boyds Mills Press. Used by permission of Marian Reiner for the author.

331 Copyright © 1999 by X. J. Kennedy. Excerpt from THE 20th CENTURY CHILDREN'S POETRY TREASURY, published by Alfred A. Knopf. Reprinted by permission of Curtis Brown, Ltd.

332 Beetles, from GOOSE GRASS RHYMES by Monica Shannon, copyright 1930 by Doubleday, a division of Random House, Inc. Used by permission of Doubleday, a division of Random House, Inc.

333 Copyright © 1993 by Walter Dean Myers. Used by permission of HarperCollins Publishers.

334, 340 Text copyright © 1993 by David L. Harrison from Somebody Catch My Homework by David L. Harrison. Published by Wordsong/Boyds Mills Press, Inc. Reprinted by permission.

335 Text copyright © 1984 by Jack Prelutsky. Used by permission of HarperCollins Publishers.

336 From THE COLLECTED POEMS OF LANGSTON HUGHES by Langston Hughes, copyright © 1994 by The Estate of Langston Hughes. Used by permission of Alfred A. Knopf, a division of Random House, Inc.

337 From THE WAY THINGS ARE AND OTHER POEMS by Myra Cohn Livingston. Copyright © 1974 Myra Cohn Livingston. Used by permission of Marian Reiner.

338 Copyright © 1974 By Evil Eye Music, Inc. Used By Permission of HarperCollins Publishers.

339 From OUT IN THE DARK AND DAYLIGHT by Aileen Fisher. Copyright © 1980 Aileen Fisher. Used by permission of Marian Reiner for the author.

342 © Noel R. Berry

343 From ONE AT A TIME by David McCord. Copyright © 1965, 1966 by David McCord. By permission of Little, Brown and Company, (Inc.)

344 "The Farmer" by Carole Boston Weatherford from the collection IN DADDY'S ARMS I AM TALL Copyright © 1997. Permission arranged with Lee & Low Books Inc., New York, NY 10016.

345 "Commas" from BING BANG BOING, copyright © 1994 by Douglas Florian, reprinted by permission of Harcourt, Inc.

351-357, 363, 385, 387 *Star Sisters* from PUSHING UP THE SKY by Joseph Bruchac, copyright © 2000 by Joseph Bruchac, text. Used by permission of Dial Books for Young Readers, an imprint of Penguin Putnam Books for Young Readers, a division of Penguin Putnam Inc.

368-371, 374-375, 377 From THE ADVENTURES OF SPIDER by Joyce Cooper Arkhurst. Copyright © 1964 by Joyce Cooper Akhurst (Text); Copyright © 1964 by Barker/Black Studio, Inc. (Illustrations). By permission of Little, Brown and Company, (Inc.)

381, 383, 386 Excerpts from TOAD OF TOAD HALL © 1929, reproduced by permission of Curtis Brown Ltd., London.

392-394, 402 Provided by NASA

406 Courtesy of Michael J. Tuttle, Copyright 2001 by the Smithsonian Institution.

407 © Google, Inc.

409 National Park Service and image of George Washington by James Peale, Inde 14171, courtesy NPS Museum Management Program and Independence National Historical Park.

496, 509 Copyright © 1998 by Houghton Mifflin Company. Reproduced by permission from *The American Heritage Dictionary*.

PHOTO CREDITS

60 Courtesy of James Monroe Museum and Memorial Library

61 bottom The National Archives

114 right, left © S. Barrow/SuperStock

118 right © Image Shop/Phototake

118 left © Grant V. Faint/Image Bank

118 center © Anup & Manoj Shah/Animals Animals

118 bottom © Charles D. Winters/Photo Researchers

119 right © Mitsuaki Iwago/Minden Pictures

119 left © Kevin Schafer/Peter Arnold

122 right © Charles D. Winters/Photo Researchers

122 left © Image Shop/Phototake

124 top © Anup & Manoj Shah/Animals Animals

124 bottom © Grant V. Faint/Image Bank

125 © Tony Arruza

130 © John Sweedberg/Bruce Coleman Inc., New York

146 left, **152** left, **153** Malhorta/HBL Photo Agency/Gamma/Liaison

147 bottom Paula Bronstein/Newsmakers/Liaison

429, 431 From BUILD OUR NATION in WE THE PEOPLE, by Hartoonian et al. Copyright ©1997 by Houghton Mifflin Company. All rights reserved.

432 Sophia Smith Collection, Smith College

509 © Corbis/Library of Congress

The editors have made every effort to trace the ownership of all copyrighted selections found in this book and to make full acknowledgment for their use. Omissions brought to our attention will be corrected in a subsequent edition.

STUDENT REVIEWERS

Marni Brown, Laurel Elementary School, San Mateo, CA

Sudie Brown, Powhatan School, Winchester, VA

Sarah Cohen, Baywood School, San Mateo, CA

Anna Ettinger, Countryside Elementary School, Edina, MN

Eric M. Fletcher, Christ the King School, Topeka, KS

Marshall Glass, La Entrada School, Menlo Park, CA

Kelsey Harrell, Clyde Hill Elementary, Bellevue, WA

Laura Hicks, St. Francis Xavier, Wilmette, IL

Lucy Marie Horton, Clyde Hill Elementary, Bellevue, WA

Devin Ingersoll, South Londonderry School, Londonderry, NH

Madeline Jaffe, Clyde Hill Elementary, Bellevue, WA

Rachel Keizer, Clyde Hill Elementary, Bellevue, WA

Anna Larson, South Londonderry School, Londonderry, NH

Matthew P. Mauro, Sunnyside Elementary, New Brighton, MN

Brett Menella, Clyde Hill Elementary, Bellevue, WA

Josh Paterson, Virginia Avenue/Charlotte DeHart School, Winchester, VA

Kelsey Perry, South Londonderry School, Londonderry, NH

Katie Pierce, Creek Valley Elementary, Edina, MN

Andy Quinn, Deer Path Middle School, Lake Forest, IL

Colby Regier, Christ the King School, Topeka, KS

Ian Rosenfield, South Hillsborough School, Hillsborough, CA

Mrs. Ryan's 5th Grade Class, Liberty Bell School, Coopersburg, PA

Lauren Schechinger, South Londonderry School, Londonderry, NH

Emily Schmar, Christ the King School, Topeka, KS

Jordan Tandowsky, Jewish Day School of the North Peninsula, Foster City, CA

Nicole Yang, McKenzie School, Wilmette, IL

Brittany Young, West Indianola, Topeka, KS

Author and Title Index

Skills and Terms Index